F

Other books by Tony Alessandra:

NON-MANIPULATIVE SELLING
THE ART OF MANAGING PEOPLE
BE YOUR OWN SALES MANAGER

Other books by Phil Hunsaker:

THE ART OF MANAGING PEOPLE

COMMUNICATING
AT WORK

TONY ALESSANDRA, PH.D.

&

PHIL HUNSAKER, PH.D.

A FIRESIDE BOOK
Published by Simon & Schuster ▪ New York London Toronto Sydney Tokyo Singapore

F

FIRESIDE

Rockefeller Center
1230 Avenue of the Americas
New York, New York 10020

FIRESIDE and colophon are registered
trademarks
of Simon & Schuster Inc.

Designed by Barbara Marks
Manufactured in the United States of America

3   5   7   9   10   8   6   4   2

Library of Congress Cataloging-in-Publication
Data
Alessandra, Anthony J.
Communicating at work / Tony Alessandra &
Phil Hunsaker.
p.   cm.
"A Fireside book."
Includes bibliographical references.
1. Communication in management.
I. Hunsaker, Phillip L.
II. Title.
HD30.3.A39   1993
658.4'5—dc20   93-12900
CIP

ISBN: 0-671-78855-8

To my loving wife, Sue, who has taught me a new dimension of the art of communicating.
—A. J. A.

To my children: Phillip, Katherine, and Sarah, who have shown me the challenge and rewards of meaningful interpersonal communication.
—P. L. H.

ACKNOWLEDGMENTS

Special thanks goes to Joyce Wycoff, who played a major role in reorganizing, reconstructing, and editing our material; to Jeff Davidson, who helped us envision the project and sell it to our publisher; to Ed Walters, our editor, who gave us guidance in envisioning the scope of the project; to Gary Alessandra, who helped us computerize the manuscript back and forth from IBM and Macintosh; to Annie Morrissey, who years ago helped design the listening and nonverbal communications materials; and to Jim Cathcart, who helped develop the concepts in many of the chapters, especially the three chapters on communication styles.

Additional thanks to Jim Burns, Joanne Coté, and the research committee at the University of San Diego who facilitated and supported much of this work.

CONTENTS

Introduction   9

PART I: INTERPERSONAL COMMUNICATION   11

  1. Future Perfect Communication   13
  2. Personal Communication Styles   20
  3. The Four Styles   34
  4. Communicating with the Four Styles   45

PART II: VERBAL COMMUNICATION   51

  5. Active Listening   54
  6. The Art of Asking Questions   69
  7. Making Sure with Feedback   78
  8. Conflict Resolution   91

PART III: NONVERBAL COMMUNICATION   109

  9. Projecting a Powerful Image   111
 10. The Power of Nonverbal Communication   120

8 • CONTENTS

11. It's How You Say It 135
12. Communicating Through Spatial Arrangements 142
13. How Your Use of Time Talks 160

PART IV: GROUP COMMUNICATION 167

14. Presentation Power 169
15. Meeting Magic 187
16. Conducting Powerful Meetings 204

PART V: WRITTEN COMMUNICATION 221

17. Putting Yourself Ahead of the Pack 223
18. It's a Matter of Style 235

Wrap Up: Putting It All Together 248

Bibliography 252

Index 261

INTRODUCTION

*Easy question: Is accurate, effective, open communication
important in managing others?*
Answer: You bet!

It's almost impossible to be productive in the workplace without
being an effective communicator. The very definition of managing
is to get things done through other people. If you cannot accurately
communicate what needs to be done, how do you expect to get
it accomplished? In addition, even if you can accurately communicate directives, you may do so in such a way that it causes
hard feelings or turns off other people. In either case, the job may
not get done at all, may not get done on time, may not get done
correctly, or may be subtly sabotaged.

Information is an asset. It is as valuable as real estate or
manufacturing equipment. Good communication is the key to
acquiring, processing, and capitalizing on that asset. Today's business environment is changing at a frantic pace, reorganizations,
down-sizings, mergers, acquisitions, new products, global mar-

kets, increasing regulations—all put tremendous pressure on our abilities to communicate new information, procedures, and processes. Good communication skills are a basic necessity for people at all levels of today's organizations.

> *Harder question: How well do you communicate with others? Are you a highly effective, powerful communicator; moderately effective; or (heaven forbid!) an ineffective communicator who is often misunderstood?*
>
> *Answer: (You'll have to evaluate your own skills. Are you getting results? Are you frustrated by communications at work? Are you satisfied with your communication skills? Even if you rated yourself moderately high or very high, there is always room for improvement and the best communicators are always honing their skills.)*

All of us, at times, are misunderstood by another person or we misunderstand the other person's message. We use words or phrases that are misinterpreted. Sometimes we create mistrust by what we say, the words we use, or the way we say it. However, the important thing to keep in mind is that these problems happen much more frequently and with much greater severity to poor communicators than to good communicators. Even if you now believe that you are not a good communicator, this book will provide you with the crucial skills to become a much better communicator. That even goes for those of you who are already pretty effective at communications. Everyone can learn to communicate better.

> *Hardest question: How do you become a powerful, dynamic communicator? How do you communicate precisely what you need to have done in a way that insures that the results will match your expectations? How do you avoid misunderstandings, mistrust, and disinterest?*
>
> Answer: Read on.

INTERPERSONAL COMMUNICATION

The most immutable barrier in nature is between one man's thoughts and another's.

—WILLIAM JAMES

Almost every problem, every conflict, every mistake, and every misunderstanding has at its most basic level a communication problem. William James saw the communication barrier as "immutable." We believe that while communication problems may never be completely eliminated, they can be reduced and often avoided.

We live in a world filled with other people. We live together, work together, and play together. In our personal lives, we need each other for security, comfort, friendship, and love. In our working environment, we need each other in order to achieve our goals and objectives. None of these goals can be achieved without communication. Communication is the basic thread that ties us together. Through communication we make known our needs, our wants, our ideas, and our feelings. The better we are at communicating, the more effective we are at achieving our hopes and dreams.

This section will lead you through an interpersonal communication model that will help you understand your own style of communication and the styles that others use. Once you understand how people prefer to communicate, you can adapt your own communications in ways that will enhance understanding and build rapport.

FUTURE PERFECT COMMUNICATION

It is a luxury to be understood.

—RALPH WALDO EMERSON

When *Star Trek*'s Mr. Spock wants a perfect transfer of information between himself and another Vulcan, he does a mind-meld. By touching skulls, information flows from one mind to another in a faultless process—free of errors, emotional content, and personal perspectives. Unfortunately mind-melding is not available to us. We have to use a much more flawed technique involving the three "Vs" of communication: verbal, vocal, and visual elements.

This chapter discusses the general communication process, including the most common places it breaks down and how you can avoid problems as you work to communicate. For simplicity and practicality, we show the communication process only from your perspective. That is the only part of the process you can, and need to, control. Of course, in successful relationships, both parties participate meaningfully in the entire two-way process. Figure 1-A presents a model of the communication process. The communication process has five basic elements: two people—the

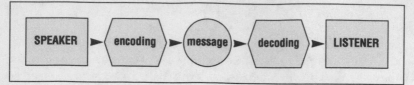

1-A *A general model of the communication process*

speaker and the listener; two processes—sending and receiving; and one message.

The problem faced in any communication is how to get ideas from one person's head to another. Since we haven't figured out how to use Mr. Spock's mind-meld method of direct transfer, we are stuck with the problem of using an imperfect system that contains considerable opportunity for misunderstandings.

The speaker starts with what he wants to say—the message. To send the message, he translates it into words and actions. Literally, he selects words that he thinks will convey his meaning and he throws in a variety of gestures, facial expressions, etc., that he believes will help transmit the message.

The message to be communicated is carried by the three "V elements"—verbal, vocal, and visual. The words we use make up the verbal element. The vocal element includes the tone and intensity of our voice and other vocal qualities that are often referred to as the "music we play with our voice." The visual element incorporates everything that the listener can see.

It might surprise you to learn that the most powerful element of communication is the visual. Dynamic visual, nonverbal communication grabs and holds onto the listener's attention.

Old story: An old codger and a young whippersnapper are on a mule trip. The youngster is having trouble getting his mule across a creek and asks the oldster for help. The wily veteran grabs a big stick and whacks the mule across the head. The mule trots meekly across the creek. The tenderfoot looks amazed and the old guy just says, "First you gotta get their attention."

Effective communication begins with getting the listener's attention through strong visual, nonverbal elements and then uses powerful vocal and verbal elements to transmit the message.

The listener "receives" the message through a series of filters: his past experiences, his perception of the speaker, his emotional involvement with the message, his understanding of the verbal content, his level of attention, etc. In a sense, he translates the message into his own words, creating his own version of what he thinks the speaker was saying.

COMMON PROBLEM AREAS
■

Problems arise in three major areas: sending, the environment, and receiving.

SENDING: As speakers, we don't send our messages perfectly. The words we choose may be ambiguous; our tone of voice may not reflect our true feelings; our gestures may not convey the importance of the message.

ENVIRONMENT: There might be too much "noise" in the environment. The message might be presented in the midst of many distractions or to a listener whose mind is wandering.

RECEIVING: The message can be garbled during reception. A word or a facial expression might be misinterpreted or a previous experience might cause the message to be translated in a way different from its intent.

While communication can break down in several places, people who understand these problem areas have more control of the process and have fewer communication glitches.

PROBLEMS IN SENDING
■

Let's consider the communication involved in a sales situation. This is represented in figure 1-B. The speaker is the salesperson and the listener is the customer. Imagine that you are the computer salesperson. As part of your sales communication, you tell the customer that the computer you recommend has 2.5 megabytes of RAM. The actual message in your head is that this computer has enough working memory to handle all the programs the customer needs to run. Your customer doesn't understand computer terminology and he doesn't receive the message you are trying to

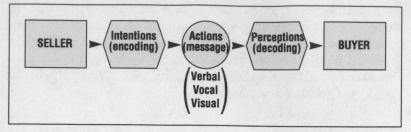

1-B *A communication model for selling*

send. This is an example of how the verbal element of communication can throw the message off-track.

Communication can also be derailed by sending inappropriate visual and vocal messages. Most speakers don't understand that the words they use are a secondary element in communication. As a matter of fact, the words used are the least important element of communication. Studies show that listeners generally attend first to the visual and then to the vocal elements of a message, finally focusing on the meaning of the words themselves.

Assume that you are a company president thinking about moving your account to a new bank. The vice-president in charge of new accounts for the bank you are considering is sitting with a messy pile of papers in front of him. His tie is stained and askew. He sits up nervously as you walk in; his handshake is timid and his palms are sweaty. He makes very little eye contact and his eyes dart around the room frequently. His voice is squeaky and he says "uh" a lot. He mumbles. His words are: "Our bank is the best in the county. Our record for return on investment is second to none. We would really like to do business with you."

We dare you to ignore the visual information and concentrate only on the meaning of his words. The visual element is that most powerful first impression, and people respond to it before, and in spite of, the words that are spoken. The vocal elements are then processed before the actual words are heard and translated.

If the vocal sounds are bothersome or detract in any way from the meaning of the words, people will react and understand less of what was intended. Imagine a vacation-travel salesperson who spoke in a monotone, or an investment counselor who said, "Like . . ." or "you know . . ." every other sentence. What if a newscaster's voice was so soft and hypnotizing that you were lulled by it? What if a speaker had a heavy regional or foreign accent? You *do* notice. You *do* respond. Sounds are recognized *before* you even get to the meaning of the words spoken.

Since visual and vocal elements are noticed before the actual words, you need to make sure that your appearance and vocal tone work in harmony with your message. Look for inconsistencies—a strong message delivered in a weak tone or with soft, flabby words; or a logical, fact-filled message presented in an emotional tone with ambiguous words.

"NOISE" IN THE ENVIRONMENT

During the message-sending process itself, numerous barriers to communication can arise. These barriers are "noise" in the communication process. Noise creates distortions of the message and prevents it from being understood the way it was intended.

Noise can come from many sources. Environmental noise such as ringing telephones, honking horns, and messy, chaotic surroundings can prevent your message from being received clearly. Another environmental factor is time—is the message being delivered at an inappropriate time? A Friday afternoon prior to a holiday weekend is not a good time to deliver a complicated, fact-filled report on a new marketing plan. Speakers who want their messages to be received clearly and accurately will remove as much environmental noise as possible. They try to present their message in a calm, distraction-free environment at a time when the listener can devote his or her full attention to the message.

RECEPTION PROBLEMS

Often it is hard to determine the listener's ability to receive a message. The listener may be inattentive or bored. If you're presenting a message to someone who has just won the state's multimillion dollar lottery, chances are good that you will be dealing with a distracted listener. The ability of a listener to receive your message is affected by his emotional state, preexisting commitments, financial pressures, and judgments he may already have formed about you and your message. Before presenting your message, you need to make sure that you have the listener's attention.

Another way of thinking about communication is to compare it to a radio station. A sender and a receiver are required to transmit the message. A powerful station can send a message to a high-quality receiver and the message comes through loud and clear. A weak station trying to get a message over a range of mountains to a 1940 vacuum-tube radio doesn't have much of a chance.

There are three requirements to getting your message through clearly:

MAKE SURE YOU ARE A POWERFUL STATION: Your words need to present your message clearly; your vocal tone needs to match and strengthen your words; and your visual appearance and gestures need to be consistent with your words and vocal tone.

CLEAR THE ENVIRONMENT: Anywhere along the process, "noise"—or static—can drown out the message. Don't try to transmit over a mountain range. Eliminate distractions, excess noise, and messy, chaotic surroundings. Present your message at a time when it can be received. A radio station that wants to reach business commuters plays its message during the rush hour, not at 3:00 A.M.

MAKE SURE THE LISTENER'S RADIO IS ON. Get your listener's attention. Find out what frequency he's tuned to and transmit on that frequency. If he's interested in facts and figures and you're giving him emotional high drama, you're transmitting on the wrong frequency.

Any time you hear people saying, "I didn't understand what you meant . . . I thought you said . . . You never told me . . . I didn't hear that . . . ," you know there was a failure in one of these areas and your message did not get through. We commonly call this a communication breakdown. However, you can get around or avoid many of these breakdowns. You can project a clear verbal, vocal, and visual signal in a way that gives your listener a better chance to receive it precisely as it was sent. The powerful communication processes presented in this book will help you develop the skills needed to filter out the noise, gain the attention of your listener, and present your message in its clearest, most powerful form. It will also help you establish a feedback process that will allow you to adjust your signal and correct errors received by your listener.

By using noise-free verbal and nonverbal skills during the sending and the feedback processes, you minimize communication barriers and establish an effective, efficient communication climate—a climate that establishes, maintains, and enhances mutual trust and credibility.

In the following chapters, we present specific verbal, vocal, and visual communication skills: questioning, listening, vocal intonations, image, body language, and feedback. You can then use these skills to send, listen, and give feedback to others as you apply the techniques of effective communication. But, before we get into the specific techniques for improving the three "Vs," it's important to understand the differences in personal communication styles. The next two chapters will give you a complete understanding of how people differ in their communication styles and how to adapt your communication effectively with each style.

2

Personal
Communication
Styles

She speaks Russian . . . he speaks English.

She wants to go to the ballet . . . he wants to go to a ball game.

They struggle to communicate and then give up in frustration. She doesn't understand him; he doesn't understand her. They don't speak the same language.

The same type of conflict happens to us almost every day. While most of the people around us speak the same language, many of us are speaking in different "styles."

Style? What do you mean by "style"?

In the last chapter we saw the overview of the communication process and learned about the three V-elements—verbal, vocal, and visual. These elements can be combined into different "style languages." Just as Spanish, French, and Italian use the same alphabet but come up with different languages, people combine the same V-elements into different communication patterns we call "style."

Because we can combine these elements into different patterns . . . different style languages . . . we often experience communication breakdowns. Misunderstandings happen because we don't understand that different people have different styles of communication. In effect, we are speaking different languages just like the language-crossed couple at the beginning of this chapter.

THE FOUR-TYPE MODEL

Throughout the ages philosophers and scientists have been fascinated with communication and communication breakdowns. They knew that much of the problem was caused by the basic differences in people. The earliest recorded efforts to understand those differences were found in astrology, where it was believed that the alignment of the heavens influenced behavior. Astrologers defined twelve signs, or types of people, that corresponded to the four elements of earth, air, fire, and water.

In ancient Greece, the physician Hippocrates studied the human psyche as well as the body and developed his concept of the four temperaments—choleric, phlegmatic, sanguine, and melancholy. He believed that temperament was shaped by body fluids—blood, phlegm, and black and yellow bile.

In the 1920s, Dr. Carl Jung was the first to scientifically study personality types. He described the four behavior styles as intuitor, thinker, feeler, and sensor.

This basic, four-type model spans all cultures—east and west, north and south. For instance, contemporary Japan still studies behavior and physical composition. A recent best-seller, *Advice on How to Form a Good Combination of Blood Types* by Toshitaka Nomi, claimed 100,000 documented cases of cross-referencing personalities with the four blood types. Nomi indicated that 40 percent of Japan's population has type-A blood, which he associates with the conscientious, hard-working behavior expected of engineers and technicians. He hypothesizes that this explains Japan's emphasis on high-technology excellence.

Today there are more than a dozen varied models of behavioral differences. They all have one common thread—the grouping of behavior into four categories. We are presenting a very simple model which has been validated with hundreds of thousands of people. It is a powerful guide you can use to improve communication and morale, build better work groups, and develop better relationships with coworkers, supervisors, customers, vendors, and others.

The personality model you will learn is simple, practical, easy-to-use and remember . . . and extremely accurate. Because it focuses on patterns of observable, external behaviors which people show to the world, you can easily learn and apply the model. The differences we see on the outside give us some real clues as to what's going on *inside* someone's head. You'll be able to pick up on the differences in people and use those differences to make any situation work for you.

TWO SIMPLE QUESTIONS
■

The four styles are based on two dimensions of behavior:

INDIRECTNESS VERSUS DIRECTNESS: this dimension describes the person's observable behavior. Directness means the tendency to move forward or act outwardly by expressing thoughts, feelings, or expectations in order to influence others.

SUPPORTING VERSUS CONTROLLING: this dimension explains the motivating goal behind our observable actions. People who are supporting tend to put relationships with others as their chief priority while the priority for people who are controlling is accomplishment of the task at hand.

In order to better understand a person's style, we need to ask two simple questions:

Is the person more direct or more indirect?
Is the person more supporting or more controlling?

Once we can answer those two questions, we will understand the dominant style of that person and we will know what *style language* to use in our communication.

DIRECT OR INDIRECT?
■

Direct people come on strong, take the social initiative, and create a powerful first impression. They tend to be assertive, fast-paced people who make swift decisions and take risks. They can easily become impatient with others who do not keep up with their pace. As active people who talk a lot, they appear confident and sometimes dominant. Direct people tend to express opinions readily and make emphatic statements. Such individuals try to shape their environment and relationships directly. "Tell McCullough that I want to talk to him ASAP!" barks a Direct person while a more Indirect one asks his secretary to find out if McCullough wouldn't mind coming to his office when convenient.

Direct people are faster paced, more assertive, and more competitive. At worst, these tendencies sometimes transform into hastiness, combativeness, or lower awareness of others' needs. More outspoken, talkative, and dominant, Direct people are extroverts who focus their attention on interests in their environment. In other words—action! They tend to work and play faster. When at a social gathering, they're the ones who introduce themselves as a natural way of seeking to influence others in their surroundings.

They prefer to make rapid decisions, becoming impatient when things don't move fast enough or don't go their way. Checking for errors is something other people can do. It's too time-consuming for Direct people. Instead of checking, they busily rush into new areas where the more Indirect may fear to tread. In fact, they often rush into so many new areas that their time seems to evaporate into thin air. That's one reason why they have difficulty consistently being prompt—because something comes up at the office or somewhere else. Meanwhile, their more punctual, Indirect friends learn to busy themselves with time-killers, such as projects or magazines, while waiting for their more easily sidetracked companions.

Direct people may enjoy risks and want results now, or yesterday. Risks are a way of life with them. Not only are they less worried about rocking the boat, they'll often tip it over and splash around in the hot water they find themselves in. They crave excitement, so they do as much as possible to get it.

Directness is measured on the horizontal axis in figure 2-A. Typical Direct people are:

- Fast-paced, assertive, take charge—Wall Street bulls
- Forceful, type-A personalities who confront conflict, change, risk, and decision-making head-on

- Outspoken communicators who often dominate business meetings
- Competitive, impatient, and confrontational; they bulldoze their way through life, often arguing for the sake of arguing
- Confident; they maintain strong eye contact and have firm handshakes
- People who thrive on accomplishment and are not overly concerned with rules and policies
- Inclined to think, "It is easier to beg forgiveness than to seek permission."
- In terms of the verbal, vocal, and visual elements, direct people tend to speak quickly in loud, aggressive tones and present a bold visual appearance.

On the opposite side of the Directness spectrum, Indirect people are more quiet and reserved. They may be seen as more easygoing, or at least more self-contained in keeping their views to themselves. Indirect people ask questions and listen more than they talk. They typically do not share their opinions or concerns. When asked to take a stand, they may make tentative statements or none at all. They often appear more objective, quiet, and indecisive. When taken to an extreme, these positive traits can be viewed as negative ones—wishy-washy, tight-lipped, unassertive behaviors. Indirect people are also less confronting, less demanding, less assertive, and less socially competitive than their Direct counterparts. They allow others to take the social initiative. For instance, when they want to go to the movies or a restaurant, they might think to themselves, "Gee, I'd like to see that new adventure movie." Then when their spouse or date suggests the latest western, they go along without mentioning their own interests.

They tend to be more risk-conscious—moving slowly, meditating on their decisions, and avoiding big changes. As a result, they often avoid taking bold chances or spontaneous actions. After all, what's the best way to keep from failing? One way is to do nothing until you're satisfied it will be an improvement. In other words, do only sure things. Those sure things result in a higher success ratio, so they are more natural for Indirect people.

When Indirect people flop, they tend to take the setback personally. They are likely to internalize or privately reassess it, often wondering if there's something wrong with them. "How could I have been so stupid?" the Indirect person asks himself after a setback. Just give a hint that something is going wrong, and reserved folks may engage in self-criticism for days. By contrast, the Direct type seldom has extra time to spend looking back and reflecting on such considerations.

Indirect people tend to move at a slower or more measured pace than Directs. They speak and respond more slowly since they are more cautious or stability-focused when considering change. If their behavior becomes too measured, detractors (usually Direct people) can view this as dragging their feet, or even lacking interest.

Predictability is more important to Indirect people, so they tend to consider the pros and cons, attend to details, and fact-find. Caught in a gray area with no clear-cut guidelines, they usually ask for clarification or permission before they take action. They seek to meet their needs by accommodating the requirements of their environment. Generally they operate according to established formats and rules, so when you make an appointment with an Indirect person, you can expect him to show up on time, or possibly to wait for you!

Indirect people tend to communicate by asking or observing instead of stating or showing. Their questions clarify, support, or seek more information. They prefer qualified statements and speak more tentatively, often taking a roundabout or step-by-step approach. "According to some sources," or "Perhaps another way of looking at this situation might be to consider . . . ," are common ways Indirects start a comment. If they don't like something, they respond subtly. "Well, your other suit does look good," is an Indirect's way of telling you she hates your suit. They reserve the right to express their opinions or keep them to themselves. But they can also act like impregnable rocks when they don't want to be cracked.

Typical Indirect people are:

- Cautious in their approach to risk, decision-making, and change—Wall Street bears
- Slow-paced, low-key, and often even meek
- Tentative, reserved communicators who hesitate to contribute in meetings. They often preface their statements with qualifi-

cations such as "I'm not sure if . . ." or "According to my sources . . ."

- Conflict avoiders. They are diplomatic, patient, and cooperative. On unimportant issues, they will conform rather than argue. When they have strong convictions about an issue, however, they will stand their ground.
- Low-profile, reserved, and gentle. Handshakes are gentle and they speak at a slower pace and lower volume than direct people.
- Slow to take the initiative at social gatherings
- In terms of the verbal, vocal, and visual elements, indirect people tend to speak slowly and cautiously, making indirect qualified statements and are generally conservative and reserved in their visual appearance.

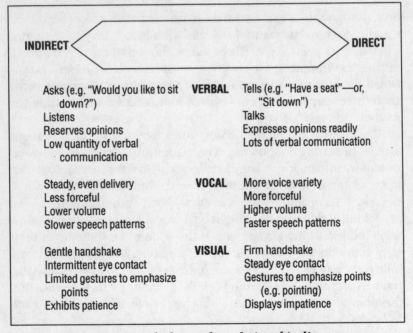

INDIRECT		DIRECT
Asks (e.g. "Would you like to sit down?")	**VERBAL**	Tells (e.g. "Have a seat"—or, "Sit down")
Listens		Talks
Reserves opinions		Expresses opinions readily
Low quantity of verbal communication		Lots of verbal communication
Steady, even delivery	**VOCAL**	More voice variety
Less forceful		More forceful
Lower volume		Higher volume
Slower speech patterns		Faster speech patterns
Gentle handshake	**VISUAL**	Firm handshake
Intermittent eye contact		Steady eye contact
Limited gestures to emphasize points		Gestures to emphasize points (e.g. pointing)
Exhibits patience		Displays impatience

2-A *Using verbal, vocal, and visual indicators to identify directness*

SUPPORTING OR CONTROLLING?

▪

We've found that the other dimension of behavior, besides that of Directness/Indirectness, is that people tend to be either Supporting or Controlling. While the degree of directness or indirectness describes people's observable behavior—how others see and hear us behaving—the second behavioral scale explains the internal goals motivating our daily actions. This dimension is concerned with *why* we do the things we do in the way we do them. When combined, the two scales show how inclined we are to reveal our thoughts and feelings plus the degree to which we tend to support other people's expressions of their thoughts and feelings.

SUPPORTING BEHAVIORS

Supporting people are motivated by their relationships and feelings. They want to get to know people and they tend to make decisions based on feelings, experiences, and relationships.

Supporting people are emotionally open and show it by displaying a wide range of verbal, vocal, and visual elements. They talk with their bodies, using more vocal inflections, making continual eye contact, and communicating in terms of feelings more than the Controlling types. Other visual clues are animated facial expressions, much hand and body movement, a flexible time perspective, and immediate nonverbal feedback. Supporting people also like to tell, or listen to, stories and anecdotes and to make personal contact. They are comfortable with emotions and openly express their joy, sadness, confusion, and other feelings.

Supporting people respond to passing interests, their own and others', even though this may take them away from the business or subject at hand. They like to make conversations enjoyable, so they often willingly stray from the subject to discuss personal experiences and interests. As long as it's in the ball park, they figure it's probably relevant. A Supporting person might say, "That reminds me of the time Uncle Jed got stuck on the Garden State Parkway for five hours . . ." And exaggeration of details just adds interest by fully depicting personal experiences.

Supporting types are also more accepting about time usage. Their time perspective is organized around the needs of people first and tasks second, so they're more flexible about how others use their time than the Controlling types. "I'm sorry I'm late," explains a Supporting person, "but my son was crying this morning because Jason broke his science project. So I had to write a note to his teacher and cheer him up before I dropped him off at school."

Supporting behaviors, when carried to an extreme, might drive some people up the wall. For example, self-disclosure can be seen as neediness, digression as inattention, animation as melodrama, acquiescence as weakness, and friendliness as patronizing. Too much of any behavior can become a liability if taken to its extreme.

The level of supporting behavior is measured on the vertical axis in figure 2-B. Typically supporting people:

- Are emotionally open, with animated facial expressions and physical gestures
- Feel comfortable expressing joy, sadness, confusion, and other emotions quickly and unabashedly to virtually anyone

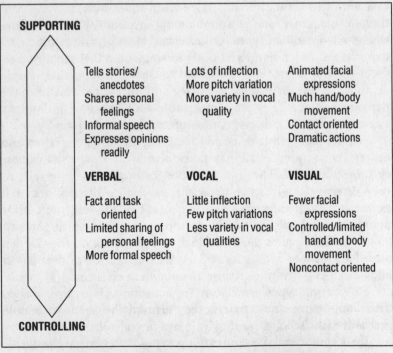

SUPPORTING

Tells stories/ anecdotes	Lots of inflection	Animated facial expressions
Shares personal feelings	More pitch variation	Much hand/body movement
Informal speech	More variety in vocal quality	Contact oriented
Expresses opinions readily		Dramatic actions
VERBAL	**VOCAL**	**VISUAL**
Fact and task oriented	Little inflection	Fewer facial expressions
Limited sharing of personal feelings	Few pitch variations	Controlled/limited hand and body movement
More formal speech	Less variety in vocal qualities	Noncontact oriented

CONTROLLING

2-B *Using verbal, vocal, and visual indicators to identify supportingness*

- Maintain a closer physical proximity; they tend to be huggers, hand shakers, and touchers
- Are informal and prefer relaxed, warm relationships
- Enjoy loose, amusing conversations, frequently tell stories and anecdotes, often about personally embarrassing incidents
- Prefer unstructured time and are seldom disturbed when other people waste their time
- Are feeling-oriented decision makers. They value their hunches and the feelings of others.

CONTROLLING BEHAVIORS

If Supporting types seem like an open book, Controlling ones tend to be more poker-faced. Controlling types like to play their cards close to the vest in order to increase their probability of getting the upper hand and decreasing the probability of appearing foolish. Controlling types are motivated by the task at hand and want to accomplish their goals. They usually like to keep their distance, both physically and mentally. They don't touch you and you don't touch them. People often comment, once they get to know a Controlling person, "He's a really great guy; but it's awfully hard to break through the thick shell."

Controlling people tend to stand farther away from you, even when shaking hands, than Supporting types. They have a strong sense of personal space and territory and hate it when someone invades it—for instance, by taking something from their desk, using personal items without permission, or calling meetings requiring their time without asking for their input.

Controlling people generally have a restricted range of verbal, vocal, and visual expression. Their faces don't often give their thoughts away, they display limited or controlled hand and body movement, and adhere to a more time-disciplined agenda. They push for facts and details, focus on the issues and tasks at hand, and keep their personal feelings private. They aren't natural touchers, and they tend to respond stiffly if anyone touches them. Unlike their Supporting counterparts, they give less wide-ranging nonverbal feedback.

By contrast with Supporting people, Controlling types typically place higher priority on getting things done. They prefer working with things or through people rather than with them or for them. Typical comments from a Controlling person include, "I can't talk now, Frank," or "I have a two o'clock deadline to meet," or "I'll let you know when I have time to do that," or "I'll get back to you later after I've had more time to think about it."

The more Controlling types like structure since they know what to expect and have more control over the results within a structured environment. When negatively motivated, they can be viewed as coercive, restrictive, or overbearing. They prefer to stick with an agenda, at least if it's their own. As more naturally independent, motivated workers, they prefer to have control of the conditions surrounding their tasks—either in terms of input and output (Directness) or the process itself (Indirectness). These more self-contained people make use of either key talent or key procedures to meet their own goals. Thus, they view the planning and supervision processes as ways of reaching goals. Direct individuals attempt to control the people around them while the Indirect types prefer to exercise control on their environments.

Because time equals money to Controlling types, they're more disciplined about how other people use *their* time. In part, this explains their tendency not to show, discuss, or willingly listen to thoughts and feelings like Supporting people do. Controlling people are more matter-of-fact, with more fixed expectations of people and situations. Just as facts place second for Supporting types, feelings take the back seat for those who are Controlling. You might say that people who are Supporting experience life by tuning in to the concerns or feeling states (of themselves and others) and then reacting to them. By contrast, people who are Controlling focus on the tasks or ideas in question and respond primarily to those stimuli.

Controlling types like to know where a conversation is going. Idle, nondirected chit-chat is not for them. If Supporting types stray from the subject, people who prefer the Controlling style find a way to bring them back on track. They usually need clarity before they move on to the next topic. If you get off the subject, they're likely to ask, "Can you sum that up for me?" or "What is the key point you're trying to make?"

Because of their different priorities, Controlling types often perceive Supporting ones as time-wasters or wishy-washy. And Supporting types may view these Controlling types as cold, unsympathetic, or self-involved. As a result, misunderstandings can quickly grow out of proportion when we don't discern and respond to the source of the differences—the inner motivating needs that drive our personal styles of behavior.

The range of behaviors between supporting and controlling are represented on the figure 2-B vertical axis with the top being supporting behaviors and the bottom repesenting controlling behaviors.

Typical Controlling people are:

- Emotionally reserved—often called poker faces.
- More rigid, physically, and less expressive than Supporting people. Tend to keep physically distant from others.
- Guarded physically, mentally, and emotionally. Seldom boisterous or rowdy.
- Task-oriented; they dislike digressions from their agendas.
- Fact-oriented decision makers. They want to see statistics and other hard evidence.
- People who prefer working alone and put little value on opinions and feelings.
- More comfortable operating in an intellectual mode.
- Champions of time management. They are the efficiency experts of the world who create and follow rigid plans and schedules.

WHICH STYLE ARE YOU?

•

As you read the above descriptions of each dimension, you undoubtedly did what everyone does: you compared yourself to the characteristics being described. Now, review the descriptions to determine where you stand on the two axes of figure 2-C. Answer the questions:

Are you more direct or more indirect?
Are you more supporting or more controlling?

Next, think of a "difficult" person with whom you would like to communicate better. Determine that person's position on the two axes and mark on those places. More often than not, you will find that people with whom you have conflicts have different personal styles from yours.

SUPPORTING
(Relationship-oriented)

THE RELATER STYLE
Slow at taking action and
    making decisions
Likes close, personal
    relationships
Dislikes interpersonal conflict
Supports and "actively" listens
    to others
Weak at goal setting and
    self-direction
Has excellent ability to gain
    support from others
Works slowly and cohesively
    with others
Seeks security and a sense of
    belonging
Good counseling skills

THE SOCIALIZER STYLE
Spontaneous actions and
    decisions
Likes involvement
Dislikes being alone
Exaggerates and generalizes
Tends to dream and gets others
    caught up in his dreams
Jumps from one activity to
    another
Works quickly and excitedly with
    others
Seeks esteem and
    acknowledgment
Good persuasive skills

INDIRECT
(Slow Pace)

DIRECT
(Fast Pace)

THE THINKER STYLE
Cautious actions and decisions
Likes organization and structure
Dislikes involvement
Asks many questions about
    specific details
Prefers objective, task-oriented,
    intellectual work
    environment
Wants to be right, so can be
    overly reliant on data
    collection
Works slowly and precisely
    alone
Good problem solving skills

THE DIRECTOR STYLE
Decisive actions and decisions
Likes control, dislikes inaction
Prefers maximum freedom to
    manage himself and others
Cool, independent, and
    competitive
Low tolerance for feelings,
    attitudes, and advice of
    others
Works quickly and impressively
    alone
Good administrative skills

CONTROLLING
(Task-oriented)

2-C *Summary of behavioral characteristics*

In determining your personal style or that of someone else, look for overall patterns. How do you act most of the time? Which descriptions of yourself did you identify with first before you started thinking, "Yes, but . . . ?"

People are not simple; they are infinitely complex. Even though everyone has one dominant personal style, they also possess some characteristics from all the styles. You may do some things in an indirect way and others in a direct way; in some situations you are supporting and in others controlling. The more comfortable you feel, however, the more you are acting in accordance with your dominant style.

FOUR BEHAVIORAL STYLES
•

The two dimensions, when combined graphically as in figure 2-C, form four quadrants. These quadrants and their unique combinations of behaviors identify four styles of relating to the world, four "style languages." Figure 2-C shows the placement of the Socializer, Director, Thinker, and Relater.

Knowing which personal style best describes you and the other people you need to communicate with is an important second step in analyzing and improving your communication skills. The next chapter will give you a description of each type and show you how each type has a different way of perceiving the world, behaving, and communicating. Once you have a better understanding of each style, chapter 4 will help you understand how best to "send" your message to each style, as well as how your intended "receiver" is likely to interpret it based on his or her personal communication style.

3

THE FOUR
STYLES

If a person is worth knowing at all,
he is worth knowing well.

—ALEXANDER SMITH, NINETEENTH-CENTURY SCOTTISH POET

Each of the four types has a different way of seeing the world and communicating with other people. Once you understand the basic differences of each type, you will be able to communicate more effectively. You will be able to speak the four different style languages.

THE SOCIALIZER

.

Socializers are direct and supportive. Interacting Socializers are friendly, enthusiastic, and like to be where the action is. They thrive on admiration, acknowledgment, compliments, and applause. They want to have fun and enjoy life. Energetic and fast-paced Socializers tend to place more priority on relationships than on tasks. They influence others in an optimistic, friendly way and focus on positive outcomes. The friendly, out-going, fast-paced Socializer can also, however, be viewed as manipulative, impetuous, and excitable when displaying behavior inappropriate to the situation.

Socializers are seldom concerned with facts and details and try to avoid them as much as possible. This disregard for details sometimes prompts Socializers to exaggerate and generalize facts and figures. It also gives them a built-in excuse when they are wrong on something. They can always say, "I didn't have all the facts!"

The Socializers are idea people who have the ability to get others caught up in their dreams. With great persuasion, they influence others and shape their environments by building alliances to accomplish their results. Then they seek nods and comments of approval and recognition for those results. If compliments don't come, Socializers may invent their own! They are stimulating, talkative, and communicative.

Socializers are generally very open with their ideas and feelings. They are sometimes seen as "wearing their hearts on their sleeves." They are animated, interactive storytellers who have no qualms about "creative exaggeration." They love an audience and thrive on involvement with people. They tend to work quickly and enthusiastically with others. They are risk-takers and base many of their actions and decisions on intuition. Their greatest irritations are doing boring tasks, being alone, and not having access to a telephone.

Socializers are true entertainers. They love an audience and thrive on involvement with people. They tend to work quickly and enthusiastically with others. They are stimulating, talkative, and gregarious.

The primary strengths of Socializers are their enthusiasm, persuasiveness, and delightful sociability. Their primary weaknesses are getting involved in too many things, being impatient, and having a short attention span, which causes them to become bored easily. Socializers may be public relations specialists, talk show hosts, trial attorneys, social directors on cruise ships, or hotel personnel. They gravitate toward glamorous, high-profile careers.

In the business environment, they like other people to be risk-takers and to act quickly and decisively. In a social environment, they like others to be uninhibited, spontaneous, and entertaining.

Certain environmental and proxemic clues indicate the presence of Socializers (proxemics is the study of personal space and the movement of people in it and will be discussed in detail in a later chapter). Socializers design and use their space in a disorganized and cluttered manner; however, they know if something is missing. Their office walls may contain awards, stimulating posters or notes, and motivational, personal slogans. Their office decor is open, airy, and friendly, and the seating arrangement indicates warmth, support, and a willingness to make contact with others.

Socializers like contact and often move to an alternative seating arrangement when talking with visitors. Socializers are touchers and don't mind a slap on the back or a warm handshake. They don't mind people getting close to them, so there is little danger of alienating Socializers by standing too close or playing with something on their desks.

To increase their flexibility and achieve more balance, Socializers need to control their time and emotions; develop more of an objective mindset; spend more time checking, verifying, specifying, and organizing; concentrate on the task; and take a more logical approach to projects and issues.

SOCIALIZERS AT A GLANCE

- need interaction and contact with people
- are enthusiastic and lively
- act and decide spontaneously
- are concerned with approval and appearances
- think emotionally
- think about the "big picture" but get bored with details
- like changes and innovations
- need help getting organized
- dislike conflict
- maintain a positive, optimistic orientation to life
- exaggerate and generalize
- tend to dream and get others caught up in the dreams
- jump from one activity to another
- work quickly and excitedly with others

- seek esteem and acknowledgment from others
- have good persuasive skills

THE DIRECTOR

■

Directors are direct and controlling. They are driven by an inner need to take charge of situations. They are firm in their relationships with others, oriented toward productivity and goals, and concerned with bottom-line results. Closely allied to these positive traits are the negative ones of stubbornness, impatience, and toughness.

Directors tend to take control of other people and situations and are decisive in their actions and forthright in their decisions. Always in a hurry, they like to move at a fast pace and are impatient with delays. It is not unusual for a Director to call you and, without saying hello, launch right into the conversation. When other people cannot keep up with their speed, they view them as incompetent.

Directors want to win, so they often challenge people or rules. They accept challenges, take authority, and plunge head-first into solving problems. They tend to exhibit great administrative and operational skills and work quickly and impressively by themselves.

Directors are high achievers. They get things done and make things happen. They are like jugglers in that they like to manipulate many projects at the same time. They start juggling three things at once, and when they feel comfortable with those three things, they pick up a fourth. They keep adding more until the pressure builds to the point where they turn their backs and let everything drop. They call that "reevaluating their priorities." After reducing their stress, they immediately start the whole process over again.

Directors have a tendency toward workaholism. Therefore, doctors would say that Directors are in the high-risk category for heart attacks. Impatient, type-A personalities may also seem like prime candidates for ulcers. Directors, however, don't get ulcers; they give ulcers to other people!

Directors specialize in being in control. They tend to be independent, strong-willed, precise, goal-oriented, cool, and competitive, especially in a business environment. They accept challenges and take authority. Directors try to shape their environment to overcome obstacles to their plans. They demand maximum freedom to manage themselves and others. Directors can have a low tolerance for the feelings, attitudes, and inadequacies of others. They use their leadership skills to become winners.

The primary strengths of Directors are their ability to get things done, their leadership, and their decision-making ability. Their weaknesses tend to be their inflexibility, their impatience, their poor listening habits, and their neglect of taking time to "smell the flowers." In fact, they are so competitive that when they do finally go out to smell the flowers, they return and say to others, "I smelled twelve today. How many did you smell?"

In a business environment, Directors like others to be decisive, efficient, receptive, and intelligent, and in a social environment they want others to be congenial, assertive, and witty. A Director's ideal occupation might be a hard-driving newspaper reporter, stockbroker, independent consultant, corporate CEO, or drill sergeant.

Directors' desks will appear busy with lots of paperwork, projects, and material separated into piles. Their offices are decorated to suggest power, for example, by having a hatchet buried in the wall. There are often large planning calendars on the wall. Directors are formal and keep their distance physically and psychologically. Their offices are arranged so that seating is formal; that is, a big desk symbolizing power separates Directors from their visitors. They don't like people talking three inches from their noses.

To achieve more balance, Directors need to practice active listening; project a more relaxed image; and develop patience, humility, and sensitivity. They need to show concern for others, use more caution, verbalize the reasons for their conclusions, identify more as team players, and be aware of existing rules or conventions.

DIRECTORS AT A GLANCE

- need to be in charge, dislike inaction
- act quickly and decisively
- think logically
- want facts and highlights
- strive for results
- need personal freedom to manage self and others
- like changes
- prefer to delegate details
- cool, independent, and competitive
- low tolerance for feelings, attitudes, and advice of others
- work quickly and impressively alone
- want to be recognized for their accomplishments
- have a tendency to engage in arguments and conflict
- have good administrative skills

THE THINKER
·

Thinkers are both indirect and controlling. They're analytical, persistent, systematic problem-solvers. They can also be seen as aloof, picky, and critical. Thinkers are security-conscious and have a high need to be right, often leading them to an overreliance on the collection of data. In their quest for information they tend to ask many questions about specifics, and their actions and decisions tend to be extremely cautious. Although they are great problem-solvers, Thinkers could be better decision-makers. They are slow to reach a decision, but given a strict deadline, they will rarely miss it.

The primary concern of the cautious Thinker is accuracy. This often means that emotions take a back seat since they are subjective and tend to distort objectivity. Their biggest fear is of uncontrolled emotions and irrational acts which might prevent the achievement of their goals. They are uncomfortable with emotionality and irrationality in others. Thinkers strive to avoid embarrassment by attempting to control both themselves and their emotions. They are careful to avoid risk.

Thinkers tend to be serious and orderly and are likely to be perfectionists. They tend to focus on the details and the process of work and become irritated by surprises and "glitches." Their theme is, "Notice my efficiency," and their emphasis is on compliance and working within existing guidelines to promote quality in products or service.

Thinkers like organization and structure and dislike too much involvement with other people. They work slowly and precisely by themselves and prefer objective, task-oriented, intellectual work environments. They are precise, detail-oriented, disciplined about time, and often critical of their own performance. They tend to be skeptical and like to see things in writing. They like problem-solving activities and work best under controlled circumstances.

The primary strengths of Thinkers are their accuracy, dependability, independence, follow-through, and organization. Their primary weaknesses are their procrastinating and conservative nature, which promotes their tendency to be picky and overcautious. They tend to gravitate toward such occupations as accounting, engineering, computer programming, the hard sciences (chemistry, physics, math), systems analysis, and architecture.

The greatest irritations for Thinkers are disorganized, illogical people. In business environments, they want others to be credible, professional, sincere, and courteous. In social environments, they like others to be pleasant and sincere.

Thinkers generally have offices with highly organized or clear desk tops and charts, graphs, exhibits, or pictures pertaining to the job on the walls. They are noncontact people who are not fond of huggers and touchers and who prefer a cool handshake or a brief telephone call. This preference is reflected in the functional but uninviting arrangement of their desks and chairs.

To increase flexibility, Thinkers need to openly show concern for and appreciation of others, occasionally try shortcuts and time savers, and try to adjust more readily to change and disorganization. They also work to improve timely decision-making and the initiation of new projects, to compromise with the opposition, to state unpopular decisions, and to use policies more as guidelines than as rigid decrees.

THINKERS AT A GLANCE

- think logically and analytically
- need data
- need to be right
- like organization and structure
- ask many questions about specific details
- prefer objective, task-oriented, intellectual work environment
- need to understand the process
- are cautious decision-makers
- prefer to do things themselves
- work slowly and precisely alone
- like to be admired for their accuracy
- avoid conflict
- like to contemplate
- have good problem-solving skills

THE RELATER

Relaters are supporting and indirect. They are the most people-oriented of all of the four styles. Having close, friendly, personal, first-name relationships with others is one of their most important objectives. They dislike interpersonal conflict so much that they sometimes say what they think other people want to hear. They have tremendous counseling skills and are extremely supportive. People feel good just being with Relaters. Relaters are excellent listeners and generally develop relationships with people who are also good listeners. As a result, they have strong networks of people who are willing to be mutually supportive. While Relaters tend to be relatively unassertive, warm, supportive, and reliable, they are sometimes seen by others, however, as compliant, soft-hearted, and acquiescent.

Relaters seek security and, like Thinkers, are slow at taking action and making decisions. This pace stems from their desire to avoid risky and unknown situations. Before they take action or make a decision, they have to know how other people feel about the situation.

The focus of Relaters is on getting acquainted and building trust. They are irritated by pushy, aggressive behavior. Their theme is, "Notice how well-liked I am." They ask about any proposal, "How will it affect my personal circumstances and the camaraderie of the group?" They are cooperative, steady workers and excellent team players.

The primary strengths of Relaters are relating to, caring for, and loving others. Their primary weaknesses are that they are somewhat unassertive, overly sensitive, and easily bullied. Their ideal occupations cluster around the helping professions such as counseling, teaching, social work, the ministry, psychology, nursing, and human-resource development. They generally make good parents.

In the business environment, Relaters like others to be courteous and friendly and to share responsibilities. In a social environment, they like others to be genuine and friendly.

As for environmental clues, Relaters' desks contain family pictures and other personal items. Their office walls have personal slogans, family or group pictures, serene pictures, or mementos. Relaters are high-touch in a high-tech world. They give their offices a friendly, warm ambiance and arrange seating in a side-by-side, cooperative way.

To increase flexibility, Relaters need to say no occasionally, to attend to the completion of tasks without oversensitivity to the feelings of others, to be willing to reach beyond their comfort zone to set goals that require some stretch and risk, and to delegate to others.

RELATERS AT A GLANCE

- concerned with stability
- think logically
- want documentation and facts
- need personal involvement
- take action and make decisions slowly
- need to know the step-by-step sequence
- avoid risks and changes
- dislike interpersonal conflict
- work slowly and cohesively with others
- try to accommodate others
- want tranquility and peace
- seek security and belongingness
- enjoy teamwork
- want to know they're appreciated
- have good counseling skills

As you begin to understand the four styles and how they act and respond to the world around them, you will be able to better understand your own style and identify the style of the people around you. The chart on page 44 offers some quick guidelines. The next chapter will help you develop more powerful communication skills as you learn even more about the communication preferences of each style.

THE FOUR STYLES AT A GLANCE

Relater
Relationship-oriented
Moves, acts, and speaks
  slowly
Avoids risk
Wants tranquility and peace
Enjoys teamwork
Good counseling skills

Socializer
Relationship-oriented
Moves, acts, and speaks
  quickly
Risk-taker
Wants excitement and change
Enjoys the spotlight
Good persuasive skills

Thinker
Task-oriented
Moves, acts, and speaks
  slowly
Wants to be accurate
Enjoys solitary, intellectual
  work
Cautious decision-makers
Good problem-solving skills

Director
Task-oriented
Moves, acts, and speaks
  quickly
Wants to be in charge
Gets results through others

Makes decisions quickly
Good administrative skills

4

Communicating
with the
Four Styles

The real value in understanding the four styles and their communication preferences is to be able to adapt your communication in a way that improves the reception of your message. When you understand your own style and the style of the person you are communicating with, you can adapt your "sending" style to better match the "receiving" style of the other person. Understanding style will help you improve your communication in all work situations—one-on-one, meetings, sales presentations, employee reviews, problem-solving sessions—as well as in personal relationships.

Knowing how to adapt your communication to each of the different styles is the key to successful communication. However, adaptability requires not only the knowledge of how to adapt to each style but the willingness to communicate in ways other than your normal, preferred mode. It requires making strategic adjustments to your methods of communicating and behaving, based on the particular needs of the relationship at a particular time. It means making the choice to speak the language of the person you are with.

Everyone can learn to become more adaptable to other people's styles. Here is a general guideline for increasing your adaptability:

If you are a . . .	Lower your emphasis on . . .	Develop and demonstrate more . . .
Director	Control of other people and conditions	Supportive skills and actions such as listening, questioning, and positive reinforcement
Socializer	Need for approval from other people or groups	Directive skills and actions such as self-assertion, conflict-resolution, negotiations
Relater	Resistance to try or seek out new or different opportunities	Directive skills and actions such as negotiation and divergent thinking
Thinker	Unnecessary perfectionism and the tendency to focus on weaknesses	Supportive skills and actions such as empathic listening, positive reinforcement of others, involvement with others with complementary strengths

Adapting your communication doesn't mean *imitating* the other person's style of communicating. It does mean adjusting your Supportingness, Controllingness, Directness, and Indirectness to be more in tune with the other person's preference. For example, if you are a Socializer speaking to a Director, your normal communication pattern will probably seem unfocused and too social. The Director might think the conversation is just "chitchat." By reviewing the Director profile, you can see that you would benefit by getting directly to the point and staying focused on the task at hand. In this example, you are both Direct so the pace of your communication is in tune but your priority preferences are different. As a Socializer, you are a Supporting person and have a relationship-orientation. The Director is a Controlling person and has a task-orientation.

ADAPTING TO STYLES

■

The most effective way to communicate is to know the style of the person you are communicating with and then adapt to his or her specific communication preferences. The following is a brief description of adaptations that can be made for each style:

SOCIALIZERS (DIRECT, SUPPORTING): Socializers talk, move, and make decisions quickly. They are relationship-oriented. Here are a few ways to communicate effectively with them:

- Supporting their opinions, ideas, and dreams
- Allowing the discussion to flow and occasionally go off on tangents
- Being entertaining and fast moving
- Being interested in them
- Avoiding conflict and arguments
- Agreeing and making notes of the specifics of any agreement
- Complimenting their appearance, creative ideas, persuasiveness, and charisma
- Allowing them to "get things off their chests"

DIRECTORS (DIRECT, CONTROLLING): Directors talk, move, and make decisions quickly. They are task-oriented. Here are adaptations that are effective with them:

- Supporting their goals and objectives
- Talking about the desired results
- Keeping your communication businesslike
- Recognizing their ideas rather than them personally
- Being precise, efficient, and well organized
- Providing them with clearly described options with supporting analysis
- Arguing on facts, not feelings, when disagreements occur

THINKERS (INDIRECT, CONTROLLING): Thinkers talk, move, and make decisions more slowly. They are task-oriented. Here are adaptations that are effective with them:

- Being thorough and well prepared
- Supporting their organized, thoughtful approach
- Supporting their need to be accurate and logical
- Complimenting their efficiency, thought processes, and organization
- Demonstrating through actions rather than words
- Being systematic, exact, organized, and prepared
- Describing a process in detail and explaining how it will produce results
- Asking questions and letting them show you how much they know
- Allowing time for deliberation and analysis
- Answering questions and providing details and analysis
- Listing advantages and disadvantages of any plan
- Providing solid, tangible, factual evidence

RELATERS (INDIRECT, SUPPORTING): Relaters talk, move, and make decisions more slowly. Like Socializers, they are relationship-oriented. Here are adaptations that are effective with them:

- Being warm and sincere
- Supporting their feelings by showing personal interest
- Assuming that they'll take everything personally
- Allowing them time to develop trust in you
- Moving along in an informal, slow manner
- Actively listening
- Discussing personal feelings in the event of a disagreement
- Discussing and supporting the relationship
- Complimenting their teamwork, their relationships with others, and their ability to "get along"

ONE-DIMENSIONAL ADAPTING

·

Sometimes you may want to adapt your communication style but you're not sure what style the other person has. Even if you only

know where he or she falls on one of the dimensions (Direct/
Indirect; Supporting/Controlling) you can move in that direction
and improve your communication effectiveness.

INCREASING DIRECTNESS: If the person is Direct (moves
and speaks quickly; readily expresses thoughts and feelings), you
can increase the directness of your communication by the
following:

- Speaking at a faster pace
- Initiating conversations and decisions
- Giving recommendations and not asking for opinions
- Using direct statements rather than roundabout questions
- Communicating with a strong, confident voice
- Challenging and tactfully disagreeing when appropriate
- Facing conflict openly but not initiating it
- Increasing eye contact

INCREASING INDIRECTNESS: If the person is Indirect
(moves and speaks more slowly; is cautious in expressing personal
thoughts and feelings and in making decisions), you can increase
your Indirectness by the following:

- Talking and making decisions more slowly
- Seeking and acknowledging the opinions of others
- Sharing decision-making and leadership
- Showing less energy; being more "mellow"
- Not interrupting
- Providing pauses to allow the other person to speak
- Refraining from criticizing, challenging, or acting pushy
- Choosing words carefully when disagreeing

INCREASING SUPPORTINGNESS: If the person is Supporting (motivated by relationships and feelings), you can increase
your Supportingness by the following:

- Sharing your feelings and letting your emotions show
- Responding to the expression of others' feelings
- Paying personal compliments
- Taking time to develop the relationship
- Using friendly language

- Communicating more, loosening up, and standing closer
- Being willing to digress from the agenda, going with the flow

INCREASING CONTROLLINGNESS: If the person is Controlling (motivated by the task at hand and accomplishing goals), you can increase your Controllingness by the following:

- Getting right to the task or the bottom line
- Maintaining more of a logical, factual orientation
- Keeping to the agenda
- Leaving when the work is done; not wasting time
- Not initiating physical contact
- Downplaying enthusiasm and body movement
- Using businesslike language

DYNAMIC COMMUNICATION REQUIRES ADAPTABILITY
·

Throughout this section, we learned some of the common problem areas of communication. But powerful communication depends on more than just avoiding the pitfalls. Dynamic communication that persuades and influences requires a speaker and a listener who are on the same wavelength. They have to be speaking the same style language. By understanding the four styles and the way they affect communication and behavior, you have the basis for expanding your communication potential. As you learn to adapt your communication to your listeners' style language, you improve your ability to communicate your ideas and feelings. You develop better relationships, avoid misunderstandings, and increase your effectiveness. You become *multilingual* in style communication.

In Part II, you will learn more about how to make your verbal communication more powerful through active listening, asking questions, and verifying communication through feedback, as well as how to resolve conflicts.

II

VERBAL COMMUNICATION

A man cannot speak but he judges and reveals himself. With his will, or against his will, he draws his portrait to the eye of others by every word.

—RALPH WALDO EMERSON

Our ability to put our thoughts, feelings, hopes, and dreams into words is the foundation of verbal communication. But, as we discussed in chapter 1, communication is a two-way process that involves both sending and receiving messages. Throughout our education process, we learn how to put our thoughts and feelings into words—how to send a message. Very little of our educational process is devoted to improving our ability to receive messages. *Receiving* is far more than merely hearing.

> *I know you think you understand what I said. But I don't think you understand that what I said is not what I meant.*

While you may not often hear the above statement in actual words, I'm sure you have experienced it. *Receiving* is about the message (both the words and the intent) being transmitted accurately from sender to receiver. *Receiving* is about listening for content and intent. *Receiving* is about asking questions and providing feedback to insure accurate transmission of the message. The communication process is not complete until you have verified the accuracy of the message received.

In the last section we discussed how to adapt the messages we send to the four styles and in the next section we discuss how to make sure we are sending a powerful nonverbal message. This section will be devoted to the skills needed to make sure we are accurately and effectively receiving the messages sent to us and that the messages we send are accurately received. In the following chapters you will learn how to improve your listening skills, how to ask questions, and how to use feedback to make sure your message is accurately received. You will also learn how to resolve conflicts effectively.

5

ACTIVE LISTENING

It is better to remain quiet and be thought a fool than to speak and remove all doubt.

—ANONYMOUS

Some time ago, a team of professors at Loyola University in Chicago participated in a study to determine the single most important attribute of an effective manager. For a year and a half, they queried hundreds of businesses across the country and finally decided that *listening* is a manager's most important skill.

Ineffective listening is one of the most frequent causes of misunderstandings, mistakes, jobs that need to be redone, and lost sales and customers. The consequences of poor listening are lower employee productivity, missed sales, unhappy customers, and billions of dollars of increased costs and lost profits. Poor listening is a factor in low employee morale and increased turnover because employees do not feel their managers listen to their needs, suggestions, or complaints. Ineffective listening is acknowledged to be one of the primary contributors to divorce and the inability of a parent and child to openly communicate. And, finally, people view poor listeners as boorish, self-centered, disinterested, preoccupied, and socially unacceptable.

So, with all these negative consequences, why don't we listen more effectively? Here are five basic reasons:

LISTENING IS HARD WORK. It's more than just keeping quiet. An *active* listener registers increased blood pressure, a higher pulse rate, and more perspiration. It means concentrating on the other person rather than on yourself. As a result, a lot of people just don't do it.

COMPETITION. In today's society there is enormous competition for our attention from advertisements, radio, TV, movies, reading material, and more. With all this incoming stimuli, we have learned to screen out information that we deem irrelevant. Sometimes we also screen out things that are important to us.

THE RUSH TO ACTION. We think we know what someone is going to say, and we want to act on his words. We jump in and interrupt, not taking the time that is required to hear people out.

SPEED DIFFERENCE. The difference between speech speed and thought speed creates a listening gap. The average person speaks at about 135–175 words a minute, but can listen to 400–500 words a minute. That difference between listening speed and speaking speed is time spent jumping to conclusions, daydreaming, planning a reply, or mentally arguing with the speaker. At least that's how poor listeners spend their time.

LACK OF TRAINING. We do more listening than speaking, reading, or writing, yet we receive almost no formal education in listening. Many people assume they are good listeners; few actually are. The average employee spends about three-quarters of each working day in verbal communications. Nearly half of that is spent on listening. Incredibly, on the average, the typical employee's listening effectiveness is only 25 percent. In other words, three-fourths of everything the employee hears is distorted in some way or quickly forgotten.

The normal, untrained listener is likely to understand and retain only about 50 percent of a conversation, and this relatively poor percentage drops to an even less impressive 25 percent retention rate forty-eight hours later. This means that recall of a particular conversation that took place more than a couple of days ago will always be incomplete and usually inaccurate. No wonder people can seldom agree about what has been discussed!

Managers who are poor listeners miss numerous opportunities. They miss current or emerging problems. They often miss the essence of the message being sent. This leads them to propose solutions that are faulty or inappropriate. Often they address the wrong problem altogether. Lack of listening by the manager creates tension and distrust in the employee. A cycle is created—if the manager doesn't listen, the employee stops listening. This downward spiral creates the potential for organizational disaster. Following any major problem, there will always be one or more people who say, "I tried to tell them." Studies of the Challenger tragedy show that there may have been eleven hundred people who knew about the potential danger of failure of the O-ring. A responsive listening organization might have heard the warnings in time to stop the disaster.

It's hard to realize that an activity as simple as listening could have such a powerful impact on an organization. Here's a recap of some of the bottom-line benefits of better listening:

IT IMPROVES RELATIONSHIPS. When you listen to somebody, it makes them feel good about you, which leads to increased trust and credibility and an increased willingness toward cooperation. In organizations, this generally means a reduction in turnover and more of a commitment to the organization's goals.

THERE ARE FEWER MISUNDERSTANDINGS. Fewer errors result in lower costs, better products and services, and higher profits.

BETTER UNDERSTANDING. Better listening improves the transfer of information, improves team work, builds morale, and leads to higher productivity.

FOUR LEVELS OF LISTENING
▪

People typically listen at one of four basic levels of attentiveness. Each category requires a particular depth of concentration and sensitivity on the part of the listener. These levels are not distinct lines of difference but general categories into which people fall. Depending on the situation or circumstance in which listeners find themselves, these categories may even overlap or interchange. As you move from the first, to the second, to the third, to the fourth level, your potential for understanding, trust, and effective communication increases.

THE NONLISTENER. At this first level, the listener does not hear the speaker at all. In fact, no effort is made to hear what the other person is saying. The nonlistener is recognized by her blank stare and nervous mannerisms and gestures. Sometimes she fakes attention while thinking about unrelated matters. The nonlistener wants to do all or most of the speaking. She constantly interrupts and always has to have the last word. She is usually considered a social boor and a know-it-all, perceived as insensitive and nonunderstanding. The nonlistener is typically disliked or merely "tolerated."

THE MARGINAL LISTENER. The marginal listener hears the sounds and words but not the meaning and intent. The message is toyed with, not really heard. The marginal listener is a superficial listener. She stays on the surface of the argument or problem, never risking going deeper. She is too busy preparing what she wants to say next to listen to what is being said to her now. The marginal listener is easily distracted by her own thinking and by outside occurrences. In fact, many marginal listeners selectively look for outside distractions, so that they have an excuse to draw themselves away from the conversation. They prefer to evade difficult or technical presentations or discussions, and when they do listen, they tend to listen only for the data, the bottom line, instead of the main ideas.

Marginal listening is hazardous because there is enormous room for misunderstanding since the listener is only superficially concentrating on what is being said. At least at level one—non-listening—the speaker receives many noticeable clues that the listener is not attending to the conversation. However, at the marginal listening level, the speaker may be lulled into a false sense of security that she is in fact being listened to and understood. This is not the case. Television sitcoms thrive on the humorous possibilities of marginal listening. In real life, it isn't funny; it's frustrating. And in the workplace, it's a source of low morale, misunderstandings, errors, and problems.

THE EVALUATIVE LISTENER. More concentration and attention are required at this level. The evaluative listener is actively trying to hear what the speaker is saying but isn't making an effort to understand the speaker's intent. She tends to be a logical listener, more concerned about content than feelings. She tends to remain emotionally detached from the conversation. She evaluates the message strictly on the basis of the words delivered, totally ignoring that part of the message that is carried in the speaker's vocal intonation, body language, and facial expressions. She is good at deciphering the verbal element, the words, facts, and statistics, but lacking in sensitivity, empathy, and the true understanding that comes from being able to understand the other "Vs"—the vocal and visual elements.

The evaluative listener believes that she understands the speaker, but the speaker does not feel understood. This phenomenon is a common byproduct of the tremendous speed discrepancy at which a human can listen and think. As discussed earlier, while a person speaks at an average rate of 120 to 160 words per minute, the mind is capable of listening and thinking at a rate up to four times that speed. The evaluative listener is using that time gap to think about his response or to notice the soup stain on the speaker's tie or to count the number of times the speaker says "you know." Because this listening speed gap is so natural to the way our minds work, this is the level of listening that people employ in most everyday conversations. It's a truly difficult habit to break.

THE ACTIVE LISTENER. This is unquestionably the most comprehensive and, potentially, the most powerful level of listening. It is also the most demanding and tiring because it requires the deepest level of concentration, attention, and mental, as well as emotional, processing effort.

The active listener refrains from coming to judgment about the speaker's message, instead focusing on understanding her point of view. Attention is concentrated on the thoughts and feelings of the other person as well as the spoken word. To listen in this manner requires our initial suspension of our own thoughts and feelings in order to give attention solely to the message and intent of the speaker. It means figuratively "putting yourself into someone else's shoes." It also requires that the listener send verbal and nonverbal feedback to the speaker indicating that what is being said is really being absorbed.

THE CARESS MODEL
•

In order to develop the highest level of listening proficiency, you need to develop six separate skills. We have combined them into an easy-to-remember model expressed by the acronym CARESS. These letters stand for the six steps that will help you become an active listener, whether you're listening to a keynote speaker, your boss, a meeting leader, your coworkers, or a friend or family member:

C—CONCENTRATE. Focus your attention on the speaker and only on the speaker. That will help you eliminate environmental "noise" and help you "receive" the message clearly.

A—ACKNOWLEDGE. When you acknowledge your speaker, you demonstrate your interest and attention. Your acknowledgment encourages the speaker and actually helps the speaker send a clearer message.

R—RESEARCH. Gather information about your speaker, his interests and objectives. This will help you understand the message, ask questions that prompt a more in-depth conversation, and respond to the speaker in a way that promotes communication.

E—EXERCISE EMOTIONAL CONTROL. Deal with highly charged messages in a thoughtful manner and wait until the entire message is received before reacting. Regardless of how provocative the message is, you must concentrate on understanding it first.

S—SENSE THE NONVERBAL MESSAGE. What is the speaker saying with his body language and gestures? Try to understand the vocal and visual messages as well as the words being spoken.

S—STRUCTURE. Structure or organize the information as you receive it. This is what you should do with the time generated by the gap between speaking and hearing speeds. By organizing the information as you receive it, you will improve your retention and understanding of the material.

CONCENTRATE
■

The first step in active listening is to concentrate completely on the speaker. The listener must eliminate noise and distractions. These distractions, or barriers to listening, come in three major categories. Each category has negative effects on listening and communication. The categories are:

- external environmental barriers
- external speaker-related barriers
- internal listener-related barriers

EXTERNAL ENVIRONMENTAL BARRIERS to listening include noises in the room, other people talking at the same time, poor acoustics, bad odors, an uncomfortable room (too cold or too hot or too humid or an uncomfortable chair), visual distractions (such as passersby or outside traffic), physical disruptions such as telephone calls or visitors, or having a radio or T.V. on while you're trying to talk or listen.

EXTERNAL SPEAKER-RELATED BARRIERS include the way the speaker is dressed, poor grooming, disturbing mannerisms (such as a nervous twitch or jiggling change in his pocket), facial expressions or body language on the part of the speaker, and the speaker's accent or speaking style.

INTERNAL LISTENER-RELATED BARRIERS include two types. One is internal *physical* barriers. If it's close to lunch or quitting time, people are going to listen less or be preoccupied. If somebody has a headache or fatigue, is under time constraints or much pressure, or is in pain or discomfort, the likelihood is that the person is not going to listen with full attention.

The second is internal *psychological* barriers, which include your inner voice that prompts you to think while another person is talking, being close-minded to new ideas or material you haven't heard before, boredom, daydreaming, personal values and beliefs that might prevent you from listening, past experiences, and future expectations. Another is physical proximity to the speaker. If somebody is either too close or too far away from you, it may make you feel uncomfortable and block your ability to concentrate.

All of these barriers create incredible distractions which prevent the message from getting from the sender to the receiver. In order to begin lowering these barriers, we have to assess whether they are within our control or not within our control.

Which of these barriers are, to a great extent, within our control? We have a great deal of control over the external environmental variables. We have little or no control over speaker-related variables. Internal psychological and physical barriers fall somewhere in between.

• • •

There are ways you can eliminate or minimize external environmental noise:

First, try to create a receptive listening environment, a place that has as few auditory or visual distractions as possible.

Second, you want to set up a private, quiet, comfortable setting, especially in terms of temperature and seating. If you're meeting with someone at his or her place of business, you have less control over the external environment, but if there are a lot of distractions, such as phones ringing or interruptions, you can recommend moving into a meeting room with more privacy. If that's not possible, look for a receptive listening environment on neutral territory such as a quiet out-of-the-way restaurant.

Third, you need to avoid violating another person's personal space. Some people are "contact-oriented" while others are "non-contact-oriented." Keep in mind that when you're talking to people, some may be very open and like to communicate in close proximity, while others may tend to be more self-contained and want to keep more physical distance. If you notice that the person you're talking with keeps backing away from you and seldom initiates physical contact like handshakes, you are probably dealing with a noncontact person. Review the material on the four styles to help you identify the person's style and know how to respond to the person's needs.

When you cannot avoid distractions, minimize them by totally focusing on the speaker, concentrating and paying attention. There are four specific techniques that will help you concentrate and focus while listening.

- **DEEP BREATHING.** When you feel that you have to interrupt the speaker for *any* reason, take a long deep leisurely breath in. Try it now, and as you're doing it, try to speak. It's impossible, isn't it?
- **DECIDE TO LISTEN.** Make a conscious decision to listen to the other person. Ralph Waldo Emerson once said that everyone was his superior in some way and he could learn something from each person. So, pay attention and look for the things in conversation that are interesting or useful.
- **PARAPHRASE.** Mentally paraphrase what the speaker is say-

ing. This will prevent you from daydreaming on irrelevant and superfluous topics. Try to echo, rephrase, evaluate, anticipate, and review what the speaker is saying so that you focus and concentrate on the speaker instead of yourself.

- **EYE CONTACT.** Maintain eye contact. It's called the hitchhiking theory: where your eyes focus, your ears follow. You are most likely to listen to what you are looking at.

So, when you cannot eliminate a distraction, use these four techniques of applied concentration to help you overcome them.

ACKNOWLEDGE
■

The second part of the CARESS model is *acknowledging* the speaker, showing her that you're listening. To understand how to acknowledge a speaker, think about how you like to be listened to.

What are the most important things that you like to see in people when *they* are listening to *you*? Here are four things most people mention:

- Eye contact
- Verbal responses and participation such as asking questions and vocal prompts such as, "hmm," "yeah," "really," "go on"
- Other acknowledging gestures like smiling, nodding of the head, leaning forward with interest, sitting directly facing the speaker, and using appropriate facial expressions and body language. All of these gestures project very positive acknowledgment and people like to see that.
- Clarifying points by asking questions or restating the point to make sure it was received accurately

When you acknowledge the speaker, you are letting her know that her message is being received. You are giving her positive feedback that you are interested in what she is saying and that you understand her message.

RESEARCH

·

The third part of CARESS, *researching,* serves many purposes. In most contexts, researching means getting information out of books or files. As a listening skill, though, it allows you to clarify a message, enlarge upon a subject, or go into a particular topic in more depth. Researching allows you to get the speaker to change the direction of the conversation or prompt the speaker to "vent" feelings of anger, excitement, enthusiasm, and so on. It also allows you to support and reinforce particular parts of a speaker's message.

In the context of listening, researching is what you do to keep a conversation a two-way flow of communication by asking questions and making clarifying statements. It uses the information-gathering techniques of questioning and feedback. This two-way flow of communication facilitates a meeting of the minds between the speaker and the listener.

The person who doesn't participate in the conversation through questions, feedback statements, and comments will make the speaker feel uncomfortable by creating an information imbalance. An information imbalance is when one person does all the talking and provides all the information while the other person simply listens and takes it all in. After a while, the speaker gets concerned that the listener knows too much about her and she doesn't know anything about the listener. This can create tension and suspicion on the part of the speaker.

The ability to ask the right questions at the right time and respond appropriately to the speaker is an essential and integral part of active listening. Skillful researching simplifies the listener's job because it gets the speaker to "open up," to reveal inner feelings, motives, needs, goals, and desires. (The next chapter gives you a detailed guide for developing the art of questioning.)

Another technique of researching is using *empathy statements.* These statements consist of three specific parts:

- tentative statement
- defining the feeling
- putting it into its situational context

An example of an empathy statement would be, "It seems to me that you're very frustrated because you can't get the product to work the way you want it to work." In this empathy statement, the phrase "it seems to me" is what we call a tentative statement. The phrase "you're very frustrated" attempts to define the feeling. And the phrase "because you can't get the product to work the way you want it to work" is putting it into its situational context— the situation that caused you to experience the feeling of frustration.

Empathy statements are a good way to get people to open up and share their feelings and thoughts with you. Why? By restating the speaker's message, the empathy statement proves you're paying attention, which provides encouragement for the speaker. The empathy statement gives the speaker an opportunity to refine, expand, or correct the message. And, by affirming the speaker's feelings, empathy statements help build an emotional bond between the speaker and the listener.

EXERCISING EMOTIONAL CONTROL
•

What causes an emotional overreaction? It's generally prompted by something about the speaker herself or has something to do with what the speaker says. Often differences in values, beliefs, attitudes, education, speed of delivery, image, and a host of other things cause a disruption in communication between the speaker and the listener.

The speaker may have certain dress or speech patterns, or other idiosyncrasies, that may totally turn off the listener or cause the listener to receive the speaker's message negatively. For instance, going to a bank for a loan dressed in too-casual clothing might negatively influence the bank manager. On the other hand, wearing a high-powered Wall Street suit might put a rural business person on the defensive against a not-to-be-trusted city slicker.

A person's accent can cause an emotional reaction in the listener. For instance, there is no doubt that many people make value judgments about the intelligence of a person with a Brooklyn accent versus someone with a Harvard sound.

Loaded words often cause severe emotional overreaction on the part of the listener. Whenever a speaker uses ethnic, racial, religious, or political words or humor, it's likely to cause an emotional reaction in many listeners.

If, as listeners, we focus on the provocative aspects of the speaker's appearance, style, accent, tone of voice, or vocabulary, we often miss the true substance of what is being said. By exercising emotional control, you can avoid blocking the meaning of the speaker's message. You do this by *recognizing* and *redirecting* your negative emotional reactions.

RECOGNIZE AND REDIRECT. You need to learn to *recognize* an emotional reaction coming on by monitoring any increased heartbeat, respiration, or facial flush—physical things that typically happen when you're getting upset about something. When your emotional reaction begins, there is an almost irresistible tendency to interrupt, to butt in, to argue. You lose your train of thought. The first step in controlling this response is to recognize it.

Then, you can learn to *redirect* your negative emotional reaction through the following techniques:

- **PAUSE.** Pause or delay your response or reaction. Counting to ten or taking in a long, leisurely deep breath can calm you down.
- **COMMON GROUND.** Try to think about what you have in common with the speaker, rather than focusing on what's different.
- **VISUALIZE CALM.** Imagine yourself calm and relaxed. Think of a time in your past when you were feeling laid back, calm, on top of the world, and feeling incredibly great. Construct a mental picture of that experience in as much detail as you can.

For more information on exercising control, see chapter 9.

SENSE THE NONVERBAL MESSAGE
■

Sensing, the fifth major component of listening, focuses on the vocal and visual parts of communication. Dr. Albert Mehrabian, author of *Silent Messages,* says that in face-to-face, social communication, about 90 percent of the message is carried through the vocal and the visual channels, with only 7 to 10 percent of the meaning carried through the actual words themselves—the verbal channel.

It is critical that we learn to recognize the nonverbal and vocal messages in our communications—the messages we send as well as the messages sent to us. The next section of this book details the use of nonverbal messages and body language.

STRUCTURE

Structuring is the last segment of our CARESS formula. This is where we listen, primarily to the verbal component—the content—of somebody's message. As we said earlier, there is a time gap created by the difference in listening and speaking speeds. We can use that time to structure the message we're listening to. Structuring revolves around three primary activities—indexing, sequencing, and comparing.

INDEXING is taking mental or written notes of (1) the topic or the major idea, (2) the key points being discussed, and (3) the reasons, subpoints, and supporting points. Indexing is made easier by listening for transitional words. Here are samples of transitional words or phrases:

> "What I want to talk to you about today is . . ." (what follows is probably the main idea, the subject, or the topic);
> "First," (generally followed by "Second," "Third," and succeeding numerical transitions for each of the following key points);
> "For example," or "let me elaborate on that," (generally tells you that a rationale, a subpoint, or a supporting point is likely to follow).

SEQUENCING is listening for order or priority. Sometimes someone tells you something in which the order is very important, or you're given instructions or directions where the order is crucial. So in sequencing, as in indexing, you want to listen for transitional words like "first," "second," "third," etc. If you have any doubt or confusion, check back with the speaker with a comment such as, "Let me make sure I understand what should be done first," or "Let me make sure I understand the order you're describing." Feedback and clarification will help you get the proper sequence.

COMPARING is trying to discriminate between what is fact and what is assumption; discriminate between pros and cons; discriminate between advantages and disadvantages; and discriminate between positives or negatives. You also want to listen for consistency, trying to determine if what the person is saying now is consistent with what was said previously, because sometimes people contradict themselves.

One demonstration of active listening and structuring is taking notes on what the speaker is saying. An excellent technique for note-taking is mindmapping, which is explained in chapter 17. This technique helps you take notes quickly without breaking the flow of the conversation.

THE ACTIVE LISTENING ATTITUDE
·

The skills needed to improve listening are relatively simple to learn and implement. Perhaps the harder task is developing the active listening attitude. You do this by first understanding that *listening is as powerful as speech*. What someone says to you is just as critical as what you have to say to them.

A second attitude you need to develop is that *listening saves time*. People who listen actively find that they experience fewer mistakes, fewer interpersonal misunderstandings, less employee and customer turnover, and fewer false starts. We can develop long-term relationships by actively listening to each other.

A third and final attitude that you need to acquire is that *listening is important and worthwhile with everyone*. When you believe that you can learn something from everyone you meet, you will approach listening with a new enthusiasm.

With active listening, you will have fewer communication glitches, your relationships will improve, and productivity and morale will go up in your organization. The payoff for improving the simple skill of listening is enormous. But, while listening skills are simple, they are not particularly easy to implement. For most of us, it means breaking a lifetime of poor listening habits.

Using the CARESS model can help you break through this barrier of poor listening. As you begin to *Concentrate, Acknowledge, Research, Exercise Emotional Control, Sense the Nonverbal Message,* and *Structure,* your ability to accurately receive the messages sent to you will improve.

6

THE ART OF
ASKING QUESTIONS

What time is it?
What do you think about this project?
Can you support this decision?
What can I do to help you?
How would you deal with this problem?
Are we in agreement on the process?
What's your objective?
How do you feel about this?
Do you have a dog?

The world is full of questions . . . good questions, silly questions, important questions, and offensive questions. Questions can build rapport and trust or foster suspicion and dislike. Questions can open up a conversation or slam it closed. Questions can generate information or send the conversation shooting off on a tangent. Questions are the heart of communication. They pump fresh life into conversations.

Asking good questions is particularly important in organizations where working together to achieve a common purpose depends upon the members of the organizations understanding each other clearly. Asking questions about how things are done, why they're done, who's responsible for doing them, or when they're due form the basis of organizational effectiveness. Imagine launching a new product, putting together a budget, improving a process, implementing a new policy, or reviewing employee performance without asking questions. The Information Age couldn't exist without questions.

Because questions are so important, our education system takes great pains to teach us the fine art of asking questions. . . . No? . . . Why not? Probably because the average three-year-old asks 4.2 questions per minute. Everyone assumes we know all we need to know about asking questions by the time we learn what a question mark is. After all, isn't that what a question is, a group of words followed by a question mark? That may be the definition of a question but comparing that to the art of asking questions is like saying that if you can spell "car," you're ready for the Indy 500.

This chapter will help you understand how to use questions to improve your communication, what types of questions to use and when to use them, and the strategies and techniques of artful questioning. Being able to ask the right question at the right time is a critical piece of the communication process.

WHY DO WE ASK QUESTIONS?

·

The standard response to that question is "Because we want to know something." But questioning has a much richer payoff than just information transfer. There's an old (but apparently true) story about a salesman who was scheduled to appear on the Johnny Carson show. As he was sitting in the green room, the producer came in and started asking him about his approach to sales. The producer, stubbornly skeptical, finally demanded: "Well, then, sell me something!" The salesman looked around the room and spied a large ashtray on the table. The following conversation occurred:

Salesman: Do you like that ashtray?

Producer: Yeah, sure.

Salesman: What do you like about it?

Producer: Well, it's big enough to hold all the ashes of the people who come through here every day.

Salesman: What else do you like about it?

Producer: Well, it's a nice color and it matches the decor in here.

Salesman: How much do you think an ashtray like this is worth to you?

Producer: I don't know . . . maybe $20.

Salesman: Sold!

With just a few questions, the salesman was able to find out why the producer would buy the ashtray and what price he would be willing to pay for it. While sales aren't always this easy, the story illustrates how powerful questions are as a tool for getting information. In fact, questions are the heart of any information-gathering process. But they can also be used for many other reasons. Here are just a few of the reasons we ask questions:

To GAIN INFORMATION—information transfer depends on questions. *Who, what, where, when, why, how, how much* are all staples of information gathering.

To STIMULATE CONVERSATION—imagine attending a social function where no one could ask a question! No: *How are you? Have you heard . . . ? Did you see . . . ? Can you believe . . . ? What do you think . . . ?* It would be a pretty strange gathering.

To GAIN THE OTHER'S VIEWS—when you need to know what someone else is thinking, ask. *What do you think about . . . ? Can you tell me how you feel about . . . ?*

To CHECK AGREEMENT—what does the other person think about what you have discussed? *Do you think we're on the right track? Can you support this decision? Are we in agreement? Do you have any objections? How does this sound to you?*

To BUILD RAPPORT AND TRUST—rapport and trust are built by showing support for the other person's goals and objectives. *How can I help you? What can I do to help you meet your objectives? What would you like to accomplish? Tell me about your goals/dreams/objectives.*

TO VERIFY INFORMATION—sometimes what you hear is not what was meant. Asking for feedback is a critical part of the communication process. *Did I understand you to mean . . . ? Can I summarize this as . . . ?*

THE TWO MAJOR TYPES OF QUESTIONS
■

There are only two basic types of questions—closed and open. Each type is very important to the communication process. Closed questions are generally simple, information gathering questions. Response to a closed question is usually a "yes" or "no" or a very brief answer.

Typical closed questions are:

What time is it?
Did you finish the project?
Are you going to the meeting?
Can you work overtime tonight?
When did you first discover the problem?

Closed questions perform the following functions:

- They allow specific facts to be gathered.
  What color do you prefer?
- They are easy to answer and seldom intimidating.
  Will you be finished by 5:00 P.M.?
- They are useful in the feedback process where someone wants to check the accuracy or completeness of the communication.
  Have I got the information right?
- They can be used to gain commitment to a position.
  Does this seem right so far?
- They can be used to reinforce positive statements.
  This seems like a good plan, doesn't it?
- They can be used to direct the conversation to a desired topic or concern.
  Do you have time to talk about the budget?

Open questions are generally more stimulative and require longer, more complex answers. Open questions are used to draw out a wide range of responses on a broad topic. They often ask for opinions, thoughts, or feelings. Typical open questions are:

How did you feel about the meeting?
What could we do to make this project better?
How can we meet our objectives?
What's your opinion on the new marketing plan?
How important is it to you?

Open questions have the following characteristics:

- They cannot be answered by a simple yes or no.
  How do you think we could make this process work better?
  Not: *Do you think we could do this process better?*
- They usually begin with "what" or "how."
  What do you think about the new benefit policy?
- They do not lead the answer.
  Where could we make improvements in the new marketing plan?
  Not: *How much do you like our neat new marketing plan?*
- They draw out ideas and feelings.
  How do you feel about the reorganization of the department?
- They encourage elaboration on objectives, needs, wants, and problems.
  What do you think about the new employee review system?
- They promote self-discovery.
  How do you think the new process will work for your group?
- They stimulate thinking about your ideas.
  Where do you think we might run into problems with this idea?
- They allow a broad range of responses and styles.
  How would you change the policy?

It's important to know which kind of question—open or closed—to use to achieve your goals. Both are useful and can help you achieve several different purposes including:

FACT-FINDING—if you are looking for specific information and data, use closed questions that ask for the detail you need. *"What did you accomplish on the project?"* will generate more detail than *"Did you get a lot done?"* Take notes and verify that you understood the information correctly.

FEELING-FINDING—to understand a person's feeling about a subject generally requires an open question. *Are you happy about the project?* doesn't get the same response as the open-ended question: *How do you feel about the project?* Used properly, feeling-finding questions generate a lot of information about attitudes, convictions, and motivations. Feeling-finding questions are extremely powerful because they are so seldom asked . . . and the answers are carefully listened to even less frequently.

CLARIFYING—closed questions are used to verify your understanding of a conversation. *Do I understand you correctly? Are you referring to . . . ? Do you mean . . . ?* are examples of questions you can ask to make sure you understand the information being given to you.

EXPANDING—open questions are used to draw out further information on a topic. *Can you give me an example? Would you tell me more about that point? What else might be causing a problem?* are questions that continue to generate information about the subject.

DIRECTING—directing questions are generally closed and point the conversation toward a particular goal. *What was the other point you wanted to make? Can we go back and talk about your first item? Couldn't we postpone the decision for a week?* With these questions, you want to direct the conversation to a different topic or to lead the person to a particular decision.

QUESTIONING STRATEGIES

All forms of communication are improved by planning and understanding the focus of the communication. Questioning is no exception. If you intend to ask someone a question, you should know what you're trying to accomplish by asking the question. If you're trying to find out how someone feels about an upcoming change, slapping them on the back and saying, "Sounds great, doesn't it?" will probably not meet your goals. Too often we think we're asking a question for one reason when we really want something else. For instance, if you ask someone what she thinks about the budget, you may actually want to know if she will support it. A question such as *Is there anything in the budget you couldn't support?* might better accomplish your objectives.

FUNNEL TECHNIQUE

One of the most fundamental questioning techniques is to start with broad, open questions and build on the speaker's responses by asking narrower, more specific questions. This is called the *funnel technique*. It's like painting a picture. You start with a blank canvas and begin filling in the background with broad brush strokes. Gradually you add more and more detail until you have a complete picture. With questions, you start out at the top of the funnel with a broad question and then as you move down the funnel, you "paint with a finer brush"—by asking closed questions that demand more exact answers—and fill in the details.

With the funnel technique, you actually begin exploring the other person's needs and expectations, problems and opportunities by using your questioning and listening skills. You start with, "Tell me about your business" or "What are your long-range goals in this position?" or "What's important to you?" A typical computer salesperson might ask a prospect what kind of computer system he currently has or what his computer needs are. The *hotshot* salesperson who has learned the funnel technique starts out by asking about the prospect's business or operation. A manager trying to locate the cause of a recurring problem *could* say, "Why does this switch keep failing?" An artful questioning manager would start on a broader level, saying something like, "Tell me about the overall process that surrounds the switch." A supervisor trying to deal with a tardy employee *could* ask why the employee is late again. Or he could sit down with the employee and ask, "How are you feeling about your job?" Broad-brush questions give you a lot of information about the situation, including important clues as to where to direct more specific follow-up questions, and give the other person a chance to relax and tell you what he thinks is important.

Broad, open-ended questions show your interest in the other person's situation. They often start with "tell me," "how," "who," "what," or "why." They are much more powerful than closed questions that require a simple answer such as "yes" or "no" or a specific piece of information. After the broad question opens the conversation and begins to build rapport, the artful questioner builds on the responses and adds to his understanding of the information being transferred. Our computer salesperson might have a client who says, "I need more control over our order system." He then builds on that response by asking a question using the most important words in the answer—*control* and *order system*. For instance, he might ask, "What aspects of your order system would you like to have more control over?" or "Could you tell me more about your order system?" When the client responds, he builds his next question around the response to that question and so on.

The broad, open questions at the top of the funnel are easy for the speaker to answer. They give the speaker the freedom to tell you whatever he wants. By the time you get to the more specific questions, he can see where you're heading with your questions and he'll be willing to share more information with you. Not only that, but most people's level of trust and willingness to share information is related directly to how much information they have previously shared.

Here's another example of building on previous responses. Imagine two people meeting on an airplane—the words that are used to build the next response are shown in *italics*:

"Hello, my name is Ellen. What do you do for a living?"
"I'm a *writer*."
"A *writer* . . . what kind of writing do you do?"
"Mostly *humor*. Occasionally I write something serious or philosophical but people seem to laugh at that, too."
"*Humor*—I've always thought that must be the hardest kind of writing to do. Tell me how you do it."
"Well, for me, it's one part sarcasm, two parts irreverence, and a dash of creativity. I shake the whole thing up and hope it doesn't explode in my face!"

Notice how the intelligent use of the funnel technique has guided the conversation from a simple, nonmeaningful declaration, "I'm a writer," to a fairly detailed, very personal expression!

Here are some general strategies to help you formulate your questions in a way that helps you meet your objectives:

1. HAVE A PLAN. Know what you want to accomplish and what type of questions you will need to use. You don't have the questions written out in advance but you should be clear about your objectives.

2. KEEP THE QUESTION SIMPLE. It's best to ask for one answer at a time. A question like: *What do you think about the marketing plan and will the new ad campaign confuse customers and would that confusion actually be beneficial to the long-term product growth?* will not produce a meaningful answer. If you ask a two-part question, people tend to either answer the second part only or only the part they were interested in or felt safe with. One question at a time!

3. STAY FOCUSED. Keep the questions on track and follow a topic to its conclusion. Any question that starts with *By the way . . .* is probably going off on a tangent. Hold the question for later.

4. STAY NONTHREATENING. Trust is a key essential in communication. The wrong question can quickly destroy trust and the relationship. *Why didn't you . . . ? How could you . . . ? Aren't you . . . ?* are all questions which generally make people defensive. Once someone throws up a wall of defense, the opportunity for exchanging information and building a relationship goes away.

5. ASK PERMISSION. If the area of questioning is sensitive, explain the need for the questions and ask permission before proceeding. *The application requires some detail about your financial condition. Would you mind answering . . . ?*

6. AVOID AMBIGUITY. Ambiguous questions generate ambiguous answers. *Could you support the budget?* does not tell you whether the person *would* support it.

7. AVOID MANIPULATION. Keep the relationship as a primary focus. Tricking someone into giving you an answer you want destroys trust and rapport. *Would you prefer to work overtime tonight or tomorrow night?* does not give a person the chance to say that he doesn't want to work overtime at all. Explaining the need for the overtime and asking if he's available has a totally different feel. Manipulation is an attempt to take away a person's control.

Mastering the art of asking questions will help you gain the information you need, build trust, stimulate the views and opinions of others, and verify information. The next chapter will show you how to add the process of feedback to your "receiving" skills.

7

MAKING SURE
WITH FEEDBACK

What do the following sentences mean to you?

I'll be there in a minute.
It isn't very far.
I need it quickly.
We'll provide you with a small number of these at no cost.
That will cost a lot of money.

You have probably already realized that most, if not all, of these statements are highly ambiguous. When used in normal conversation, there is a high probability that these statements will be misinterpreted—unless they are clarified. For instance, a person says: *Call me later and we'll discuss it.* Does he mean fifteen minutes from now, one hour from now, tomorrow, or next week? These statements, in addition to thousands of others not mentioned here, can have a variety of meanings. They generate misunderstandings.

Unfortunately, we frequently use these statements in everyday conversation and expect the other person to understand clearly what we mean. The same is true when other people are communicating with us. Unless statements such as these are clarified and confirmed between the two communicating parties, there is great likelihood the message received will not be the same as was intended. This is the foundation of errors, misunderstandings, and strained relationships. Through the simple use of feedback skills, these highly ambiguous statements can be transformed into specific, effective communications.

The lack of feedback shows up in the workplace as errors, botched plans, political in-fighting, lost productivity, lost profits, and, ultimately, lost jobs. If that seems extreme think about the errors that you see every day . . . shipping errors or delays, delivery of the wrong parts or the wrong paperwork, budget overruns, marketing plans that miss the target, new products that flop, employees who don't live up to their potential. Studies show that the lack of clear communication is a major factor in *every* organizational problem. Feedback and clarification can take the ambiguity out of promises, agreements, schedules, policies, and procedures.

The use of feedback in communication is often taken for granted. In the management process, no other communication activity is so widely used yet so misunderstood. Feedback may be the most important aspect of interpersonal communications if conversation is to continue for any length of time and still have meaning for the parties involved. Without feedback, how does each person "really" know what the other person is talking about and communicating? The effective use of feedback skills helps insure the accurate transmission of your message.

Whenever you verbally, vocally, or visibly react to what another person says or does, or seek a reaction from another person to what you say or do, you are using feedback. Effective two-way communication depends on it. This chapter explores the feedback skills you can use to communicate effectively and clearly with your colleagues, supervisors, employees, contractors, and customers.

TYPES OF FEEDBACK

▪

Feedback comes in a number of forms. There is verbal, nonverbal, fact, and feeling feedback. Each serves a specific purpose in the communications process.

VERBAL FEEDBACK. Verbal feedback is the type we are most frequently aware of and most often use. With verbal feedback, you can accomplish a number of favorable objectives: 1) You can use verbal feedback to ask for clarification of a message. 2) You can use verbal feedback to give positive and/or negative strokes to the other person. 3) You can use verbal feedback to determine how to structure a presentation that will be meaningful and effective for the other person.

To improve the accuracy and clarity of a message during a conversation, use clarifying feedback statements such as the following:

- Let me be sure I understand what you've said.
- Let's see if I can review the key points we've discussed.
- I hear you saying . . .
- I think I hear you saying that your central concern is . . .
- As I understand it, your major objectives are . . .

Clarifying feedback statements can also end with the following:

- Did I understand you properly?
- Did I hear you correctly?
- Was I on target with what you meant?
- Were those your major concerns?
- Can you add anything to my summary?

Using feedback for clarification is probably the most critical use of feedback in the workplace. There is only one way to know if the message you're receiving is the same as the message being sent. That is by asking for clarification, or restating the message in your own words and asking for verification of your understanding. Obviously you can't clarify or verify everything that is said during the day. If your coworker says that he's going to get a cup of coffee and you ask for clarification, the results you get probably will not be positive. You need to know when to use feedback. Some typical times are: when you have any doubt about the meaning of the message or about how to proceed, when the message is highly complex, when you're dealing with an important process or project, and when the message deals with information that is new to you.

Verbal feedback should also be used to give positive and negative strokes to others. When a person does something positive, that behavior needs to be positively reinforced. Simple statements are in order, such as: "The project report you did was clear and concise—Nice job"; "You made it really easy for the committee to understand the issues"; "I really appreciate the extra effort you put in"; and "You're doing an excellent job staying within budget." Tell the person specifically what you recognize and appreciate.

Given in a timely and consistent manner, this type of feedback lets the person know what kind of performance is required. It encourages them to continue with similar performance.

On the other hand, when behavior requires negative feedback, offer it in a private, constructive environment. Ignoring inappropriate performance tends to prolong it, as silence is construed as tacit approval. No one likes to be criticized, so negative feedback should be directed only at the performance—rather than the person. Whenever possible, negative feedback should be sandwiched between positive feedback.

For example, use phrases such as: "It's obvious that you put in a lot of effort on this report. The issues are so complex that it would help if we had a one-page summary." "Your work is extremely accurate but when you come in late, it puts us all behind schedule." "I appreciate your help folding the brochures. Since they will be going to customers, it's important that they are extremely neat. Could you redo these?" Make sure you give the person enough specific information so that he can correct his performance in the future.

By asking simple questions, you can determine whether a presentation is working—whether to proceed in the current direction or modify your approach. For instance, if you think you are going a bit too fast for the other person to comprehend your message, you might simply ask: "I sometimes get carried away with my enthusiasm and move along too quickly on this topic. Would it be more helpful to you if I covered these issues a bit more slowly?" The same can be done if you are getting the impression that you should speed up your presentation. Questions such as, "Shall we explore that issue some more?" allow you to determine the other person's interest and understanding of the conversation. Answers can help you avoid capriciously cutting the topic too short or dragging it on too long. You are simply asking for direction. "Would you like me to go into the details of this project, or do you have some other questions that you'd like to ask me first?" allows you to determine the person's present state of mind and level of receptivity. Without this information, you may get into the details of the project when, in fact, the other person does have a number of questions she would have liked to ask first. In this situation, the person is probably dwelling on her questions and not paying attention to what you are explaining. Through questions such as the preceding, you can determine how to tailor your delivery style and presentation to fit the needs of each individual person. Although this takes a bit more time in the short run, it saves much time in the long run, because it prevents communication problems and improves receptivity, understanding, and productivity.

NONVERBAL FEEDBACK. Many of us can remember when the word "vibes" was in vogue. Both good and bad vibes are the result of a direct form of nonverbal feedback. By using their bodies, eyes, faces, postures, and senses, people can communicate a variety of positive or negative attitudes, feelings, and opinions. You do this consciously or unconsciously, just as others do with you. The sensitive, perceptive communicator uses the nonverbal feedback he or she is getting from the other person to structure the content and direction of the message. The outcome is a positive continuance of the interaction and increased trust and credibility in the relationship.

The amount of nonverbal feedback you receive and send is not as important as how you interpret it and react to it. Nonverbal signals help you realize when you are losing the other person's interest. With this sensitivity to and perception of the person's nonverbal feedback, you can react by changing your pace, topic, or style to recapture the person's attention, interest, or trust.

Nonverbal feedback is extremely important in the manager/

employee relationship. Too often ineffective communications between managers and employees result in "mixed messages." This simply means that while one message is being verbalized, something totally different is being stated through vocal intonation and body language. These mixed messages force the receiver to choose between the verbal message and the intent signaled by the body language. Most often, they choose the nonverbal aspect of the message. When a person receives mixed messages from you, it immediately creates tension and distrust. Rightly or wrongly, the person feels that you are purposely hiding something or that you are being less than candid. Unfortunately, managers and employees often do not realize they are sending mixed messages to each other. The resulting miscommunication takes a terrible toll on work relationships. It is extremely important to keep your nonverbal feedback and your verbal feedback in sync.

In an earlier chapter on listening skills, we mentioned the process of acknowledging. This is nothing other than projecting nonverbal (and verbal) feedback to the speaker. It lets the person know that her message is getting through to you, and it also lets her know how you feel about that message. People do not like to speak to people who do not respond or show any emotion. They want and seek feedback. Make a concerted effort to give them that feedback, especially in nonverbal ways.

FACT FEEDBACK. In an earlier chapter on questioning skills, we mentioned the fact-finding question. This type of question is meant to elicit specific data and information. If the facts are worth asking for, they are certainly worth being heard accurately. This is where fact feedback comes into play. There are also times when you are relating specific information which needs to be received as accurately as possible and, again, fact feedback can help. Fact feedback is asking a specific, closed question or making a specific statement of the facts as you know it and asking for verification.

When you are depending on other people's facts and they are depending on yours, it is critical to get and give the information exactly. When you want clarification, agreement, or correction, fact feedback is called for. Fact feedback is also used in translating messages and interpreting words or phrases. The following messages contain words or phrases that are unclear. They are perfect candidates for fact feedback statements.

- Due to recent layoffs, all employees are expected to work harder.
- There will be a short wait for a table.
- Don't spend too much time on that job.
- In this company, we are liberal and democratic.
- Major credit cards are accepted.
- We will be visiting Philadelphia and New York City. We expect to open our first unit there.

Examples of requests for fact feedback would be:

- What exactly do you mean by "working harder"? Should we plan on putting in longer hours?
- How long is the wait? Will the wait be more than 15 minutes?
- How much time should I spent on the job? Is there a deadline?
- What do you mean by "liberal and democratic"?
- Which major credit cards do you honor? Do you take Visa?
- Which city will have the first unit?

If something can be misunderstood, *chances are it will be.* Use fact feedback to keep your messages clear and make sure you are receiving the message as it is intended.

FEELING FEEDBACK. A firm understanding and clarification of the words, phrases, and facts of messages are obviously important. However, this increased accuracy in communications still only stays on the surface of the discussion. It is also important to know why the person is saying the things she is saying. What are the underlying causes and motivations behind her message and her facts? How much personal feeling does her message carry for her? How does she really feel about what she is saying to you? Does she know whether her message is really getting through to you—at the feeling level? Is she aware that you really care about what she is saying to you?

All these questions underscore the importance of feeling feedback in two-way communications. Feeling feedback is especially important in organizations . . . perhaps because it is so seldom requested. The old school of business etiquette believed that feelings had no place at work. Personal lives, feelings, and emotional involvements were to be taken care of outside of the workplace. Now we know that it is impossible to put our feelings in a little box as we walk into the office and to pick them up again as we leave. Research has shown that one of the most effective ways to handle organizational change is to let the people "chat" about how they feel about the change. Just the process of talking about how they feel helps them adapt to the change.

Organizations are a complex web of people working to achieve a common purpose. As organizational life becomes more complex and more demanding, it requires the full commitment of each member to achieve the organization's goals. Full commitment requires an environment of trust that allows each person to express his or her thoughts and feelings openly. Organizations that request, and provide, a high level of feeling feedback understand that the feelings of each person are a critical part of the communication process. It is as important to understand the feelings inherent in a message as it is to understand the facts of the message.

Feeling feedback should be two-directional. You need to make a concerted effort to understand the feelings, emotions, and attitudes that underlie the messages that come to you. In addition, you should clearly project feeling feedback to the other person to let her know that her message has gotten through to you—at the feeling level. The following statements are candidates for feeling feedback questions:

- I'm tired of all the politics around here.
- My last review was a joke.
- "Quality" is just another management fad.
- No one cares about my problems.
- Another reorganization . . . probably just another name for a layoff.

Examples of requests for feeling feedback would be:

- How are the "politics" here affecting you?
- What's bothering you about your last review?
- Why do you feel that management isn't committed to the quality program?
- What would make you feel like the organization cared about your problems?
- How do you feel about the reorganization?

Fact feedback is simply a meeting of the minds, whereas feeling feedback is a meeting of the hearts. Feeling feedback is nothing more than the effective use of empathy—putting yourself into the other person's shoes so that you can see things from her point of view. When you can really experience the other person's true feelings and understand where she's coming from and at the same time project this emotional awareness to her, it serves to reinforce rapport, lower interpersonal tension, and significantly increase trust. Probing questions, supportive and understanding responses, and an awareness and projection of appropriate nonverbal signals are the key tools used in sending and receiving feeling feedback. Often, until you and the other person understand how each other truly feels, the "facts" don't matter at all. Improve the accuracy of communications through fact feedback—and improve the rapport of your relationships by practicing empathy through feeling feedback.

THE KEYS TO EFFECTIVE FEEDBACK
·

If you took a few moments and really thought about it, you could probably recall numerous times you could have smoothed over problems in communications simply by using the forms of feedback that we have discussed. Effective communication between two people is not easy. You really have to practice to make it work. The proper use of questioning skills helps. Using active listening helps. Sensitivity to nonverbal behavior helps. Without feedback, however, all of these skills are for naught. Through the effective use of feedback skills, you can create a good communication climate. The following general guidelines will help you use your feedback skills more effectively.

GIVE AND GET DEFINITIONS. The interpretation of words or phrases may vary from person to person, group to group, region to region, or society to society. When people believe or assume that words are used for one and only one meaning, they create situations in which they think they understand others but really do not. The words you use in everyday conversations almost inevitably have multiple meanings. In fact, the 500 most commonly used words in our language have more than 14,000 dictionary definitions. For instance, according to Webster's, a person is considered "fast" when she can run rather quickly. However, when one is tied down and cannot move at all, she is also considered "fast." "Fast" also relates to periods of not eating, a ship's mooring line, a race track in good running condition, and a person who hangs around with the "wrong" crowd of people. In addition, photographic film is "fast" when it is sensitive to light. On the other hand, bacteria are "fast" when they are insensitive to antibiotics.

The abundance of meanings of even "simple" words makes it hazardous to assume to understand the intent of a message without verifying and clarifying that message. These assumptions often lead to subsequent misunderstandings, breakdowns in the communications process, and decreased trust. Therefore, during the process of questioning and listening, use feedback. Give and get definitions.

DON'T ASSUME. Making assumptions invariably gets you into trouble. During interpersonal communications, it is dangerous to make the assumption that the other person either thinks or feels as you do at that moment. The other person may have a frame of reference that is totally different from your own. She reacts and perceives according to what she knows and believes to be true, and that may be different from your reactions, perceptions, and beliefs.

Do not assume anything in communications. If you do, you stand a good chance of being incorrect. Don't assume that you and the other person are talking about the same thing. Don't assume that the words and phrases you are both using are automatically being understood. The classic phrase of people who make assumptions is: "I know exactly what you mean." People who usually use that statement without ever using feedback techniques to determine exactly what the other person means are leaping into a communication quagmire.

Use more feedback and fewer assumptions, and you'll be happier and more accurate in your interpersonal communications.

ASK QUESTIONS. Questions have many uses. We've discussed a number of these in the previous chapter. Remember to use questions to test for feedback. A good rule of thumb is: "When in doubt, check it out." One of the best ways to check it out is through the effective use of questioning skills. Clarifying questions, expansion questions, direction questions, fact-finding questions, feeling-finding questions, and open questions can be used freely during conversation to test for feedback.

SPEAK THE SAME LANGUAGE. Abstain from using words that can easily be misinterpreted or mistranslated, especially technical terms and company jargon. These terms, which are so familiar to you, may be totally foreign to the people with whom you talk. Simplify your language and your technical terms so that everyone can understand you, even when you think the other person knows what the terms mean.

STAY TUNED IN. Constantly be on the lookout for and recognize those nonverbal signals that indicate that your line of approach is causing the other person to become uncomfortable and lose interest. When this happens, change your approach and your message accordingly. This fact was stated earlier, but it is so important that it cannot be repeated too often. Observe the other person. Be sensitive to the feelings they are experiencing during your interaction; above all else, respond to those feelings appropriately.

GIVE FEEDBACK ON THE BEHAVIOR, NOT THE PERSON. This relates to the appropriate use of positive and negative strokes. When someone does something especially well, give positive feedback, and relate it specifically to the action or behavior that was performed. When people do something especially badly, give them negative feedback specifically directed toward the action or behavior that you would like corrected. Do not under any circumstances criticize the person personally because of an inappropriate action or behavior. This is not only degrading but also counterproductive. Many ineffective managers, upon learning that one of their employees has done something wrong, criticize that employee personally: "You're an idiot"; "That was really stupid"; "You can't do anything right, can you?" These statements constitute inappropriate feedback. After a while, the employee starts believing these statements, and they become self-fulfilling prophecies. How can an employee improve performance on a particular task or behavior unless she knows specifically what behaviors or actions she must improve? So, direct your praise and punishment specifically toward your employee's behavior and actions, not toward the employee personally.

WITHHOLDING FEEDBACK. There are times when it's best

not to give feedback. Bite your tongue and restrain your body language and facial expressions in these situations. A few months ago, one of the authors was visiting a married couple. While waiting for the husband to finish getting dressed for an appointment, the author was chatting with the wife in the dining room. All of a sudden, the husband came into the dining room in what appeared to be a huff. In a loud and harsh vocal intonation he asked his wife, "Where did you get this shirt cleaned?!" While "asking" this assertion, he was shaking the collar of the shirt and seemed to be peering at his wife. The initial interpretation of this occurrence was that the husband was rather upset about the condition of his shirt. Most spouses would tend to act rather defensively, and some would even counterattack. His spouse was rather expert in withholding inappropriate feedback while at the same time asking for feedback. In a gentle voice with no disturbing body language, she simply told her husband: "I got it done at XYZ Cleaners. Why do you ask?" His reply almost floored me. He said it was the first time that any cleaner had done his shirt properly. He told his wife to take his shirts to that specific cleaner from now on. Clearly, there are times when it is best to withhold inappropriate feedback until you use effective feedback to clarify the intent of another person's message.

Feedback can reduce interpersonal tension and create a sense of trust and credibility between you and your supervisors, employees, customers, suppliers, and other coworkers, if used properly. Use feedback to help clarify messages, uncover an important need or problem, provide feedback to others, and to make sure your presentation is being clearly received. Use feedback to improve your relationships by letting the other person know what is going on in the relationship. Most of all, use feedback to improve your part of the conversation.

Feedback is an important part of communication in the workplace. As you develop these skills, you will find them an important part of every aspect of your professional life, including negotiations with bosses, employees, and customers; personnel issues; interviewing; problem-solving sessions; and building consensus to insure efficient implementation of decisions.

Through feedback, you can determine which areas to spend more time on and which ones need less time. It is important to confirm all uncertain verbal, vocal, and observable cues through feedback. The proper and effective use of feedback skills leads to improved communication. This increased sense of mutual understanding will lead to less interpersonal tension, increased trust and credibility, and higher productivity. Everyone wins when communications are clear and open.

CONFLICT
RESOLUTION

*What concerns me is not the way things are, but rather
the way people think things are.*

—EPICTETUS

Most of us long to have conflict-
free relationships in our working environment and in our personal
lives. But unless we are transported to some Orwellian future
world where all of our minds and emotions work in perfect uni-
son, freedom from conflict will never happen. And it would be a
mistake to attempt to completely erase disagreement from our
lives. People naturally disagree about what to do and how and
when to do it. That interaction of ideas and opinions sparks new
ideas and leads to better solutions and plans of action. However,
when differences of opinion are accompanied by too much emotional commitment to one point versus another, the resulting conflict can be damaging. When we become emotionally locked into
one idea and believe that it is the only one that can meet our
needs and objectives, we enter into conflict with only two options:
fight or flight. This chapter will help you identify the sources of
conflict and understand how to encourage healthy disagreement
without spiraling down into a negative conflict. It will also give

you tools that will help you break out of a conflict routine once it has begun.

THE NATURE OF CONFLICT

Conflict arises from the clash of perceptions, goals, or values in an arena where people care about the outcome. You see it your way, he sees it his way, and tension ignites. Conflict can cause a complete breakdown of a relationship if one person thinks that his only options are to continue the conflict or give up a valued objective.

Conflict can also lead to productive growth if it is properly managed and resolved. The process of recognizing and working through a conflict can only happen in an environment of open communication. The old saying, *What doesn't kill us makes us stronger,* is appropriate for conflict. Conflict left under the surface festers and can be lethal. When it is recognized and brought out into the open, its resolution can bring people closer together as they grow in their understanding of each other. Communication is the key element affecting conflict: both its cause and remedy. Open communication is the means by which disagreement can be prevented, managed, or resolved. The lack of open communication can drive conflict underground and create a downward spiral of misunderstanding and hostility.

Organizations depend on a group of people working together to achieve a common purpose. This results in a built-in breeding ground for conflict as people disagree on what the common purpose is, how to achieve it, as well as how to achieve their individual goals within the organization. Competition for limited resources, both internally and externally, feeds the conflict. The ability to manage the conflicting goals and methods within a limited-resource environment is critical. Unresolved, or unmanaged, conflict can quickly escalate and halt organizational progress as people worry more about the conflict than the organization's goals.

By definition, conflict occurs when two or more people have a strong disagreement that is driven by a clash of goals, perceptions, and/or values. The three basic components of conflict are:

1. Two or more persons are involved.
2. There is a *perceived* incompatibility between ideas, actions, beliefs, or goals.
3. The opposing sides see their way as the only way to achieve their goals or objectives.

This chapter will give you a simple model that will help you resolve conflict but also help you to understand the causes of conflict. A great deal of conflict can be avoided by wise handling of change in these areas. Here are some of the common sources of conflict within organizations:

RESPONSIBILITY LEVELS: If levels of responsibilities are fuzzy, there will be numerous occasions for conflict to arise over decisions made or actions taken in the disputed territory. For instance, if the sales department designs and produces a product-description brochure, the marketing department may take offense because brochures are their responsibility. Clear job descriptions and organization charts can help prevent these disputes, but in a rapidly changing organization, responsibility issues will be a frequent source of conflict.

LIMITED RESOURCES: Almost all organizations lack the resources to achieve all the objectives of each person within the organization. Manufacturing may want to replace some obsolete equipment while finance wants a new computer for the accounting system and marketing wants to increase advertising. The typical organizational division along functional lines makes it easy to lose sight of the overall organization goals as each department tries to maximize its own results.

CONFLICT OF INTEREST: Since all individual goals cannot be achieved, goals and objectives have to be ranked and some may have to be eliminated. Individuals may fight for their personal goals and lose sight of the organizational goals. The salesperson whose compensation is based on sales may bend credit requirements while the collections department would forgo sales in order to reduce bad debt. Each individual in an organization needs to know how his own goals and efforts fit within the organization's goals and efforts.

COMMUNICATION BARRIERS: Communication barriers exist at the interpersonal and organizational levels and include: differing perceptions, language, ineffective listening, "style" differences, and power and status barriers. Overcoming communication barriers requires extensive opportunity for interaction and an organizational commitment to training. The computer systems operator who never has a chance to talk to one of the salespeople will probably never understand the goals, needs, and frustrations of the sales department. Only by training people at every level of the organization in effective communication techniques can the organization hope to break down communication barriers.

INTERDEPENDENCY: Increasingly, our ability to accomplish our goals and objectives depends on the cooperation and assistance of others. This interdependency increases the opportunity for conflict. Accounting needs information from the sales department in order to complete financial reports; sales needs product information from manufacturing in order to make sales; manufacturing needs the right parts from purchasing; marketing needs information from customer service for a new advertising campaign. Organizations are an interrelated web of departments, teams, and individuals. No one in an organization can do his job without the input of someone else. When that someone else is late, has a different view of priorities, misunderstands directions, or is playing politics, conflicts are created.

INCREASED INTERACTION: The more people interact, the more potential there is for conflict. The trend toward increasing levels of participation and team work indicates a higher level of conflict and a greater need for conflict resolution skills. While interaction helps eliminate conflict as we begin to have a better understanding of another person's needs and priorities, it also increases conflict as we discover new areas of differences. In the old style organization, the assembly person might be isolated, with relatively little opportunity for conflict with other departments. Now, if he is made part of a special project team, he'll start to understand certain points of view, but also find new areas of conflict. Increased interaction creates the need for special training in communication and conflict resolution.

COMPETITION: When there is competition for rewards such as promotions, recognition, contest prizes, etc., conflict is a natural outcome. If only one person can become the new supervisor of the department and more than one person wants the position, the state is set for conflict. If the organization rewards the person who breaks all barriers to achieve a particular reward, interpersonal conflict increases. It is almost impossible to emphasize individual goals and rewards without diminishing the organization's goals. Achieving the organization's goals requires people to work together. Setting up competitions to stimulate individual achievement can be self-defeating for the organization. For example, if an organization sets challenging assembly quotas and rewards the fastest worker with a special bonus, there is no incentive for anyone to stop and look at quality or for a way to improve the process. If salespeople are rewarded only on sales volume, how interested will they be in the profitability of those sales?

There is no way to avoid conflict in today's rapidly changing environment but conflict can be managed. People can be taught communication techniques and conflict resolution techniques that help them avoid conflict or work through it once it is recognized.

THE FOUR PHASES OF CONFLICT

Organizational conflict can occur at several levels: between individuals, between groups, and between organizations. While we will focus on interpersonal conflict, the principles and ideas discussed here are also valid for intergroup and interorganizational conflicts.

Conflict typically proceeds through four stages even if each step is not recognized as such. The phases identified by theorist Louis Pondy are as follows:

PHASE 1: LATENT—When two or more parties must cooperate with one another in order to achieve a desired objective, there is potential for conflict. Latent conflict is often created whenever change occurs. Examples are a budget cutback, a change in organizational direction, a change in a personal goal or value, a new crisis project added to an already overloaded work force, or an expected occurrence (such as a salary increase) not happening.

PHASE 2: PERCEIVED—This is the point at which members are becoming aware of a problem, even if they are not sure where it comes from. Incompatibility is perceived and tension begins.

PHASE 3: FELT—The parties begin to focus in on differences of opinion and interests, sharpening perceived conflict. Internal tensions and frustrations begin to crystallize around specific, defined issues and people begin to build emotional commitments to their particular positions.

PHASE 4: MANIFEST—The outward display of conflict occurs when the opposing parties plan and follow through with acts to frustrate one another. Conflict is very obvious at this point.

As conflict proceeds through the stages, resolution becomes more difficult. People become more locked into their positions and more convinced that the conflict must be a win-or-lose situation. The ideal is to recognize conflict early and work for a resolution that is a win for each of the parties.

STRATEGIES FOR MANAGING CONFLICT
▪

Each strategy for managing conflict has its advantages and disadvantages. One strategy might work better for a particular situation than another. Each option varies in regard to concern for self (the degree to which a person tries to protect his own interests) versus concern for others (the degree to which a person wants to satisfy the view of others).

In any case, familiarize yourself with these conflict management options so that you feel comfortable using them or guiding others in their use.

AVOIDANCE—Avoidance is an instinctive, simple response to conflict. By not confronting the problem neither party is labelled winner or loser. However, avoidance rarely works, because it does nothing to make the conflict go away. The ostrich approach doesn't resolve the problem and it may actually allow the conflict to escalate to the next stage. Avoidance often takes the form of physical flight, falling asleep, or mentally withdrawing. You can recognize avoidance when someone changes the subject, tries to redefine the conflict so that it no longer seems to exist, abruptly leaves the scene of the conflict, or tunes out. If the problem is inconsequential, avoidance can be an appropriate option as with a manager who avoids getting involved with a minor employee dispute.

ACCOMMODATION—Accommodation happens when someone "gives in" without actually working through the conflict. A supervisor wants an employee to do something a new way. The employee says, "Oh, all right—but I really think it's better my way." The employee has accommodated the supervisor but there is no real resolution.

Although accommodation includes cooperative effort, it still requires sacrifice, turning conflict into a win-lose situation. Because assertiveness is not involved, there is a tendency for the "losing" party to repress its point of view. At least one of the parties involved plays down its differences while emphasizing common features. This exploitation of cooperative elements is beneficial when the accommodating party feels little personal involvement with the issue, or has little to lose by giving in to the other. Accommodation may also ensure positive future relations. In the case with the supervisor and employee, the supervisor may really appreciate the employee's willingness to try a new way and, if it works, the employee may feel good about the supervisor's abilities and be more willing to accept guidance in the future.

Accommodation provides a quick solution which is, however, often temporary because the base issues are left unresolved. Frequently, the relative power of the parties influences the outcome more than the legitimacy of complaints or the wisdom of each option. Accommodation responds to emotions but does not manage them. In our example, the supervisor didn't convince the employee of the superiority of the new method and he didn't listen to the employee's reasons for wanting to stay with the old method. The conflict might stay at the latent stage but additional pressures could cause it to escalate.

DOMINATION—This win-lose strategy involves a struggle for power and domination over another party. The most powerful party, in some cases the manager, imposes a solution. Domination has its benefits: it resolves conflicts quickly and it is effective when the parties recognize and accept the power relationship.

Unfortunately, this strategy can create resentment among involved parties if overused, because goals may be reached at others' expense. Consistent "losers" might feel that their needs will never be met and begin to withdraw from the conflict altogether. Domination fails to treat the root of the conflict, making it only a temporary solution.

NEGOTIATION—this is a compromising strategy that involves moderate levels of cooperation and assertiveness. Both sides state their positions and try to reach an acceptable compromise. In salary negotiations, every dollar the employee "wins," the company "loses." Most negotiations attempt to minimize losses while maximizing gains or creating a situation where everyone partially wins and partially loses. This can lead to a situation where no one is completely satisfied. In sensitive negotiations, it is easy for the parties to tip the scale into a more assertive mode and wind up in a stand-off.

COLLABORATION—collaboration requires a high level of co-operation and assertiveness. Rather than just negotiating salary, the employee and the supervisor might discuss at length the employee's goals and objectives and how they fit in with the organization's goals and needs. The process might reveal that the employee needs flex-time more than additional salary or that the employee's long-term goal includes an advanced degree, which would require a reduction in work hours. Collaboration takes time and effort, but it addresses the underlying issues of the situation or conflict. This makes collaboration a generally long-lasting and productive conflict resolution strategy. Through face-to-face assertiveness and confrontation, involved parties work through the conflict cooperatively.

Rather than depending on negotiation or compromise, collaboration relies on creative problem-solving to identify solutions which will meet the needs of all the parties. Through open communication and identification of the goals and objectives of each of the parties, new avenues of exploration can be identified and often totally unexpected solutions appear.

Obviously, if it is important to you to resolve a conflict positively in a way that enhances the relationships involved, collaboration is far more effective than avoidance or the other strategies of conflict resolution. There are four basic components of collaboration: understanding and respecting the goals and objectives of each of the parties, assertiveness, creative problem-solving, and confrontation.

UNDERSTANDING AND RESPECTING—Collaboration assumes an equality in the standings of the parties. Even if there are differences in the power or status of one or more of the parties, for the purpose of this conflict resolution exercise, the goals and objectives of each person are presented equally. After presenting the goals and objectives, there may be a need to rank and evaluate them logially but it is done with the participation of all of the parties. Each member of the group tries to stay focused on the organization's goals rather than on individual objectives.

ASSERTIVENESS—For a collaboration to succeed, each person must feel safe in expressing his ideas and opinions. Each position needs to be presented as powerfully as possible. People often confuse assertiveness with aggression. Aggression is assertiveness without regard for the needs of the other person. Assertiveness says: *Here's my position . . . what's yours?* Aggression is: *Here's my position . . . take it or leave it.*

CREATIVE PROBLEM-SOLVING—Good creative problem-solving skills can help define a solution that results in a win for each person. It is important to focus on the problem rather than on specific solutions. Spend time identifying as many potential solutions as possible before proceeding with evaluation. Avoid dwelling on the history of the problem, which often involves placing blame.

CONFRONTATION—This is a specific communication strategy, a way to change behavior through constructive feedback. During an emotionally charged conflict resolution session, it is often necessary to use confrontation to break through a communication barrier. For example, two coworkers have competing priorities which have created conflict between them. Worker #2 consistently is late delivering necessary information to Worker #1. Worker #1 may decide to confront #2 by telling him what impact his behavior is having on the organization. Confrontation is a useful strategy but it has to be done skillfully or it can escalate the conflict. The next section gives you a model, the "confrontation continuum," for handling different levels of conflict through confrontation.

THE CONFRONTATION CONTINUUM

▪

The confrontation process allows you to get at the root causes of the conflict in a productive manner. You are indirectly trying to say, "Let's exchange ideas—pleasantly and comfortably. I will try to hear you and will take your opinion into account before I state mine. Then I want you to hear my opinions and take them into account. Once we have exchanged our opinions, we will decide on the best option. This is not a contest for superiority."

Anyone who has been involved in a confrontation of this kind knows that there are many levels of confrontation—at the beginning, there may be a simple misunderstanding or a sense by one party that he is not being heard by the other. At the other end of the confrontation "continuum," the conflict may be so severe that it jeopardizes the organization's goals. At the beginning of the continuum, we need to achieve understanding. At the other end, we must demand a change in behavior. As you move along the continuum, different confrontation strategies can be used to resolve the conflict.

The following confrontation strategies make up a progressive series which can be used to resolve escalating conflicts. As the conflict moves from being merely a matter of achieving understanding to a need for a behavior change, the confrontation can incorporate more aggressive strategies.

REFLECTION—In this stage you demonstrate your sincere desire to understand the person's feelings and needs. You gather

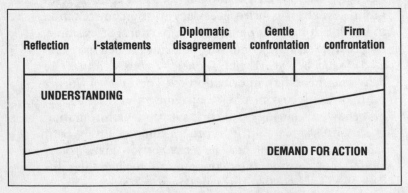

8-A *Confrontation continuum*

data and build rapport with the person. By reflecting the feelings you hear the person expressing, you give him a chance to correct your impression and to elaborate on your comment. The form of this statement is generally:

> "I understand that you feel/think _____ because _____."
> Example: *I understand that you feel unappreciated because you are not invited to the weekly staff meetings.*

I-STATEMENT—With I-statements you reveal your feelings, asserting your own needs and objectives in a nonjudgmental fashion. You want the other person to understand your feelings and reasons. These statements follow this general form:

> "I feel _____ when you _____ because _____."
> Example: *I feel angry when you ignore the safety rules because you and others might get hurt.*

DIPLOMATIC DISAGREEMENT—In the diplomatic disagreement stage you try to achieve understanding in a gentle, tactful manner. You want the other person to understand your reasoning and you try to understand his. You want the person to know that you value the relationship. The format for this stage includes reflection and an I-statement.

> "You feel/think _____."
> "I appreciate your position and understand that _____."
> Example: *I understand that you think we need a new computer.*
> *I appreciate your position and realize that you think it will improve our productivity.*
> *I believe we should wait because a new model is about to be released.*

GENTLE CONFRONTATION—In gentle confrontation you try to cause a change in behavior and build the relationship at the same time. You want to suggest the change in a tactful, somewhat tentative fashion. The format includes reflection, an indication that the other person is valued, an I-statement, and an indication of consequences.

"You feel/think _____."

"I appreciate your position and understand that _____."

"I feel _____because _____."

"If this continues it will cause _____."

Example: *You think the accounting department should pay our vendors immediately.*

I appreciate your position and understand that it helps you negotiate better prices.

I feel frustrated, however, because I am trying to manage our cash flow as well as our profits.

If you continue to pressure the accounting department, it will make it much more difficult for me to manage the cash flow and investments. That could result in vendors going unpaid and a reduction in profits which could impact our profit sharing.

FIRM CONFRONTATION—In the firm confrontation you try to clear up disagreements and cause a definite change in behavior. The change in behavior is your primary objective. The added statement is in the format:

"I would appreciate it in the future if you would _____."

Example: Same as Gentle Confrontation above, plus:
In the future I would appreciate it if you would come to me for any special early payment requests.

Throughout the entire confrontation process, there are some basic guidelines that will help make the process more productive:

TIMING—Is the person ready to listen? If you're trying to tell someone why showing up late for work every day isn't in his best interests, doing it right after he checks in probably isn't a good time. He knows he's late and he knows you know he's late. He's probably feeling defensive. Wait until you have something positive to say about his performance. Then you can tell him how his tardiness is affecting the overall perception of his commitment and performance.

FOCUS ON CURRENT SPECIFICS—Talk about behavior

that is happening today, not something that happened last week or last month.

STATE YOUR FEELINGS—When you tell someone how you feel, you are keeping the conversation open rather than focusing it only on the other person. "When you come to work late, I feel really angry because the rest of us have to wait for you before we can start on the project."

Confrontation is a powerful conflict resolution strategy which requires a great deal of skill and practice. Most of us are relatively unfamiliar with the process and it may take training and role-play practice before everyone in the organization acquires the skills necessary to use the individual strategies included on the confrontation continuum. However, once everyone in the organization learns to be more sensitive to timing, to focusing on current specific behaviors, and to state their own feelings about the behaviors, a large percentage of conflicts can be resolved more productively.

It's also important to remember that people only change when it is in their best interest to do so. You cannot make another person change, no matter how persuasive your argument, but you can increase his motivation to do so by appealing to his self-interest.

If you are irritated by a coworker's behavior, for instance, focus less on how he affects you and more on how your reaction affects him. Tell John that you are less motivated to work with him on his project because of the way his put-downs make you feel. Let John look at himself in the mirror, so to speak, so he can consider what his behavior is costing himself.

In essence, you are saying: "John, when you put me down, it makes me angry and I don't feel like working with you on your project." You are telling him how his behavior makes you feel and what that behavior costs him.

Often people are afraid to be confrontational and assertive because they are unsure of the reaction they will get. Most of us try to avoid confrontations which might create anger, defensiveness, or rejection. You can avoid this reaction and still be assertive, through the sensitivity with which your express your concerns. The confrontation continuum gives you a series of strategies to help you assert yourself in a way that reduces conflict rather than accelerating it.

For instance, only someone completely ignorant of the conflict resolution strategies we've discussed would accuse another person based on personality ("You are lazy, ignorant, and mean!"). This is labelling and it is hazardous not only because it can be wrong but also because it puts the other person on the defensive. Most of us do not have the expertise to know or understand another's intentions. When we attack a perceived attribute of a personality, we are hitting the core of that person. A very normal response is to react defensively or to deny the accusation. The conflict resolution guidelines and the confrontation continuum strategies help us achieve understanding or a change in behavior without destroying the other person's morale.

STRATEGIES TO AVOID
•

Sometimes it's not enough to know what we should do. We need to be able to recognize what we shouldn't do. In a conflict situation, emotions may be extremely sensitive and we may offend without intending to. Here are some strategies that generally escalate a conflict rather than resolving it:

MINIMIZATION—Sometimes we do not recognize the seriousness of an action or perception and we make light of it through humor or sarcasm. When this happens the other person feels unvalued or belittled. Often the person takes your minimization as a personal attack. When someone brings a problem to our attention, the first thing we need to do is acknowledge it. Which of the following responses is more effective?

Situation:
  Engineer—*I'm afraid the O-ring might fail at low temperatures.*
  Manager 1—*That's not your problem. Worry about how we're going to meet our next deadline.*
  Manager 2—*I appreciate your concern. What makes you think that?*

BLAME—While blame can often be attached to the last person who touched a situation, most problems are too complex to be totally caused by one person or one factor. The focus should be on preventing future problems rather than placing blame.

Situation:
    Salesperson—*We didn't get the Smith account.*
    Manager 1—*What did you do wrong?*
    Manager 2—*What could we have done better?*

UNLOADING—When people have worked together for a long time, there are often numerous small grievances which have gone unmentioned. When a larger problem sparks a conflict, the temptation to unload that past baggage is often overwhelming. While it might make the person unloading feel better, this is not a productive conflict resolution strategy. The other person might legitimately complain that you should have brought those problems up when they occurred.

Situation: Employee arrives at work late.
    Manager 1—*Not only are you late but last week there was an addition error in the report you submitted and you never have turned in the Murphy proposal that was due over a month ago.*
    Manager 2—*Is everything ok? I know you were only a few minutes late but you normally seem so committed and recently you've seemed to be distracted. Is there anything I can do?*

LOW BLOWS—As we work with people, we begin to understand their sensitivities. Hitting one of those emotionally touchy areas can escalate a conflict out of control and make it very difficult to regain the lost ground.

Situation: Employee misses a meeting.
    Coworker 1—*No wonder you were fired from your last job. Obviously you're incapable of managing your time.*
    Coworker 2—*I really needed your support in this morning's meeting. You know I took a time management*

course that really seemed to help me get organized. Maybe you should take it next time it's offered.

MANIPULATION—Using personal charm or approval to get someone to do something you want done without regard to the other person's needs or objectives. This also includes withholding approval or rewards in order to get the desired action.

Situation: Manager wants an employee to work overtime.
Manager 1—*If you'll work overtime tonight, I'll remember it when review time comes up.*
Manager 2—*I'm sorry to ask you at the last minute, but we have a crisis with the ABC project. If we don't get it finished tonight, the company may lose the whole project. Could you possibly work tonight?*

FORCE—This is the "I don't care what you want, do it my way, now!" approach. If all you want is to get an immediate action, it works. And if it's only used on extremely rare occasions, it's an effective way to get something done immediately. But it's demoralizing to the other person because it does not acknowledge his worth or his ideas.

Situation: Manager wants to change the work schedule.
Manager 1—*From now on our hours are 10:00 A.M. to 7:00 P.M.*
Manager 2—*Studies show that the prime hours for our customers are 10:00 A.M. to 7:00 P.M. We need to develop a system that will allow us to give the best possible service to our customers during those hours. Do you have any suggestions?*

CONFLICT RESOLUTION BEHAVIORS
·

There are five basic behaviors which will help you resolve conflict in almost any situation you encounter. They will allow you to benefit from positive disagreement without having those disagreements escalate into out-of-control personality conflicts that damage the morale and productivity of the organization. These basics are:

OPENNESS—State your feelings and thoughts openly, directly, and honestly without trying to hide or disguise the real object of your disagreement. Don't attribute negative statements about the other person to unknown others. Use I-statements and talk about how you feel and what you want. Focus on current specifics and on identifying the problem.

EMPATHY—Listen with empathy. Try to understand and feel what the other person is feeling and to see the situation from her point of view. Demonstrate your understanding and validate the other person's feelings. Comments such as *I appreciate how you feel . . . I understand your feelings . . . I'm sorry I made you feel that way . . .* let the other person know that you are sincere in understanding her views.

SUPPORTIVENESS—Describe the behaviors you have difficulty with rather than evaluating them. Express your concern for and support of the other person. Let him know you want to find a solution that benefits both of you. State your position tentatively with a willingness to change your opinion if appropriate reasons are given. Be willing to support the other person's position if it makes sense to do so.

POSITIVENESS—Try to identify areas of agreement and emphasize those. Look at the conflict as a way to better understand the entire situation and to possibly find a new and better solution. Be positive about the other person and your relationship. Express your commitment to finding a resolution that works for everyone.

EQUALITY—Treat the other person and his ideas and opinions as equal. Give the person the time and space to completely express his ideas. Evaluate all ideas and positions logically and without regard to ownership.

Conflicts offer many benefits if we can resolve them productively. Healthy disagreement can have a positive, generating effect. As people are forced to work through a problem to its solution, they get a chance to better understand the point of view of others. Successful resolution of small conflicts can diffuse the possibility of more serious conflicts and result in better working relationships.

The process of exploring problems collaboratively can lead us to acquire more information, new perceptions, and new ideas.

Issues can be clarified. Sometimes it's only through the conflict resolution process that organizations identify and highlight key issues which were rumbling under the surface and needed a healthy debate to become apparent. How well we manage conflict resolution can be a critical skill in effective communications.

III

Nonverbal Communication

How effective would your communication be if every other word you said was eliminated? (How . . . would . . . communication . . . if . . . other . . . you . . . was . . . ?) Not very effective? Studies show that over half of your message is carried through nonverbal elements—your appearance, your body language, and the tone and pace of your voice. You could use powerful, clearly understood words; you could have excellent listening skills; you could be an expert with feedback . . . but if you don't understand nonverbal communication, your communication might be less effective than you would like.

We all understand the importance of "first impressions"—but first impressions happen every time we initiate a communication. Before the person we're speaking to processes our verbal message, she has taken in our appearance, she has registered our enthusiasm and sincerity, she has noted our tone of voice and she has processed all of those together into a nonverbal message. That message is then compared to the content of our verbal message. If the two message sources complement and reinforce each other, we have delivered a powerful message. If the two messages don't match, they may cancel each other out resulting in no message delivered.

The next five chapters will help you understand how to create a powerful nonverbal message that will support your verbal content. You will learn how to build a powerful image, how to interpret and use body language to deliver the message you intend, how to project a vocal quality that matches your message, how to use space to intensify your message, and how your use of time sends part of your message.

9

PROJECTING A POWERFUL IMAGE

Have you ever seen yourself on TV or videotape?
Have you ever heard your voice on a tape recorder?

How did you look and sound? How would you *like* to look and sound? The difference between the answers to those two questions is your "image gap." If you have an image gap, this chapter can help you understand how to develop the image you would like to project. Projecting an image that is consistent with the person you want to be significantly improves your ability to develop trust and rapport with others. They will feel much more comfortable and much more at ease around you when your image is appropriate, thus making it easier for you to communicate with them. If your image is inappropriate to the other person or the situation, however, it will create a roadblock that will hamper effective communication.

While it's sometimes easy to discount the importance of image, it can be critical to your success. It's definitely a key element of communication. The dramatic impact of image was quite evident during the Nixon/Kennedy debates. Kennedy won the debates, not primarily through what he said, but because of the image of warmth, intelligence, youth, and vigor that he projected. Those debates were the turning point in the election. Image meant the difference between being president and not being president.

As irrational as it may seem, people do judge a book by its cover. It is the unusual person who can put aside a bad initial impression and allow the other person to reveal his genuine assets and skills hidden behind the bad first impression. People react in a fairly predictable manner to visual clues . . . our "image." They expect one image from an executive and quite a different image from a rock musician. In today's music environment, stardom would probably elude a new rock musician who wore a three-piece suit and short hair. At the same time, most conservative bankers would have trouble considering a tattooed candidate in ragged jeans and a tie-dyed T-shirt.

An image which does not match your message—which is somehow "inappropriate"—creates noise in the communication process. It becomes difficult for the other person to hear what you're saying because of the distraction of your image. On the other hand, an image that is appropriate smooths the communication process and makes it easier for your message to be "heard." When a clerical worker applies for a job looking neat, clean, and energetic, the interviewer has the positive first impression that this person is ready to sit down at a word processor and go to work.

The total image you project to others consists of many things. Among these are: the first impressions you project, the depth of your knowledge, the breadth of your knowledge, and your enthusiasm. These four areas are the critical components of image. Let's examine them in detail.

First impressions are lasting impressions. You've probably heard that saying before, but have you ever given it serious thought? What are the ramifications of your first impressions on other people? Your first impression is the initial impact you make on another person. It includes dress, voice, grooming, handshake, eye contact, and body posture. The way you choose to adjust each of these factors has a profound effect on how other people will initially perceive you. Positive first impressions make communications with other people much easier and more comfortable.

Negative initial impressions can cut off a relationship before it gets started. Some people can overcome a poor first impression, but it is very difficult. Many people give up rather than trying to reverse another person's negative first impression.

Have you ever judged another person's personality and/or competence solely on the first impression they made on you? What is the first thing that comes to mind when you think about a person with a heavy Brooklyn accent? What about a weak handshake? Or sloppy grooming, poor hygiene, bad vocabulary, poor posture, or ill-fitting clothing? You may think that none of these potential weak spots apply to you. Don't kid yourself! We have met few people who could not do with some improvement in the initial impressions they project to others.

One of our friends from graduate school initially had a difficult time landing a job. He was interviewed at a number of universities for a faculty position, but something elusive stood in the way of his getting a solid job offer from any of them. It had nothing to do with his competency. He was truly a brilliant individual. Nobody questioned his credentials. At one of the universities, a particular department head took a personal liking to him. Although our friend did not get the job offer there either, the department head did him an extremely big favor that no one else had done. He took our friend to the side and told him that his image had caused some problems in his interviews. Other faculty members in the university wondered if he really would "fit." You see, our friend did not create the most favorable first impression. Once you got to know him, he was friendly, warm, and helpful; but his appearance put up a barrier. First, his clothing selection was atrocious. He wore cheap, poorly made clothing and indiscriminately combined stripes with plaids and colors that clashed. That was only the beginning. His shoes were run down and scuffed. His hair was always greasy and messy. His handshake was cold and limp, and when he spoke, it was in a low, monotone voice. He seldom maintained eye contact with the person he was speaking to.

We do not tell this story to be cruel to our friend. We truly respect him professionally and cherish him personally. Our friendship, however, has gone beyond the initial impression stage. We know how he thinks and acts and feels and treats other people. Unfortunately, because of the image he projects with his first impression, a number of other people will never allow a meaningful relationship to develop with him. Thus, they never get to know and appreciate him the way we do. Our friend vividly demonstrates the unfortunate truth of first impressions: most people judge a book by its cover and probably always will.

Research has shown that you can change others' reactions to you simply by changing some aspects of your image. For instance, you can easily work on your handshake. This should be firm but not bone-crushing. People who develop painful "power-grips" evoke as negative a response as do those who are limp as a dishrag. In addition, make sure you do not hold the other person's hand too long. The other person may feel uncomfortable or question your intentions. Establish good eye contact with the other person while you are shaking hands. This helps get the relationship started.

Many times, before you even get the chance to shake somebody's hand, she has an opportunity to see how you sit or walk. She also gets to see the way you dress and how you are groomed. When it comes to sitting and standing body postures, the only thing we recommend is that you avoid extremes. People who walk with a strut, a shuffle, a bounce, or even with hunched shoulders project an image that may or may not be positive. Likewise, when you sit slouched in a chair or with one of your legs over the arm of the chair or in any other unusual posture, you again may be projecting an unflattering image. Avoid extremes. Sit and walk straight and relaxed.

Volumes have been written about personal hygiene and grooming; yet they are still often neglected. How many people do you see in your organization, regardless of where they are in the hierarchy, with dirt under their fingernails? How about dandruff on their collar or jacket? Have you ever seen any of your male coworkers with too much hair coming out of their ears or nostrils? How about any female coworkers with too much hairspray, makeup, or perfume? After lunch, have you ever spoken with people who had a strong odor of tuna fish, onion, garlic, or alcohol on their breath? Have you ever noticed an odor coming from a suit, shirt, blouse, dress, or shoes that a coworker wore once too often? Are you completely innocent of all these grooming violations? Be concerned and aware of the impressions you project to people through personal hygiene and grooming. You can and ought to improve them immediately if necessary.

The manner in which you dress has a profound effect on your acceptance by others. Clothes may not make the person, but they make a lasting statement about who the person is. Therefore, understand what you are saying to other people about yourself simply through your mode of dress.

Clothing is a powerful image maker. Through skillful dressing, you can evoke positive responses to your personality. This enhances your chances of success in interactions with other people. Most organizations have their own cultural dress codes which often vary by department and by status in the organization. If you're a manager, you may walk a clothing tightrope trying to project an aura of authority and success in order to move up in the hierarchy while not putting too much distance between you and your employees. An outside consultant or supplier might have to deal with conservative, three-piece-suit-type people and hands-on, shirtsleeve engineers in the same call. Factory workers required to handle greasy machinery might have trouble maintaining an appearance that would make a favorable impression on supervisors and managers. And women employees have the additional complication of trying to establish the right image without losing their feminine identity. All of this sounds like a tough order, but it can be done.

Think through the image that you want to project and the cultural environment of your organization. If you want to rise in the organization, there's no point in wearing expensive suits if the CEO is a casual, shirt-sleeve type. A general dress guideline is that if you want to project authority and success, dress in a conservative manner. Buy clothing made of natural fibers. Although this will cost you a little more at first, it will last longer and look much better. This includes wool or cotton suits; cotton shirts; silk blouses, ties, and scarfs; and leather shoes, belts, and briefcases. The colors, patterns, and styles of your clothing need to also be conservative. Whites, blues, and soft pastels are recommended for shirts and blouses, as are conservative plaids and pinstripes. Effective colors for suits are all shades of gray, blue (except light blue for males), and beige. Proper styling and fit are imperative in all your clothing. Of course, if you are working in a highly creative environment such as an advertising agency, you would move somewhat away from conservative colors and patterns. You might actually get points for flamboyance.

We have seen people who, even though they followed all the aforementioned rules, still projected a poor first impression because they didn't know how to put it all together. You, too, have probably seen a person wearing a pinstripe suit with a plaid shirt and a patterned tie. To complete the image you are trying to project to other people, learn how to combine your clothing properly. Make sure the colors you wear are complementary to each other. Your tie or scarf should pick up some of the color in your suit and/or in your shirt or blouse. Men's socks should blend with shoes and/or suit. A long-sleeve shirt or blouse is recommended with a suit to put the finishing touches on that successful, authoritative image. Jewelry and accessories should be simple and functional.

If your height, weight, or age is creating an emotional problem or an image problem for you, use clothing to help alleviate those problems. For instance, a tall person might soften the impact of his height by wearing soft colors and textures while avoiding dark, heavy, overpowering clothing. Short people create more visual impact by doing the opposite. They might want to wear more authoritative clothing, such as dark pinstripe suits, vests, solid white shirts, and wing-tip shoes for men; for women, dark-colored, tailored suits and plain, high-quality blouses. Heavy people can wear dark suits and outer clothing to de-emphasize their weight, whereas thin people can wear lighter clothing to make them look a bit heavier. Young people, who may need to project more power and authority, can follow the same guidelines as those recommended for shorter people. Older people, whose age already carries power and authority, can follow the same advice as that recommended for taller people.

Normally, a style of dressing that projects a conservative, authoritative, and successful image will increase your upward mobility. If you are a manager, there is no doubt that this image will prompt your employees to take you more seriously. Recommendations and instructions are much more likely to be carried out promptly and accurately when you project an authoritative and successful image. When you need to relate to your employees on their level, simply alter your image with minor adjustments. You can loosen your tie or scarf, unbutton the top button of your shirt or blouse, and take off your vest and/or jacket. This projects a much more relaxed image and will make it easier for your employees to communicate openly with you. When meeting with a superior and an employee at the same time, you need to make a value judgment on what image you need to project with those people in that situation.

Your clothes, voice, grooming, handshake, and body postures make a significant difference in the reception you receive from other people. First impressions do count and if you do not present an appropriate image to create a positive impression with other people, those impressions will count against you. Do the best you can to make it count for you.

DEPTH OF KNOWLEDGE. This refers to how well you know your subject—your particular area of expertise. How well do you know your company? How well do you know your industry? Are you current on your company's strengths and weaknesses relative to your competitors? Are you familiar with the skills and techniques of being a good manager within your company? Do other people come to you with questions about your company and your industry because they respect your expertise? Or do your employees, peers, and superiors turn to others when they need answers? Does the depth of your knowledge project credibility and command respect from your employees and fellow workers, or can you hear them thinking: "I could do her job as well as she can"?

The depth of your knowledge has a profound effect on your image. Make every effort to learn as much as possible about your company and your industry. Be thoroughly familiar with your firm's policies and procedures. Get to know your products and personnel as well as possible. Study the current situation and trends within your industry, and find out how you rate within the industry compared to your competitors. Take advantage of any training programs your company may offer. By increasing the depth of your knowledge, you will command respect from your employees, fellow workers, and superiors by projecting an image of intelligence and credibility.

BREADTH OF KNOWLEDGE. This area deals with your ability to converse with others in fields outside your area of expertise. What are the latest developments in world events? Are you familiar with the latest popular books and movies? Can you converse with people about things that are of interest to them?

By increasing the breadth of your knowledge, you will be able to develop rapport more easily with others. Not restricting the topic of conversation to something you alone find interesting allows people to be more comfortable in conversing with you. Some will go out of their way to talk with you. They will feel that you share something in common. Research has shown that the more people feel they have in common, the better they like each other. By increasing the breadth of your knowledge, you can increase your circle of influence with various types of people.

The responsibility for increasing the breadth of your knowledge falls on your shoulders. Regardless of your age or background, options abound for increasing the scope of your knowledge. We recommend that you read a local newspaper every day, front to back. Read, or at least scan, it all, not just the sports, funnies, fashion section, or the classifieds. Also, read one of the major news maagzines weekly. This will give you a good background in national and international events, as well as some additional knowledge in education, the arts, sports, books, movies, etc. Make an effort to read at least four books a year outside your normal area of interest, and try to mix fiction and nonfiction.

Make optimum use of typical nonproductive time, such as when bathing, shaving, putting on makeup, driving to and from work, cooking, cleaning, waiting in line, and so forth. You can make use of this nonproductive time by watching a morning or evening television news show, listening to radio news, or listening to books and/or educational materials on audio cassettes. Finally, even if you are not knowledgeable about another person's topic of conversation, show interest in it by asking questions. This is one of the best ways to learn. Remember that increasing the breadth of your knowledge comes most easily from reading, listening, and interacting with other people.

ENTHUSIASM. Who's your favorite entertainer? Let's make believe that you are going to a benefit concert tonight to see your favorite entertainer. The tickets cost $75 per person. By the time you and your date get to the concert and are seated, you are out $150 without ever seeing a thing. The entertainer comes out, and the house thunders with applause. She immediately begins to sing and sings as well as you have ever heard her sing, but without a trace of a smile—or any emotion. Wouldn't you feel cheated if she did not talk to the audience, did not make any gesture to the audience or attempt to build rapport, and did not show any enthusiasm at all? Would it improve your opinion of her performance if you knew that prior to coming out on stage, she had had an argument with her business manager about an advertising contract? Again, if you're like most people, these revelations would not in any way change your feeling of being cheated. If the entertainer had shown a bit more enthusiasm and warmth toward the audience, you'd probably feel much differently. You might even feel enthusiastic yourself.

When you show a lack of enthusiasm for your job, your company, or your personnel, do you think your fellow employees really know or even care why you are not enthusiastic? Won't they have the same feelings toward you as you had toward the concert singer? Wouldn't they feel cheated by a colleague or manager who lacked enthusiasm, just as you felt cheated by the entertainer who lacked enthusiasm?

Most people like to work with others who are enthusiastic about their work. Enthusiastic people seem to work harder, longer, and more accurately than those who are not enthusiastic. If you want your coworkers to have enthusiasm, try to project that quality yourself. It doesn't just happen. Enthusiasm spreads—it's catching—positive or negative. When you outwardly show enthusiasm about yourself, your colleagues, and your company, the same attitude will rub off on everyone around you. They will be enthusiastic, too. If you show a lack of enthusiasm, it, too, will eventually be projected to those around you; and they, in turn, will show a lack of enthusiasm about themselves, their fellow workers, their jobs, and their company. The choice is yours— bitterness or enthusiasm. Which do you choose?

The response you receive from the world around you is a measure of your success in interpersonal relations. The image you project will help to maximize or minimize your interpersonal success. From the beginning to the end of every transaction with another person, you are on stage. Every word, gesture, expression, and impression will be seen and evaluated, consciously or subconsciously, by that other person. Therefore, go through great pains to ensure the image you project, in each and every transaction, is one that helps facilitate and foster open, honest, trusting communications.

10

THE POWER OF
NONVERBAL
COMMUNICATION

Suppose that you have called one of your employees into your office. He is not aware that you intend to talk to him about a recent discipline problem that you recently discovered. You are determined to get to the bottom of this problem here and now. The employee enters your office, and you cordially ask him to have a seat. As you open the conversation on a social note, your employee is looking at you with his head slightly tilted, legs and arms uncrossed, and suit jacket unbuttoned. He is leaning slightly forward in his chair with his hands open and relaxed.

Midway through a difficult discussion, you notice that the employee's arms and legs are tightly crossed. His body seems rigid, his lips are pursed, and his fists are clenched. He is also maintaining little eye contact. As he tells you his side of the story, he still fails to maintain eye contact and even resists your glances. All during his end of the conversation, he seems to be squinting, rubbing his nose, and casually covering his mouth with his hands. As you listen, you occasionally peer over the rims of your glasses at him, sometimes giving him sideways glances, and intermittently raising an eyebrow. Toward the end of the conversation, you tell your employee that you intend to keep an open mind about the situation and will objectively look into the matter further.

As the employee is leaving your office, you lean back in your chair with your fingers laced behind your head and your feet on the desk. You have a funny feeling that something else went on during the conversation in addition to the words that were spoken, but you can't put your finger on it. You didn't believe a word he said because of the way he was acting, but you didn't want to let on to him that you were suspicious. That's why you told him that you would keep an open mind and be objective in this matter.

Little do you realize that both you and the employee were openly communicating with each other, not through words, but through body language. Your body movements, facial expressions, and gestures revealed much more about your attitudes and emotional state than your words. If you, the manager, only knew how to read body language, your interview with the employee might have gone in an entirely different direction, and the problem could have been resolved on the spot.

In this situation you read the employee's body language—crossed legs, rigid body, pursed lips, clenched fists, little eye contact, nervous gestures—as an attempt to withhold information or actually distort the information given. The employee reads your nonverbal responses—peering over glasses, sideways glances, raised eyebrows—as distrust. Your body language makes him nervous and he starts withdrawing. His body language makes you think he isn't telling the truth and you start distrusting him.

Body language is certainly not a new phenomenon. People have known about it and used it since the beginning of time. Before people developed language as a communications tool, they used body language to make their needs and desires known to other people. Also known as kinesics, body language describes human interaction excluding the use of written and spoken words. This broad definition encompasses everything from the most subtle raising of an eyebrow to the precise movements of the sophisticated sign languages used by the deaf.

Some nonverbal gestures are universal symbols. The chair at the head of the table has long been reserved for the leader of the group. More recently, this position of honor has also been extended to the host of the table. It is a custom that was honored as far back as the time of King Arthur, when the round table was developed as an attempt to administer democracy by eliminating the appearance of having one leader. Another universal gesture is raising the hands above the head, which has long symbolized surrender and submission.

Some gestures are even more expressive than words. Conjure up the image of a person slapping his forehead. This may be accompanied by an audible groan. Don't you already know that he has remembered something he was suppose to do? Implicit in this gesture is a rebuke to himself for his oversight.

Other well-known gestures are saluting, tipping one's hat, shaking hands, shrugging shoulders, waving good-bye, forming an O with thumb and forefinger, and blowing a kiss.

Nonverbal communication in the form of body language translates almost instantaneously. Research has substantiated that even when exposure to a situation is reduced to 1/24 of a second (the time it takes to show a single frame of film), people often grasp what it means. At 3/24 of a second, comprehension goes up dramatically, and there is increased understanding up to slightly more than one second of exposure.

Ability to understand body language is apparently not related to I.Q., the ability to take tests, or the grades one makes in school. Practice tends to improve the ability to understand body language. People tested for body language comprehension generally score higher on second and subsequent tests than on their first tries.

Researchers in the area of nonverbal communications claim that as much as 90 percent of the meaning transmitted between two people in face-to-face communications can come via nonverbal channels. As such, only 10 percent of the meaning we derive from others comes through words alone. If these figures even come close to reality (and research supports that they do), then the importance of our nonverbal communications is overwhelming.

We have a plethora of courses and seminars that teach us how to write and speak better, but have relatively few available in the study of nonverbal communications and body language. This chapter will give you a guide to developing a more thorough understanding of nonverbal communication techniques.

Sigmund Freud, an early believer in the utility of body language, distrusted the spoken word and based much of his work on the assumption that words hide more than they reveal. Freud believed, as do many researchers, that although we cannot rely on the truth of words, nonverbal behavior often does project truth.

Through kinesic behavior, people express their conscious and subconscious emotions, desires, and attitudes. Body language, which is stimulated by a subconscious need to express inner feelings, is more reliable than verbal communication and may even contradict verbal expressions. Body language is an outlet for your feelings and can function as a lie detector to aid a watchful observer in interpreting your words. To the observant, our body language communicates our sincerity and commitment.

In organizations, the communication of ideas is of primary importance. Unless we understand nonverbal body language, we are losing as much as 50 percent of the message that is being communicated. By increasing your awareness of kinesic behavior, you can read the emotions and attitudes of fellow employees, supervisors, customers, and others you interact with inside and outside your organization. As a result, you will have a greater feeling for and awareness of all your interpersonal transactions. This increased rapport with, and understanding of, others leads to increased trust and productivity.

The study of body language can also help improve others' understanding of you. The better you are able to transmit messages so that they are received by others as they were intended, the more effective you will be. Therefore, be acutely aware of the nonverbal messages you are projecting. You can increase tension and decrease trust simply by projecting negative body language or by lacking sensitivity in observing the nonverbal communication of others. The "bad vibes" that result can be disastrous to present and future relationships.

LANGUAGE GESTURES

■

Body language and nonverbal communication are transmitted through the eyes, face, hands, arms, legs, and posture (sitting and walking). You can tell a great deal about others, and they about you, simply by noting body gestures. However, each individual, isolated gesture is like a word in a sentence; it is difficult and dangerous to interpret in and of itself. As individual words have definitions, individual gestures have some meaning. Unless it is a one-word sentence, it takes more than one word to provide full meaning. Therefore, consider the gesture in light of everything else that is going on around you. When individual gestures are put together in clusters, they give a more complete and exact meaning of what the other person is feeling and thinking. Gesture clusters are the combined messages transmitted by the eyes, face, hands, arms and legs, and postures. But before we look at the attitudes and meanings projected by gesture clusters, we need to look at each individual nonverbal transmitter.

EYES. The eyes, known as the windows of the soul, are excellent indicators of a person's feelings. The expressions *shifty eyes, beady eyes,* and *look of steel* demonstrate the awareness people have for this area of the body. It is a long-held belief that the honest person has a tendency to look you straight in the eye when speaking. Recent work in this area has shown that there is some scientific basis for this belief. It has been discovered that speakers who were rated as "sincere" looked at their audience an average of three times longer than those speakers who were rated as "insincere."

People avoid eye contact with another person when an uncomfortable question is asked. Be aware of this and steer clear of topics that result in the avoidance of eye contact. Try to reduce tension and build trust rather than increase the tension.

Eye gestures are often easily interpreted. The raising of one eyebrow shows disbelief, whereas two eyebrows raised show surprise. Winking can be flirtatious or sometimes indicative of agreement, especially when accompanied by a nod or smile. Be sensitive to the body language of an employee who looks upward with a fixed expression while blinking rapidly. Chances are that what you are talking about is being seriously considered by the employee. In fact, a favorable decision may have already been made on the big issue, and the employee may simply be meditating on the details. Patience on your part is needed here. Refrain from further intense discussion until the employee's thought process is complete.

Some interesting work has been done with eye direction. People look either to the right or to the left, depending on what thoughts dominate their mental activity. Most people are classified as right lookers or left lookers. Left lookers are found to be more emotional, subjective, and suggestible; whereas right lookers are more influenced by logic and precision.

THE FACE. The face is one of the most reliable indicators of a person's attitudes, emotions, and feelings. Facial expressions sometimes betray emotions and states of mind. By analyzing facial expressions, interpersonal attitudes can be discerned and feedback obtained. "You can read his face like an open book" is a common statement used to describe a person whose facial expressions are demonstrative. Sometimes facial expressions are guarded in order to not betray a position prematurely by expressing a nonverbal opinion. The term *poker face* describes an attempt to keep others from knowing your true emotions. Common facial gestures are frowns (unhappiness, anger), smiles (happiness), sneers (dislike, disgust), clenched jaws (tension, anger), and pouting lips (sadness).

THE HANDS. Tightly clenched or wringing hands usually indicate that the person is experiencing undue pressure. This person will usually be difficult to relate to, as he is highly tense and in strong disagreement with you. "Steepling," joining the fingertips together and forming what might be described as a church steeple, indicates a smugness and great self-confidence. Superiority and authority are usually indicated when you are standing and joining your hands together behind your back.

A number of attitudes and emotions can be conveyed by what a person does with his hands around the face or head. For example, rubbing gently behind or beside the ear with the index finger usually shows signs of doubt. Casually rubbing the eye with one finger also usually means the other person is uncertain about what you are saying. Of course, it may also indicate that the other person has an itch or a "sleeper" in the eye. Rubbing the back of the head or palming the nape of the neck typically indicates frustration with the other person or the situation. Leaning back with both hands supporting the head usually indicates a feeling of confidence or superiority. Cupping one or both hands over the mouth, especially when talking, may well indicate that the person is trying to hide something. Boredom is often communicated by placing your head in your open palm and dropping your chin in a nodding manner while allowing your eyelids to droop. Putting your hand to your cheek or stroking your chin generally portrays thinking, interest, or consideration. On the other hand, pinching the bridge of your nose with your eyes closed, or placing your forefinger near your nose with your chin resting in the palm of your hand and your fingers bent across the chin or below the mouth most often shows that critical evaluation is taking place.

THE ARMS AND LEGS. Crossed arms tend to signal defensiveness. They seemingly act as a protective guard against an anticipated attack or a fixed position for which the other person would rather not move. Conversely, arms open and extended toward you generally indicate openness and acceptance.

Crossed legs tend to signal disagreement. People who tightly cross their legs seem to be saying that they disagree with what you are saying or doing. If people have tightly crossed legs and tightly crossed arms, their inner attitude is usually one of extreme negativity toward what is going on around them. As long as they are in this position, it is unlikely you will get their full agreement to what you are saying or doing.

POSTURE: SITTING AND WALKING. Sitting with a leg over the arm of a chair usually signals an uncooperative attitude. Sitting with a chair back facing forward and straddling the seat with your arms on the chair back tends to express a dominant, superior attitude. Sitting with your legs crossed and the elevated foot moving in a slight circular motion indicates boredom or impatience. Interest and involvement are usually projected by sitting on the edge of the chair and leaning slightly forward.

Generally, people who walk fast and swing their arms freely tend to know what they want and to go after it. People who walk with their shoulders hunched and hands in their pockets tend to be secretive and critical. They don't seem to like much of what is going on around them. Dejected people usually scuffle along with their hands in their pockets, heads down, and shoulders hunched over. People who are preoccupied or thinking usually walk with their heads down, hands clasped behind their backs, and pace very slowly.

INTERPRETING GESTURE CLUSTERS

Certain combinations of gestures are especially reliable indicators of a person's true feelings. These combinations are called gesture clusters. Each body language gesture is dependent on others, so analysis of a person's body language is based on a series of signals to ensure that the body language is clearly and accurately understood. Interpreting gesture clusters ensures a more meaningful analysis of the person's state of mind if the individual gestures that make up the cluster are congruent. In other words, all the individual gestures fit together to project a common, unified message. When they do not, you are faced with a case of incongruity. A good example of incongruity is the nervous laugh. A laugh traditionally signals amusement and relaxation. Yet when it sounds strained or nervous, and when the entire body shifts as though it were trying to escape an unpleasant situation, you know that the laugh does not mean amusement or relaxation. The laughter is probably there to try to cover up discomfort and possibly fear. So, in reading body language, make sure that you focus on gesture clusters and congruency. Remember that body language may augment, emphasize, contradict, or be totally unrelated to the words that someone is speaking. Therefore, reading body language is a continuous process of analysis. Let's look at some of the more common gesture clusters and their associated meanings.

OPENNESS. Several gestures indicate openness and sincerity, such as open hands, unbuttoned coat or collar, removing coat or jacket, moving closer, leaning slightly forward in the chair, and uncrossing arms and legs. When people are proud of what they've done, they usually show their hands quite openly. When they are not, they often put their hands in their pockets or behind their backs. Carefully watch the hands of a child the next time one is trying to hide something. When people take their coats off, unbutton their collars, or extend their arms toward you, they are generally beginning to feel comfortable in your presence. These are all positive signs.

DEFENSIVENESS. People who are defensive usually have a rigid body, arms or legs tightly crossed, eyes glancing sideways or darting occasionally, minimal eye contact, lips pursed, fists clenched, and a downcast head. What's the first thing that comes to mind when you think of a person with arms tightly crossed over his chest? A baseball umpire, right? Picture the manager rushing out of the dugout, arms swinging or stuck in his back pockets. As the manager approaches, the umpire crosses his arms. He has already nonverbally signaled his intention to defend his decision. As part of this cluster, the umpire may curtly turn his back on the manager, saying nonverbally, "You've talked enough." Arm gripping and tightly clenched fists are more extreme forms of the crossed-arm gesture. Especially watch for tightly clenched fists. They show that the other person is really turned off.

When someone puts his leg over the arm of a chair, it might seem to suggest relaxation and openness. It does not. Research has shown that when this happens, that person is dropping out of the conversation. You can't expect much more participation from this person unless you can reverse his attitude. Straddling a chair also might look informal and open, but it is not. It is domineering. The person has raised his defenses. Quite often in work situations the boss will do this to an employee. It is defensive, and you won't get anywhere dealing with a person in this posture.

EVALUATION. Evaluation gestures say that the other person is being thoughtful or is considering what you are saying—sometimes in a friendly way, sometimes in an unfriendly one. Typical evaluation gestures include the tilted head, hand to cheek, leaning forward, and chin stroking. Have you ever seen Auguste Rodin's famous statue *The Thinker?* Isn't this the model of a person deep in thought? In addition to the hand-to-cheek gesture, a person who tilts his head and leans slightly forward is usually considering what you are saying. A gesture indicating serious contemplation of what is being said is the chin-stroking gesture. Many say that this gesture signifies a wise person making a judgment.

Sometimes evaluation gestures take on a critical aspect. In this posture, the body is usually more drawn back. The hand is to the face, but the chin is in the palm of the hand with one finger going up the cheek and the other fingers positioned below the mouth. This is generally an unfavorable gesture. The typical delaying gesture to give a person more time to evaluate the situation is removing one's glasses and putting the earpiece of the frame in the mouth. People who smoke cigarettes sometimes light one to gain time. However, the classic stall gesture is pipe smoking. With little effort, this can be turned into a ritual of delay. The pipe has to be filled, cleaned, tapped, and lighted. Pipe smokers generally give the impression that they are more patient and moderate than cigarette smokers, who sometimes look like sprinters as they fish for a cigarette. If you are dealing with someone who is going through these stalling evaluation rituals, it is usually a good idea to let the person have the time needed to think things through. A person who pinches the bridge of his nose, closes his eyes, and slumps his head down slightly is expressing self-conflict. He is probably trying to decide if he is in a bad situation or not. Don't try to reason him out of it. Give him time. A final negative evaluation gesture is a person's dropping his eyeglasses to the lower bridge of the nose and peering over them. This gesture usually causes a negative emotional reaction in other people. Those on the receiving end feel that they are being closely scrutinized and looked down upon. Sometimes this gesture is made unintentionally by people who have ill-fitting glasses or granny glasses for reading.

SUSPICION, SECRECY, REJECTION, AND DOUBT. These negative emotions are communicated typically by sideways glances, minimal or no eye contact, shifting the body away from the speaker, and touching or rubbing the nose. When a person won't look at you, it could mean that he is being secretive, has private feelings in opposition to what you are saying, or is hiding something. A sideways glance sometimes registers as suspicion and doubt. It is sometimes called "the cold shoulder." Have you ever tried to help someone across the street who really preferred to proceed alone? You quickly discovered what the cold shoulder means. The individual may cross the street with you but turn away from you at a forty-five-degree angle. It is a gesture of rejection toward your "helping" hand. Shifting your body away from a person who is speaking or sitting so that your feet are pointing toward the door usually means that you wish to end the meeting, conversation, or whatever is going on. Touching or slightly rubbing the nose, as opposed to scratching the nose, may indicate puzzlement, doubt, or concealment.

READINESS. Readiness is related to the goal-oriented high achiever with a concern for getting things done. It communicates dedication to a goal and is usually communicated by placing your hands on your hips or sitting forward at the edge of a chair. The most common of these gestures is hands on hips. Athletes standing on the sidelines waiting to enter a sporting event often take this position. At a business meeting, it is usually assumed by someone who wants and expects other people to follow. A young child takes this position when challenging a parent's authority.

If you are about to sign an agreement you are pleased with,

you would sit at the edge of your chair. If you did not like the agreement, you would sit back. Salespeople are frequently taught that a person sitting on the edge of the seat is usually ready to make a purchase decision. These are positive gestures and are not to be feared. The individual is merely saying nonverbally that he is ready and able to take action. However, be careful when you project these gestures to others. You may give the appearance of being overly anxious.

REASSURANCE. This is usually conveyed by someone pinching the fleshy part of the hand; picking at fingernails; gently rubbing or caressing some personal object such as a watch, ring, or necklace; or chewing on some object such as a pencil, pen, or paper clip. We usually see these gestures quite vividly when people from the audience participate on a TV program. Many people are afraid of the television camera for numerous reasons. They think it will make them look heavier or older or will reveal some strange idiosyncrasies in their behavior. During the actual video-taping and the subsequent playback of the tape, people make all kinds of gestures to reassure themselves.

FRUSTRATION. The next time you watch a football game, pay close attention to what happens after a quarterback fades back and throws a pass that goes into and then out of the hands of his teammate. You will probably see the teammate kick the ground, slap the side of his helmet, or even do a double karate chop in the air. These are all frustration gestures of an extreme kind. More common frustration gestures are tightly clenched hands, rubbing the nape of the neck, hand wringing, and running one's hands through the hair. These are all negative gestures. If someone is doing this in your presence, immediately back away from whatever you are doing, and give her some more breathing room. If you don't, the frustration level will keep increasing until it eventually explodes.

CONFIDENCE, SUPERIORITY, AND AUTHORITY. These emotions are usually conveyed through relaxed and expansive gestures, such as steepling, feet up or on the desk, leaning back with fingers laced behind the head, and hands together at the back with chin thrust upward.

NERVOUSNESS. Clearing one's throat is a typical nervous gesture. Speakers often do this before they talk in front of an audience. Chain smoking is another gesture of nervousness. Yet when a smoker is extremely nervous, the first thing the person does is put out the cigarette. Covering the mouth while speaking is a nervousness gesture that police officers often see during interrogations. They report that this gesture means anything from self-doubt to lying. Other nervous gestures include twitching lips or face, fidgeting, shifting weight from one foot to the other, tapping fingers, pacing, jingling pocket change, and whistling.

SELF-CONTROL. Gestures such as tightly locking ankles and gripping your wrists behind your back usually mean that you are holding back. Do you do this in a dentist's waiting room? The Army has an old phrase—"keeping your heels locked." It means holding back and not disclosing anything; self-control.

BOREDOM OR IMPATIENCE. These unproductive feelings are usually conveyed by the drumming of fingers, cupping the head in the palm of the hand, foot swinging, brushing or picking at lint, doodling, pointing the body toward an exit, or looking at your watch or the exit.

ENTHUSIASM. This is an emotion that you love to see in other people and they in you. Enthusiasm is conveyed by a small upper or inward smile, an erect body stance, hands open and arms extended outward, eyes wide and alert, a lively and bouncy walk, and a lively and well modulated voice.

USING BODY LANGUAGE

■

The ability to project favorable body postures and to read the body language of others is undoubtedly a special asset in organizations. Here are some of the more common situations where the ability to read and project body language is especially useful:

EMPLOYEES AND MANAGERS. Body language is especially important between employees and managers because of the closeness of the relationship, the constant need for clear communication, and the need to accomplish objectives by working together. Employees tell managers how their words are being accepted by expressing their emotions and attitudes nonverbally. Managers express their emotions and feelings to employees nonverbally: they show agreement by nodding their head slowly or perhaps bobbing it enthusiastically. Disagreement may be evident when an employee or manager shakes his head or raises his eyebrows to indicate amazement or doubt. Nonverbal gestures transmit the intent of the verbal message before the person has finished speaking.

NEGOTIATIONS. People who can read body language accurately know when the negotiations are going well and when they are going off-track and need to be redirected. They know when people are ready to agree on a deal and how they feel about the deal. If someone loosens his collar, leans forward with his arms and legs uncrossed, he is displaying an openness to what is being discussed in the negotiations. If, however, the other party to a negotiation avoids eye contact and shifts his body away from you, he may have suspicious or secret feelings in opposition to what you are saying.

CUSTOMER SERVICE. Many customer service people are receiving specific training in body language in order to do a better job of making the customer happy. The service person who can read body language has a better feeling for the extent of the customer's unhappiness and what it will take to make the customer happy. If a customer service person sees tightly clenched hands, rubbing of the back of the neck, hand-wringing or running the hands through the hair, he would know that these signs of frustration mean he hasn't succeeded in making his customer happy.

SALES. Top salespeople have always been able to read body language even if they didn't realize that was what they were doing. When a prospect sits on the edge of his seat, it generally indicates a readiness to buy. By closely observing nonverbal clues, a good salesperson knows exactly when the sale is made even before the prospect has verbally indicated a purchase commitment.

Commitment is often indicated by body language, whether it's commitment to a negotiated compromise, commitment to a new action plan, or commitment to purchase a new product. The most obvious commitment clues are signs of relaxation—unlocking of ankles, palms and arms extending outward toward you, and movements toward the front of the chair—all of which indicate that the person is listening to you and tuning in to your message. If, on the other hand, the person crosses his legs, folds his arms tightly across his chest, and continues to lean back in his chair, you are probably not being effective. He is not being receptive to what you are trying to say, and a change in approach is necessary to win him back.

When someone starts to nod his head with you and copies your gestures, especially to the degree of leaning forward in the chair and balancing on the balls of his feet, you have someone who is really on the same wavelength as you. It is important to recognize these signals early and proceed with the commitment process. Otherwise, you may keep talking beyond the point of appropriateness and eventually bore the person into changing his mind. By carefully reading body language, you will know when to continue along the same line of conversation and when to change the subject, ask for a commitment, or totally end the conversation.

In addition to the other person's body language, what about your own body language? You are sending out signals of your own. Even if the other person is not trained in kinesics, he will still be affected by your body projections. Even though people may not consciously interpret nonverbal signals, they will react to them nonetheless. What makes it worse is if your body language and your words are not saying the same thing, which often happens. This can create an enormous credibility problem for you. It may condition others to look for double messages in their conversations with you.

Defensiveness, anger, or frustration can result from your projection of aggressive, dominant, or manipulative body language. Political games and deterioration of the trust result from these postures. You can create either beneficial or dangerous emotional climates through body movements. Research shows that people who sit in open, relaxed positions are seen as more persuasive and active and are better liked than those who sit in a tight, closed manner. Managers who sit in an open, relaxed way are able to affect greater opinion change in their employees than those who do not. These tips can help you maintain or increase cooperation from your coworkers, supervisors, customers, and others.

The relevance of reading body language is by now obvious to you. Studies have demonstrated that people who exhibit "expressionless stimuli"—blank face, aloofness, no interest—produce low levels of self-expression in others. A simple nod of the head in agreement seems to offer more feeling of expression, and a combination of head nods and warm smiles encourages others to express their own feelings fully.

As already discussed, body language is an essential part of interpersonal communications. Proficiency with reading and projecting body language is an integral part of your communication success. The mastery of this skill allows you to perceive the needs and desires of others and is also an aid in your own self-expression. However, body language is an inexact science. Gesture clusters are clues to the attitudes and emotions of another person, but they do not provide conclusive evidence. Test and validate your understanding of a person's body language rather than jeopardize your position with that person by making snap decisions. Body language provides the basis for making assumptions that ought to be tested and validated, not for concluding facts.

If all else fails, you can always revert to the use of words.

IT'S *HOW* YOU SAY IT

You can hear Sarah speaking. You can't understand her words, but she is speaking rapidly in a loud tone. Is she:

a. Excited?
b. Sleepy?
c. Angry?
d. Bored?

       You might say that she's either excited or angry but you really don't know for sure. Generally when someone is bored or sleepy she doesn't speak rapidly in a loud tone. But Sarah may naturally speak loud and fast . . . even when she's bored! Maybe she came from a large family where she had to speak loud and fast to be heard. So what can we tell by a person's tone of voice? A great deal—when we combine the person's vocal tone with her body language and her words. A person's vocal tone is a key communication clue. Taken by itself it might mean nothing or even be misleading but combined with the rest of the communication clues, you can put together a very accurate picture of not only *what* the speaker is saying but her *intent* in saying it. In this chapter, we take a closer look at the many different emotions people can project through their tones of voice.

Vocal intonation is a form of nonverbal communication. Vocal information is that part of the meaning of a message that is lost when speech is written rather than spoken. The verbal and vocal parts of messages do not always communicate the same meaning or feeling. Simple changes in voice qualities can change the meaning or emotion of the same group of words from one thing to another. A good example is an acting teacher who can verbalize the word "oh" eight different ways.

Exclamation—Oh! I forgot to make the check.
Excitement—Oh! Wow!
Question—Oh? Is that right?
Passion—Oh . . . I *love* opera.
Disgust—Oh, not peas again!
Pain—Oh, my arm hurts.
Disbelief—Oh, yeah?
Boredom—Oh. How interesting.

By simple changes in vocal qualities, the actor can convey eight totally separate and unique feelings and emotions to the audience. A simple two-letter word can be used to demonstrate the critical importance of vocal intonation in communications. A lack of emotional sensitivity to voice tones can create communication problems with your coworkers, managers, employees, friends, and family members. When paying attention to voice intonations, concentrate primarily on changes in the voice qualities of the person you are listening to.

VOICE QUALITIES. Some people naturally speak slowly, loudly, or clearly. When these people change their normal voice qualities, they are communicating something extra to you. It is up to you to know what these vocal qualities are, when they are changing, and what to do about these changes. The seven major vocal qualities are as follows:

1. RESONANCE—The ability of one's voice to fill space; an intensification and enrichment of the voice tone.

2. **RHYTHM**—The flow, pace, and movement of the voice.

3. **SPEED**—How quickly the voice is used.

4. **PITCH**—The tightening or relaxing of the vocal cords; the highness or lowness of sound.

5. **VOLUME**—The degree of loudness or intensity of the voice.

6. **INFLECTION**—The changes in pitch or volume of the voice.

7. **CLARITY**—The crisp articulation and enunciation of the words.

The way someone says something can have a great effect on what meaning is being communicated. An example of this is sarcasm, where the information being transmitted vocally has quite a different meaning from what is being transmitted verbally. That is why it is important for managers to learn what different voice intonations mean, how to identify them, and how to use them effectively to get their message across. A good example of how differing vocal intonations can totally change the meaning of the message was depicted in a video on nonverbal agendas. In the video, a manager has to relate verbatim the same message to three of her staff. She has ambivalent feelings toward one of the employees, dislike for one, and friendship for the other. The three scenarios clearly show that although the manager's words were the same with all three employees, her feelings, likes, dislikes, and biases were clearly projected in her vocal intonation as well as other observable behavior. Although the manager did not consciously realize what she was doing, the subconscious vocal message was clearly communicated to and identified by each of the three employees.

By learning more about vocal behavior and voice intonations, you will have a much better idea of the true feelings and intent of the people around you. In addition, you will have a better understanding of how others perceive you through your voice intonations.

PROJECTING EMOTIONS VOCALLY. The way in which a person varies any or all of the seven vocal qualities in conversations can significantly change the feeling or emotion of the message. By having the knowledge and awareness of the combinations of these vocal qualities and the respective emotions and feelings they project, you will be able to respond appropriately to these silent messages communicated to you through the vocal behavior of others. Listed next are twelve common feelings and emotions that can be communicated simply through changes in voice qualities.

AFFECTION—Upward inflection, resonant, low volume, slow speed.

ANGER—Loud volume, terse speech, irregular inflection.

BOREDOM—Moderate to low volume, resonant, somewhat slow speed, descending inflection, little clarity.

CHEERFULNESS—Somewhat high volume, fast speed, irregular inflection.

IMPATIENCE—Normal to high pitch, fast speed.

JOYFULNESS—Loud volume, fast speed, ascending inflection.

ASTONISHMENT—Ascending inflection.

DEFENSIVENESS—Terse speech.

ENTHUSIASM—Loud volume, emphatic pitch.

SADNESS—Low volume, resonant, slow speed, descending inflection, little clarity.

DISBELIEF—High pitch, drawn-out words.

SATISFACTION—Ascending inflection, little clarity.

Keep two things in mind about the vocal qualities of other people. First, you need to identify the other person's habitual vocal qualities. When it comes to vocal qualities, what is characteristic for one person is not necessarily characteristic for another. Second, noting the changes from that characteristic vocal quality, both in kind and direction of change, will give you clues as to the feeling state of the speaker. Try to recognize how the other person typically speaks in relationship to the seven vocal qualities, and during your conversation, note any changes from that characteristic style. When changes do occur, the person is probably communicating something extra that isn't carried in the words alone. It may indicate a point of emphasis, something of importance or concern, or a shift in the way that person is feeling. If you are aware of and sensitive to these clues as they are happening, you can respond to the changes and alter your communication if appropriate.

Developing the skill to understand vocal tones refines your interpersonal communications ability. It helps in building and improving solid, long-lasting working and personal relationships.

CHANGES IN VOLUME AND SPEED. Generally speaking, upward changes in a person's volume and speed indicate a positive change in attitude. But if the rhythm is clipped, it could project anger. Downward changes in volume and speed, greater resonance, and lessened clarity usually project a change in a negative direction. However, they could also indicate affection or satisfaction. Any changes in rhythm usually mean a change in mood, which also can be positive or negative. With any of the foregoing changes, first be aware of their occurrence. Then use your clarification skills to determine specifically what those changes are indicating. Your responsibility is to rely on your listening, probing, and feedback skills to get at the root of the change. Once you have determined the exact nature of the change, you can do something about it. If it's positive, you can capitalize on it. If the change is negative, you have an immediate warning that something needs to change—either adjust your message or explore the reasons for the change in the other person. When using your feedback skills for confirmation, make sure that you speak in terms of how the message is coming across to you, not in terms of the specific vocal qualities you are hearing. You are trying to exhibit sensitivity skills, not analytical skills.

USING YOUR VOCAL QUALITIES

"Don't speak to me in that tone of voice!" is a familiar comment in interpersonal conflict. Your tone of voice often has more impact than your actual words, communicating an important part of you and your personality to others.

Vocal quality is especially important over the telephone. You might find it a worthwhile exercise to tape-record only your half of several phone calls. After each call, replay the tape. How are you coming across to yourself? How does it sound? Are the volume and speed appropriate? What about the rhythm, inflection, resonance, and clarity? Do you feel that you were accurately communicating to the other person the emotions that you meant to communicate to him? By analyzing and constructively critiquing several of these phone calls, you can determine if any of your vocal qualities need improvement. As soon as you can identify these, think about how to improve them so you can start projecting the type of voice you would like to have.

Language can be interpreted in different ways, but through the use of vocal qualities you can clarify the intent of your message and communicate your feelings, likes, and dislikes. By varying tone, you can reinforce what you are saying verbally. For most people who work in an organizational environment, creating a vocal quality that conveys competence and assurance is important. Five aids to developing an assured voice are as follows:

1. Project a strong, full, but not overwhelming resonance.
2. Use your mouth and lips to speak clearly and distinctly.
3. Show enthusiasm by using the appropriate pitch, volume, and inflection.
4. Be interesting by varying your vocal qualities—avoid speaking in a monotone voice.
5. Speak naturally and at ease rather than adopting vocal qualities that do not fit who you are.

Your part of the conversation can't be monotonous, or you will be boring. On the other hand, do not vary your intonations in the same manner every time and risk coming across like a machine. A mechanical voice is boring and sounds canned. Both the uninteresting voice and the voice that follows a mechanical pattern are monotonous. You can avoid this monotony by simply varying your vocal qualities as the situation requires.

Speak rapidly when the subject matter permits; then emphasize an important point by speaking more slowly. By watching facial expressions and other nonverbal communications, you can determine the listener's degree of involvement. Emphasize points that apparently interest the listener and then pause to let the idea sink in. As you can see, timing in speech can be highly informative and effective to both you and your listeners.

A study at Yale University showed that the more errors a person made while speaking (errors meaning poor tone, volume, monotony, etc.), the more that speaker's discomfort and anxiety increased. Through practice and awareness, you can reduce these errors. By doing this, you will become much more comfortable with your speaking voice. This in turn will make your listeners

IT'S *HOW YOU SAY IT* • 141

more comfortable and they will listen more intently. You will have more credibility with them.

Carelessness in enunciation is likely to be taken as an indication of carelessness in other areas. Poor enunciation is also likely to result in the listener misunderstanding what you are saying. It can easily lead to a breakdown in the communication process. Good enunciation clarifies communication which tends to strengthen and build relationships.

The foregoing vocal suggestions can be effective if they are used appropriately. Overuse or overemphasis of these methods can annoy your listeners and take their attention away from the conversation. Your use of these vocal skills must seem natural and spontaneous, or you will appear insincere. By using the proper vocal intonation, you can draw attention to those areas of your message that impact and benefit your listeners.

Most people know the importance of using effective vocal behavior when speaking to coworkers, employees, upper management, clients, and customers. An awareness of the subtle nuances, feelings, meanings, and emotions of vocal behavior is critical. It allows you to be aware of what you are (nonverbally) communicating to others and what they are (nonverbally) communicating to you. It can make or break working relationships. It can dramatically impact an organization's productivity as it affects the communication process of people working together. Becoming more aware of and sensitive to your vocal intonations and those of others can help you improve your credibility, and help you develop stronger working and personal relationships. That payoff seems well worth the effort.

COMMUNICATING THROUGH SPATIAL ARRANGEMENTS

Have you ever had someone stand so close to you that you felt threatened or uncomfortable? How do you feel when you return to your office and find a colleague sorting through your filing cabinet? What is your reaction when you return to a meeting after a break and find that someone else is sitting in "your place"? The uncomfortable feelings most of us experience in such situations result from violations of our personal space. Answers to these types of questions offer clues as to how to use proxemics—space and the movement of people within it—to communicate with others. At least six aspects of proxemics help explain how we use space for communicating with others: territory, environment, things, proxemic zones, dyad arrangements, and group arrangements.

TERRITORY
.

Your reactions to the foregoing questions probably confirm the conclusion of anthropologists that human beings are territorial animals with inherent compulsions to possess and defend space as exclusive property. Your office is a fixed feature territory with unmovable boundaries such as walls and doors. When you enter a meeting, you establish a semifixed feature territory, bounded by movable objects such as your notebook, coffee cup, and the jacket hanging on your chair. Although you have no legal rights to certain geographic areas just because you arrived there first and staked out your claim with your jacket, notebook, and coffee cup, your immediate reaction in returning to the meeting and finding someone else in your seat is probably a feeling of loss, followed by anger and a desire to regain your space.

People like to protect and control their territory. This is easier to do with fixed feature territories, where it is possible to shut your door or even lock it. In semifixed feature territories, the best protection is your physical presence. If you are absent for a while, your only protection is other people's respect for honoring your territory. If it is a desirable territory, you may return and find that someone else has claimed it.

There are times when others invade even our fixed feature territory or cause us to lose control over it. This is a more severe social violation than ignoring semifixed boundaries, and your angry feelings are apt to be even greater. If you have your door closed and someone walks into your office without knocking and without being invited, the tension between you will skyrocket. Similar reactions would probably occur if a visitor sits in your chair, uses your pen, or grabs your personal appointment book to check a date for a future meeting.

In attempting to establish a good working relationship with coworkers or employees, don't violate their territory, even if you're the boss. When dealing with territory, mutual respect is the norm, and mutual trust is based on honoring it. People value their privacy and need to protect and control their personal territory. Studies have even demonstrated that if you are talking to someone and inadvertently violate some aspect of his personal space, he may be so upset that he doesn't hear another word you say.

ENVIRONMENT

■

Architects have long been aware that the design, color, and placement of objects such as furniture, plants, and pictures in an environment can facilitate or hinder the quality of communications and productivity of interactions among coworkers. Several commonly accepted feelings about the use of space in work environments have been identified by Dr. Anthony Athos. Attention to the environmental clues can help you understand what others are trying to say or why they react as they do to this important form of nonverbal communication. Awareness of these variables can also facilitate the breadth and clarity of your own communications.

MORE IS BETTER THAN LESS. One way to communicate to others their importance is by the amount of space assigned to them in the total organizational environment. Presidents of companies usually have larger offices than middle managers, and so forth. Space is a limited resource, so the more space people are assigned for their personal territory, the more valuable and important they are assumed to be.

People not only desire large offices but offices with a view. Although there may be practical reasons for windows such as ventilation or lighting, views also provide the illusion of greater space. In any event, if you check out office assignments in most organizations, you will surely find that newer and lower-status employees occupy the inside offices without windows or desirable views. Higher-status persons with more power and assumed importance will usually occupy larger offices with nicer views. When you notice an incongruence in this pattern, it may be worth your time to check out what is being communicated.

PRIVATE IS BETTER THAN PUBLIC. Another way of communicating status is by assigning someone personal territory (not public) that can be closed off for privacy out of the sight and sound of others. In most organizations, to go from open, public space—characterized as a semifixed feature territory—to a private office, which is an enclosed fixed feature territory—is a signal of increased importance and status. Think of most administrative offices you have visited. The typists are usually situated in a common "pool" area and sometimes do not even have the same table or typewriter to use every day. The executive secretaries often have assigned fixed feature territories characterized by partitions giving them some privacy. The manager of the typists and secretaries probably has a private office with a door and other fixed feature characteristics.

If we have private space, how we use it communicates to other people. If some people are invited into our office for a closed-door meeting, they are assumed to be privileged and to have access to important information denied those not included. It is better to be with the "insiders" than with the "outsiders." Those without the privilege of private space aren't considered important enough to need a door or the option of privacy. Important assumptions are attributed to this nonverbal communication concerning factors such as trust and importance of function.

Taking privacy away is often perceived as a territorial violation. If inadvertent, the trespasser may not understand why such tension has been created. Such a case occurred when a group of filing clerks were moved to a new work space shared by another group of workers. They were used to their own private environment and thus suffered decreased morale and productivity and increased errors and turnover. Intentional territory violations are sometimes used by "aware" supervisors as a form of punishment. While collective bargaining was in process, a group of workers engaged in a work slowdown procedure including much longer breaks than formally allowed. When supervisors started policing the break area to enforce the standard time allowable, the workers began to spend much longer periods of time in the rest rooms with reading material. Management's reaction to this ploy was to remove the doors from the toilet stalls. Although effective in shortening rest room breaks, this action brought a much greater response than anticipated from the workers. When a space is designed for activities close to our bodies, we value its privacy all the more. A related example that supports the common acceptance of this aspect of privacy as associated with status is the usual assignment of rest room space. Top executives often have rest rooms within their own offices. Managers have shared, but private, rest rooms in the hallways, which may be locked and made private. Workers usually share a common rest room area designed to be public and serve many at one time.

HIGHER IS BETTER THAN LOWER. Remember the childhood game of King of the Mountain? We have all probably played a version of this game at one time, with the objective of being higher up in space than others. As adults, we play the same game but of a much more serious nature. The wealthy people are called the "upper class," and the poor are the "lower class." As we advance, we "climb up the organizational ladder." The executive offices are usually on the top floor, and the work area is on the bottom floor. If you're higher than others, you "look down" on them. Although there are specific exceptions, it is a sign of higher status to occupy higher territorial space than others.

Knowledge of this form of nonverbal space communication can be helpful in assigning space to organization members in a fashion congruent with their expectations. It can also be helpful in interpersonal situations when you might appear to be talking down to someone if you remain standing over them when they are seated. You can probably think of several more applications.

NEAR IS BETTER THAN FAR. It is usually a sign of higher status to be assigned space close to the top executive rather than space far away. Being near the boss allows for more exposure and the chance of being noticed. It also allows for increased interaction potential and more opportunities for being in on important information and decisions. The territory assignment itself, being formally situated close to the boss, is a sign of importance.

This principle sometimes works in reverse. If, for example, you don't like the boss, or if you're trying to catch up on some work before you are noticed, being located far away may be more desirable than being near. Even if you like the increased status of being assigned space near the boss, it is a mixed blessing. It is an opportunity for recognition and advancement but also a responsibility always to appear on top of everything and to cope with the associated pressures.

One common procedure for using space to communicate rank is through the assignment of parking spaces. The lowest ranked employees may not even have a parking area available but have to use public streets or pay for parking outside. Those with a little more status usually have access to the company parking lot, and their cars are designated by a "hunter's permit" that allows them to find a space on a first come, first served basis. Upper-level managers and executives have their own private area and usually specially designed spaces with their names on them.

At a large, urban, state-supported university where one of the authors was once employed, lip service was paid to the importance of the students in the educational community, but nonverbal communications told another story. Although administrators and faculty had access to either faculty/staff parking lots or private spaces according to status differentials, students had no formally designated parking area on campus. They had to compete for metered lots and public street parking or ride the university bus from their formally assigned parking lot, which was located five miles from campus. The author is now associated with a private university that also expounds on the importance of the student in its educational community. In this case, for philosophical and financial reasons, the importance of and respect for students is real, and space assignments communicate a congruent message. Only one type of parking permit is issued, and faculty and students share the parking facilities equally.

IN IS BETTER THAN OUT. This principle is closely related to the concept of near being better than far. The difference is one of a fixed boundary versus a matter of degree. Higher status people are usually located within the main office building; but within that building, additional differences in rank are indicated by nearness to the boss, which floor you're on, and how much space your office has.

People are usually more satisfied and productive if they are working within their own office or work area than when they are required to work in an unfamiliar area. This phenomenon is similar to sports teams that usually prefer to perform on their own turf than to have to adjust to their opponent's arena.

THINGS
■

The kinds of things that are in your assigned territory also communicate meaning about your status in the organization. As the various aspects of space interact to present combined status communications (e.g., a small but private office near the boss), so do the type and use of things within our space. Several commonly accepted generalities about the value of different aspects of things are mentioned next.

BIGGER IS BETTER THAN SMALLER. Higher-level executives usually have larger desks and larger pieces of furniture in their larger offices than lower-ranking managers. The president of a company often drives a large car or a large-price luxury car, whereas the vice-presidents drive medium-sized or medium-priced cars, and managers are allowed the use of economy cars from the car pool when needed for business engagements.

MORE IS BETTER THAN FEW. Top executives often have two offices, two secretaries, two telephones, and more furniture and decorations in their offices than their lower-ranking associates. Higher-ranking organization members also usually have access to more privileges, such as club memberships, expense accounts, and dining facilities. Not only do they have more things assigned for their own private use, but they also usually have access to the facilities made available for their underlings.

CLEAN IS BETTER THAN DIRTY. White collar workers generally have their offices cleaned by a janitorial staff while blue collar workers usually have to keep their areas clean themselves. People who work in the clean environment of an office are expected to maintain a meticulously clean appearance while shop workers dealing with machinery or grimy materials are not expected to maintain the same level of cleanliness. On the status ladder, clean is higher than dirty.

NEAT IS BETTER THAN MESSY. Most high-ranking officials have neat and orderly desks, at least in their public offices where they meet with others. A clean desk communicates efficiency, whereas a messy one indicates disorganization and confusion. Clean and neat reception areas communicate that the organization cares enough about its visitors to keep their environment pleasant. The same message is communicated by the condition of visitors' rest rooms and dining areas.

EXPENSIVE IS BETTER THAN CHEAP. This is a truism, evidenced every day in the kind of clothes people wear, the furniture in offices, the cars we drive, and the food we eat. Although in some subcultures, "economical" may be of value, "expensive" is usually the signal of status in organizations.

VERY OLD OR VERY NEW IS BETTER THAN RECENT. Offices furnished with antique or modern furniture are usually more impressive than those with contemporary furniture. The same is true of antique cars and new ones versus late model cars.

PERSONAL IS BETTER THAN PUBLIC. Your own personal desk or chair is a sign of status when others have to compete for public facilities. The same is true of your own versus company provided trophies, pens, photographs, and other decorations. Finally, expense accounts and other special funds assigned exclusively to you are of higher status than those to be shared with others.

USING TERRITORY AND ENVIRONMENT TO FACILITATE COMMUNICATION

▪

Based on the preceding discussion, there are several ways to utilize feelings about territory and environment to facilitate communication and relationships. It is always best, for example, to arrange for meetings in an attractive location so that participants will feel comfortable and important. If they enjoy their surroundings, they will probably have more desire to continue their activities and do a good job worthy of the setting. The meeting place should, of course, be a neutral location so that territorial problems won't intimidate those meeting on another's turf. Finally, flexible seating is encouraged to allow participants to establish their own semi-fixed territories and appropriate spatial arrangements.

If a supervisor wants to establish more intimacy in relationships with employees, it sometimes helps to have one-to-one meetings in employees' offices or in a neutral place. The supervisor also needs to apply appropriate body language during the conversation. Standing or leaning over someone who is seated conveys power and can be intimidating and uncomfortable for the person sitting. On the other hand, leaning back and appearing too casual can also convey a feeling of superiority and create a negative reaction in the employee.

The way you arrange your office furniture communicates the degree of formality you wish to maintain in your interactions with visitors. If your chair is behind your desk, which creates a barrier between you and your visitors, the outcome will probably be relatively short and formal interactions. A chair closer to the visitor, without the barrier of a desk, creates a much more informal and relaxed atmosphere, which encourages longer and more open interactions.

PERSONAL SPACE

Another aspect of space that we use to communicate to others is air space around us. We assume that this is our personal territory, much like a private air bubble. We feel a proprietary right to this space and resent others entering it unless they are invited. The exact dimensions of these private bubbles vary from culture to culture and with different personality styles, but some generalities can be useful in helping us receive and send messages more clearly through the use of this medium. How many times have you sat next to a stranger on an airplane or in a movie theater and jock-eyed for the single armrest between you? Since touching is definitely a personal space violation in our culture, the more aggressive person who is not afraid of touching someone usually wins the territory.

INTERPERSONAL SPACE

Research in proxemics has revealed that adult American business people have four basic distances of interaction. These are defined next and are illustrated in figure 12-A.

INTIMATE ZONE—ranges from actual physical contact to about two feet.

PERSONAL ZONE—ranges from approximately two feet to four feet in distance.

SOCIAL ZONE—extends from nearly four feet to roughly twelve feet.

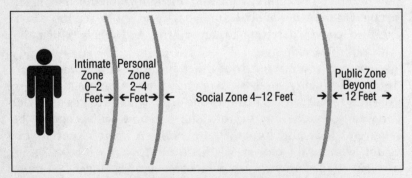

12-A *Proxemic zones*

PUBLIC ZONE—stretches from twelve feet away to the limits of hearing and sight.

People are not necessarily conscious of the importance of maintaining these distances until violations occur. This can easily lead to increased tension and distrust.

How you feel about people entering these different zones depends upon who they are. You might feel quite uncomfortable and resentful if a business associate entered your Intimate or Personal Zone during a conversation. If the person were your spouse, however, you would probably feel quite good, even if he were so close as to touch you. Manager/employee relationships usually begin in the Social Zone of four to twelve feet, although they often move to the Personal Zone over time after a high level of trust has developed.

People can generally be classified into two major proxemic categories—contact and noncontact. According to Edward Hall, Americans and Northern Europeans typify the noncontact group due to the small amount of touching that takes place during their transactions. On the other hand, Arabs and Latins normally use much contact in their conversations. In addition, although Americans are considered a noncontact group in general, there are obviously significant numbers of Americans who are "contact" people.

When these two major patterns of proxemic behavior meet, their interaction normally ends in a clash. The contact people unknowingly get too close or touch the noncontact people. This leads to discomfort, tension, distrust, and misunderstanding between the two. A commonly used example is that of the South American and North American businessmen interacting at a cocktail party. For the South American, the appropriate zone for interaction was Personal to Intimate and included frequent touching to make a point. This was about half the distance minus touch that the North American needed to be in his comfortable Social Zone. The South American would step closer, and the North American backward, in a strange proxemic dance until both gave up the relationship as a lost cause because of the other's "cold" or "pushy" behavior.

Contact and noncontact people have conflicting perceptions of each other based solely on their proxemic behavior. The noncontact people are seen as shy, cold, and impolite by the contact people. On the other hand, noncontact people perceive contact people as pushy, aggressive, and impolite. Often people are bewildered by interactions with other persons displaying different proxemic behaviors. When a proxemic violation occurs, a person generally has a feeling that something is not right but may not be able to focus directly on the cause. Attention usually focuses on the other person and why the other person is not behaving in the "proper" manner. Attention may even be focused on yourself, causing you to become self-conscious. In either case, attention shifts to the behavior of the two transactions and away from the conversation at hand and interferes with effective communication.

Most business relationships are impersonal and begin at a social distance. After the relationship has been established and trust is developed, the distance will usually decrease, and interactions will take place in the Personal Zone without any discomfort for either party. Even within the North American business culture, however, proxemic violations occur because of the different personality styles of the participants. A warm Relater or Socializer executive who feels comfortable touching the arm or shoulder of a Thinker or Director employee, for example, may create considerable discomfort for the latter. Again, the keys are being able to read the styles of others and behavioral flexibility.

INTERPERSONAL SPACE STRATEGIES

•

Because we become uncomfortable when someone violates our personal space, we develop specific behaviors to reduce tension and protect ourselves from further invasion. Charles and Marie Dalton have summarized several interpersonal space strategies. Perhaps the most commonly used strategy is simply to move away and create a greater distance until the intruder is in a more comfortable zone. Other strategies include avoiding eye contact or placing an object between yourself and the other person, such as a footstool, your leg, or an elbow. The most comfortable position for any given conversation will depend upon the nature of the other person and the situation.

DYAD ARRANGEMENTS. When two people, or a dyad, are interacting in a casual conversation in which both feel at ease with the topic and each other, a corner-to-corner arrangement is often preferred. As illustrated in figure 12-B on page 154, this position allows for unlimited eye contact and maximum use of other nonverbal signals such as facial expressions and gestures. Side-by-side seating arrangements are often preferred for cooperative task interactions where both parties intend to concentrate mainly on the work they are doing.

As figure 12-C shows, the reading of nonverbal expressions is difficult in the side-by-side position, and the physical proximity is closer than usually tolerated. Because the participants are concentrating on the task and intend to cooperate with each other, the associated assumed trust makes these disadvantages tolerable for the task at hand.

Figure 12-D illustrates the across-the-table arrangement, which is sometimes used for casual conversations but is almost always used for competitive situations. It permits close monitoring of nonverbal clues and provides the safety of a barrier between the participants.

When participants are in the same location but are working independently, the coaction position illustrated in figure 12-E on page 155 is preferable.

Coaction seating provides a kind of privacy within semifixed boundaries for shutting the other person out so that one can be alone with the work.

GROUP ARRANGEMENTS. We have seen how the nature of the interaction affects the positions of participants. Although more complex, the same type of phenomenon operates within groups and affects things like the communication pattern, leadership, and quality of the decisions.

Leaders usually sit at the end of a table, which is a position conducive to active participation no matter who occupies it. As can be determined in figure 12-F on page 156, the individual at the end of the table probably has high status in the group and will tend to be the most active participant. Since more communication will be sent in his direction, this individual will be more influential in any decision that is made and will probably enjoy the discussion more than those seated at the sides of the table. A formal leader usually will assume a position at the head of the table. In a group of "equals," the person occupying that position

12-B *Corner-to-Corner seating position*

12-C *Side-by-Side seating position*

12-D *Competitive seating position*

12-E *Co-Action seating position*

has the best chance of becoming the most influential person because of the advantages in giving and receiving both verbal and nonverbal communications.

To balance the influence of a dominant leader, other group members sometimes bunch together, as illustrated in figure 12-G on page 157. Although this grouping is most often an unconscious reaction, it does allow for easier reading of nonverbal clues between the leader and other group members. It explains the usual void of bodies in the chairs immediately adjacent to formal leaders when formal meetings are held.

Research has also provided several other interesting points about individual location in group situations. Conflict is more likely, for example, between people sitting opposite each other. Also, when a person stops talking, someone across the table is more likely to pick up the conversation than someone sitting on the side. Side-by-side conversations are often attempted to pool power or gain support before making a verbal commitment.

12-F *Group with dominant leader seating arrangement*

SPECIAL ARRANGEMENT DETERMINANTS

∎

Many factors are involved in determining the special arrangements between people in dyads or groups, among them: angle of approach, personality, previous relationship, race, and sex.

ANGLE OF APPROACH. Women tend to permit closer approaches at the sides than at the front. This is in contrast to men, who permit others to approach closer frontally than from the sides before becoming uncomfortable. Women also use the side-by-side seating arrangement when talking to others more than men, and they are more prone to talk to others seated next to them during group discussions. Also, as a passing note, women seem to be more comfortable with the closer physical presence of others, in general, than men.

PERSONALITY. Extroverts prefer closer interpersonal distances than do introverts. Also, individuals who feel that they have control over their lives like closer distances to others than

12-G *Seating arrangement balancing dominant leader*

do people who feel that their lives are controlled externally. With respect to learning style, some people prefer working closely with others, whereas others prefer distance and minimal contact. Finally, with respect to decision-making situations, some people are better at working closely, while others prefer to keep their distance and not interact at all (except maybe over the phone) if possible.

PREVIOUS RELATIONSHIPS. People who have interacted successfully with each other in the past prefer closer distances than individuals who do not feel comfortable with each other. The same is true for people who are attracted to each other or desire to communicate positive feelings to one another, as opposed to those who are indifferent or hostile to each other.

RACE. In general, people prefer greater distances between themselves and others of different races than others of the same race. When people of the same race are interacting, black females prefer more intimate distances, followed by black males, then white females, and finally white males, who like the most distant positions from each other.

SEX. It will probably come as no surprise that men and women like to be closer to others of the opposite sex than to others of the same sex. When interacting with members of the same sex, however, females are capable of tolerating less space between each other than males are comfortable with when interacting with other males. Research has demonstrated that male employees permit female supervisors to get closer to them than male supervisors. For female employees, on the other hand, there was no difference in the space they permitted between themselves and their supervisors, whether female or male.

SPATIAL IMPLICATIONS FOR ORGANIZATIONS

By watching your own behavior and checking your feelings to see how you use your own space and react to others who behave differently, you can learn a lot about what the use of personal space means to you. You can become more skillful at communicating your message to others as well as understanding others' messages to you. Sometimes communication seems to get off course for no apparent reason. Looking at how space is being used and what message is being sent by the person's use of personal space may give you a clue as to what is going wrong.

If someone violates a person's proxemic zones without verbal or nonverbal invitation, it most likely will lead to an increased tension level and a decreased trust level. The relationship often becomes nonproductive, with little or no cooperation. In attempting to build trust, be careful not to offend a person by intruding on their proxemic zones or territory. This is especially true if you are a supervisor or manager as the employee might feel that she had no recourse to the intrusion. People value their privacy and do not appreciate clumsy attempts to invade it. There are detrimental consequences for people who are insensitive to the proxemic rules of behavior: an increase in tension, a decrease in credibility, and a reduced chance of gaining commitment or agreement on the subject of the communication. An extreme example would be a salesperson who walks into the office of a prospect, sits down on the edge of the prospect's desk, and leans over into his face to deliver the "pitch." That salesperson might be doing everything else perfectly: he may look exactly right, he may have a great product, or he may know the best way to present the benefits to the prospect. Chances are though that he will not make this sale because he has badly violated his prospect's personal space.

Understanding the concepts of proxemics helps the communication process with everyone you encounter. It is perhaps most important in the supervisor-employee relationship only because that unequal-power relationship is so often subject to tension, conflict, and mistrust. The supervisory process has been described as initially meeting the employee face-to-face at a social distance and slowly moving one hundred eighty degrees to a side-by-side personal distance. You move closer (not only in a relationship sense but in an actual proxemic sense) only as trust is built. Care should be exercised in not moving too fast (increasing tension) or too slow (refusing your employee's invitation). Good communicators respect, understand, and effectively use the concepts of proxemics. The payoff for them is more attention, more trust, better communication, and a better chance for productive working relationships.

13

HOW YOUR USE OF TIME TALKS

You have a meeting with Sam. He arrives fifteen minutes late, pulls a chair up so close your knees are touching, and starts speaking loudly, shaking his finger in your face.
How do you feel?

You have a meeting with Sarah. You go to her office five minutes early and wait for her to invite you in. You sit in the chair furthest from her desk and speak so softly she has to ask you to repeat several comments.
How are you feeling?

As you have no doubt realized by now, everything we do—every action we take, everything we wear, every movement of our body, every tone of our voice— communicates our message. In the little vignettes above, we instantly get a sense of what's happening before we have heard the first word. The way we use time and the space around us are two very powerful, nonverbal communication tools. The last chapter gave you a guideline to understanding and using space in order to make your message more powerful. This chapter will explore what your use of time says to other people.

HOW YOUR USE OF TIME TALKS
·

How do you feel when you are kept waiting for an appointment to discuss something with your boss? When a colleague or employee is chronically late to meetings? When someone arrives early for a meeting with you? When you are asked to work overtime during the weekend? When your boss stops talking with you as much as usual and begins spending more time with a coworker?

The foregoing examples are meant to demonstrate that how we use time communicates things to people about how we feel about them—especially feelings of liking, importance, and status. Time is a continuously and irreversibly scarce resource. Thus, who you give it to, how much you give, and when you give it are important variables in communicating your feelings to others.

Professor Anthony Athos has identified accuracy, scarcity, and repetition as three major variables that we use to assign meaning to time. Although the rules about how time is used, with respect to these three variables, vary from one situation to another, our use of time to communicate speaks very loudly.

ACCURACY
·

In our Western culture, concern for time accuracy is enormous. Watches are advertised as not being more than a few seconds off a year, and we literally strap them to our bodies so that we can know exactly what time it is and be able to stay precisely on schedule. Because of our concern for accuracy, deviations from accuracy communicates a powerful message to other people.

Think back to your first date. Many men probably arrived early and drove around the block for a while so as not to communicate their eagerness. It would not be unusual for a woman, on the other hand, to wait in her room for a few minutes after her date arrived to mask her anxiety. If either party had been late, however, an explanation would have been necessary in order to erase a presumption of indifference. Similarly, it is not uncommon for a manager to assume that an employee who is frequently late to department meetings doesn't care, and that manager may well get angry as a result. Employees also tend to assume that managers who are late to meetings don't care much. Consequently, how accurate we are with time often broadcasts a message about our level of caring, even if that is not the message we intend.

Time can also be used to tell how we feel about others in terms of their relative status and power. If the president of the company calls a junior manager to her office for a meeting, the manager will probably arrive before the appointed time. Because of the difference in status, most managers would probably feel that any inconvenience in waiting ought to be theirs. The president's time is regarded as worth more and, therefore, is not to be wasted, as opposed to the less expensive time of others.

Time use is also a mechanism for defining relationships. If two managers of equal status are very competitive, one might try to structure the other's time to demonstrate greater status and power. Assume that one manager calls the other and asks her to come to her office for a meeting later that morning. First, the initiation indicates a higher status. Second, specifying the place and time diminishes the other's influence. Third, the immediacy of the intended meeting implies that the other has nothing more important to do. If she agrees, the chances are high that the invited manager will not arrive for the meeting exactly at the agreed-upon time. She will probably be a bit late and offer no apology. This is enough to irritate her colleague but not enough to represent an open insult. The silent message is: "Now we've each got one put-down. My time is equal to yours, and I'm at least equal to you."

Using time to manipulate or control others is common, although we are not usually aware of it, whether we are on the initiating or the receiving end. When we allow others to structure our time, it is usually in deference to their relative greater status or power. This is especially true when we would rather be doing something else. Private time is becoming more and more valued, as evidenced in the growing reluctance to work overtime in the evening or on weekends.

The longer we keep people waiting, the worse they are likely to feel. Imagine a middle manager summoned to a meeting with the president at 1:00 P.M. who arrives at a "respectful" 12:50. She remains comfortable until 1:10, when she asks the secretary to remind the president that she is there. If the secretary checks and conveys that the president will be right with her, the manager will probably remain comfortable until around 1:25. By 1:45, however, she is likely to be quite angry and assume that the president doesn't really care about seeing her. If the president then has the manager sent in and proceeds directly to the business at hand without offering an explanation, the manager may appear somewhat cranky and irritable. This may negatively affect the meeting and the relationship. If the president apologizes for being late and shares some inside information with her explanation, the manager is more apt to forgive the boss because, after all, her time is more important.

In general, the longer a person is kept waiting, the more stroking is required to neutralize the feelings of hostility that gathered during the waiting period. Awareness of this process can help you understand your feelings better when you are the person who is waiting. It also can increase your skill at helping others not feel put down when they have to wait for you because of some legitimate commitment.

SCARCITY

■

Time and money are two of our most limited resources. However, while we can often work harder or smarter and make more money, nothing we can do will change the amount of time allotted to us. Each of us has the same 10,080 minutes a week to work with. The way we spend our money tells others what we value, and who we spend our time with and what we spend it doing tells people who and what we value. If we choose to spend time going to a little league game rather than working overtime, it is a signal of our sentiments and what we think is important. If we choose to spend time perfecting the budget rather than listening to an employee's problem, it sends a message. While some demands on our time seem to limit our control, we are constantly broadcasting to the world our likes and dislikes by how we use our time.

Sociologists have discovered that liking increases with interaction, although you can probably think of several exceptions.

On the other hand, people may read withdrawal or decreases in frequency as an indication of a lessened regard. Again, however, there may be a more relevant alternative explanation, such as involvement in other important activities. Assumptions about your level of regard happen all the time by the people around you who are continuously monitoring your use of time even when they aren't doing it consciously. Problems arise when their interpretations are incorrect or differ with respect to who, or what, you consider important.

You may, for example, find that you need to spend a larger amount of time than usual with a particular employee or coworker because of a new procedure or special problem. If this causes your time with other coworkers to be temporarily reduced, they may feel that you care more about the project you're working on and less about them and their projects.

The "cost" of your time varies from moment to moment, depending on how much you have to do and how much time you have to do it in. Communications may be strained, for example, when you are in a big hurry to complete a report and a coworker drops in to chat for a while. If, on the other hand, the time being spent has approximately the same value for both participants (e.g., neither has anything else better to do), the chat will probably lack this stress. This type of tension can contribute to a deterioration in your relationship if seen as noncaring, or: "You're not OK, and I don't want to waste my time with you." The tension can sometimes be avoided by explaining your situation and why you're in a hurry. It also helps to make a date in the future to make up the time if necessary.

In general, since time is viewed as a scarce resource, who we spend it with is often taken as a signal of who we care about. Being aware of this can help you build more productive relationships by simply stating out loud what the meaning is for you of spending your time as you do. It can help others from jumping to the wrong conclusions and prevent you from having your own feelings hurt because you have responded to conditioned reactions without checking out your automatic assumptions.

REPETITION

∎

Time also has meaning for us in its repetition of activities. Most of us become irritated when someone interrupts a pattern to which we have become accustomed. Examples are having to miss a customary 10:00 A.M. coffee break or having to work late and miss dinner with your family.

Our reactions to the seasons—another pattern of time—and how we use them also varies. People become accustomed to certain activities and feelings associated with different seasons and holidays. Christmas is usually thought of as a time set aside for ritual, being with friends and family, and expressing warmth and affection. Usually there is less work done during the Christmas holidays, and trying to get people to work overtime during this season can be deeply resented.

Any disruption of established patterns of activities will be experienced as a deprivation, and if you are perceived as the source of the disruption, hostile feelings will be directed your way. Consequently, use care when planning changes in work load, especially during holiday seasons. Also use your questioning skills to determine unique individual patterns and expectations.

Because our use of time is such an expressive language, being aware of its meanings can facilitate our communications and relationships with others. This is especially true for managers because of the tendencies of employees to watch them intensely for nonverbal feedback.

The "rules" regarding time are simple and well-known, although they don't seem to be followed as often as they should be. In order to avoid negative communications through your use of time, be punctual. Let others know if you can't meet a prearranged time commitment. Don't keep people waiting, but if you do, plan to deal with their feelings of hostility about the wait. Don't impose unusual schedules that will obviously conflict with personal schedules or holidays. Don't change the amount of time you spend with a person without giving him a reason for the change. Being considerate with our use of time and openly stating the reasons for changes or "rule" violations can go a long way in avoiding misunderstandings and building more trusting and productive relationships.

IV

GROUP COMMUNICATION

The first three sections of this book have dealt primarily with one-on-one communication. This section will help you apply those skills to group communications. For most adults, the abilities of speaking in public and leading effective meetings can mean the difference between high levels of professional success or a career that stalls out at the midway point.

There is nothing magic about the ability to

speak in public or lead meetings that are productive. Both forms of group communication require high levels of organization and the communication skills you learned in the first sections of this book. The time you spend developing these skills will pay long-range dividends in personal effectiveness and career enhancement.

The next three chapters give you specific, easy-to-follow techniques for developing your group communication skills. You will be able to put many of these techniques to work immediately.

14

PRESENTATION POWER

My father gave me this advice on speech making: Be sincere . . . be brief . . . be seated.

—JAMES ROOSEVELT, SON OF FDR

THE #1 FEAR . . . THE #1 SUCCESS PREDICTOR

The number one fear of most adults (even above death) is speaking in public. Yet the ability to communicate to groups of people is a skill which can make a critical difference in our careers and in our ability to share information, ideas, experience, and enthusiasms with others. A study conducted by AT&T and Stanford University revealed that the top predictor of success and upward mobility, professionally, is how much you enjoy public speaking and how effective you are at it.

Actually, almost all of our speaking (outside the shower anyway) is public speaking . . . it's just the size of the audience that changes. Public speaking can take many forms: presentations to a large audience in a public forum, presenting a proposal to a conference room of board members, or addressing one other person in a formal environment, such as a sales presentation.

If a presentation is boring and unprofessional, it can leave you with nothing but a weak round of applause, or even worse, a lessened reputation in the professional community. On the other hand, good presentations can provide opportunities for growth in power, control, recognition, and prestige. The effective public speaker establishes himself as an expert to whom individuals can turn for advice.

Most of us have experienced more than our share of boring presentations. After what seems like hours, we still don't know what message we were supposed to get. Maybe the speaker put us to sleep with his monotone presentation or we couldn't read the small writing on the transparencies, which didn't seem to match up at all with what the speaker was trying to say.

To avoid being the source of a "sleeper" presentation, you need to build your presentation skills. This chapter will give you some simple guidelines for overcoming stage fright, preparing for a successful presentation, and using audiovisual aids effectively.

TRAINING THE BUTTERFLIES
•

Almost every speaker, actor, musician, and performer experiences stage fright . . . that feeling of sweaty palms, jelly knees, and a stomach filled with butterflies. While the fear never goes away entirely, professionals know that you can make the butterflies fly in formation. In other words, you can learn to manage your fear.

First you must understand that stage fright is a very normal reaction. Cicero, the brilliant Roman orator, wrote, "I turn pale at the outset of a speech and quake in every limb and in all my soul." It even affected Sir Winston Churchill, who compared his prespeech anxiety to the sense that a nine-inch block of ice was sitting in the pit of his stomach.

If these famous speakers were so affected by speech anxiety, it makes sense that, for the novice public speaker, the audience might as well be made up of cannibals. The clues to the speaker's terror include: a quaking voice, trembling knees, lack of eye contact, erratic pacing or rocking, stomach butterflies, pronounced monotone, and a blank facial expression. These conditions are evidence that the speaker is so overwhelmed with self-consciousness that he has lost control of the communication process.

You can overcome stage fright if you are ready to approach it with the right attitude. The way you look at yourself, the audience, the subject, preparation and delivery, and the anxiety itself has a direct impact on how you will feel when you walk toward the podium. Developing this attitude can help you convert the grinding fear which paralyzes you and makes you ineffective into a positive anxiety which keeps you sharp and motivates you to be the best you can be.

DEVELOPING THE ATTITUDE OF A SUCCESSFUL PUBLIC SPEAKER

Remember that stage fright is normal and be open about it. Sometimes just admitting that you are feeling anxiety helps relieve it. You should also remember that you are the expert. The reason you are in a position to speak publicly is because of your knowledge of the subject. The person who asked you to speak believes that you have something of value to share. The people attending the meeting believe that they will receive information of value.

Therefore, your primary duty is to understand what your audience needs to know and prepare the message and supporting materials in a way that delivers your message clearly and powerfully. Make a strong, whole-hearted commitment to your audience. Concentrating on them and their needs will help you forget about your own self-consciousness.

Here are ten additional tips for overcoming stage fright:

- Know your material well. Be the expert.
- Practice your presentation. Do a pilot test, and if possible, videotape yourself.
- Get the audience to participate.
- Establish rapport by using names and eye contact.
- Always check the facilities and audiovisual equipment in advance.
- Research your audience. Get acquainted with at least one person in the audience.
- Relax. Breathe deeply. Visualize yourself successfully presenting your message to the audience.
- Dress comfortably and appropriately.

- Use your own style. Don't imitate someone else.
- Use audiovisual aids—to prompt you and make a visual impact on the audience.

CHARACTERISTICS OF EFFECTIVE PUBLIC SPEAKERS
■

We've all experienced presentations from the audience side and we've seen the whole range, from the dynamic, mesmerizing speaker to the person who reads his notes in a never-ending droning. What is it that makes one presentation better than the next? Here is an overview of the characteristics of an effective speaker:

- Understands the needs of his audience
- Attempts to meet those needs as effectively as possible
- Is the expert on his subject and his breadth of knowledge in other areas
- Constantly grows and improves in his understanding of his areas of expertise and his ability to present his material effectively
- Is enthusiastic about his subject and sincere about conveying his message to the audience
- Has a pleasing voice and appearance
- Uses examples, illustrations, analogies, and stories to make information more interesting and exciting
- Paces the program to keep it lively and interesting
- Uses an appropriate level of humor and drama
- Encourages group involvement and participation
- Makes information as practical as possible, telling people how to use the information
- Uses depth and breadth of knowledge to answer a broad range of questions thoroughly
- Helps listeners understand and retain the information through the use of attention-getting verbal and visual devices such as repetition, graphics, and audience participation
- When appropriate, asks the audience for a commitment to change

While it may not be possible to possess all these characteristics completely, the following guidelines will help you incorporate these traits into your speaking career.

PREPARING FOR SUCCESS—PLANNING

■

The success of your public speaking is determined primarily by the time you spend preparing before you step in front of your audience. A good presentation requires careful planning and lack of planning is always apparent. Sure clues are speeches that are too long, too detailed, confusing, vague, boring, or off-track. You can spend less time producing short, powerful presentations if you systematically prepare beforehand.

The often-overlooked first and most critical step in preparation is understanding the "what" and the "why" of your presentation: its purpose. Your purpose should be the broad general outcome you want the presentation to achieve. Here are three questions you can ask yourself to clarify the objective of your presentation:

- Why am I giving this presentation?
- What do I want the audience to know or do at the end of the presentation?
- How do I want the audience to feel?

It often helps us prepare for a presentation when we understand the different types of presentations. Here are four basic types that differ primarily in the amount of detail presented and the level of persuasiveness required to meet the object of the presentation:

SALES—Use the sales presentation to sell an idea or suggestion to clients, upper management, coworkers, or employees. You may also use the sales presentation to persuade an audience to take a particular action or adopt a belief. This type of presentation uses a lot of persuasive skills and seldom requires extensive detail.

EXPLANATORY—The explanatory presentation is best used to familiarize, give an overall perspective, or identify new developments. It should rarely involve heavy detail, but should offer the audience new or renewed information and understanding. It does not require extensive persuasive efforts.

INSTRUCTIONAL—When you want to teach others how to use something, such as a new procedure or a piece of hardware, use the instructional presentation. There is usually more audience participation and involvement with this presentation format. It generally involves extensive detail. This is a persuasive presentation because you are convincing your audience to use a new technique or to adopt a new method of doing something.

ORAL REPORT—Oral reports bring the audience up to date on something with which they are already familiar. These generally focus on facts, figures, and other details and involve little persuasive efforts.

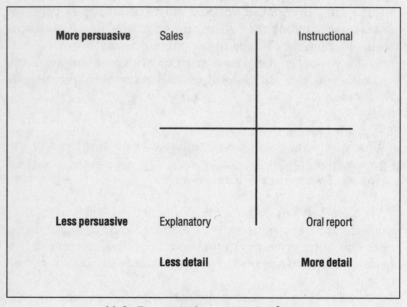

14-A *Presentation-type quadrant*

KNOW YOUR AUDIENCE
·

After you have a statement of purpose and understand the type of presentation you will be giving, you must consider the particular audience you have in mind and how to mold your presentation to fit the specific characteristics of that audience. The more time you devote to analyzing your audience beforehand, the less you will have to do "on the spot."

Here are some ways you can acquire information in advance regarding your audience:

ASK THE PRESENTATION HOST for information about the audience. Find out general demographics such as age, sex, professional level, specific interests, and needs. Also ask what the group has responded well to in the past. What presentation styles were well received?

TALK TO MEMBERS OF THE AUDIENCE. If possible, arrive early enough to survey one or more members of the audience to find out what they expect and what they would like to hear.

TALK TO OTHER SPEAKERS. If you know other speakers who have spoken to the same group, ask them what worked and what they would do differently with the group.

Here are some questions you should ask yourself to help you analyze the needs of each particular audience you will address.

- Why should they listen to you?
- How does what you say affect them?
- What's in it for them to listen to you?
- Why is it important for the audience to hear what you have to say?

WHAT IS THE SPECIFIC OBJECTIVE OF THE PRESENTATION?

The next step in the preparation process is determining the specific objective of your presentation. This is essentially the desired change in a participant at the end of the session. Describe your objective from the audience's point of view, and make it is as specific as possible. For example, assume you are speaking to the board of directors and you want their approval on your new marketing plan. Here are two possible objectives for the board:

- To thoroughly understand the new marketing plan.
- To vote to approve the new marketing plan.

There is a tremendous difference in these objectives. While the board will need to thoroughly understand the plan in order to vote for it, if your presentation was focused only on their understanding, you might never ask for their approval. Be clear about what you want.

To make your presentation truly effective, you must also make your objective realistic. Ask yourself these questions:

- Can you accomplish your objective in both the available preparation time and presentation time?
- Does your audience have the necessary knowledge and background to achieve your desired results?
- Do the audience members have the authority to make the decisions you may want them to?
- Are resources available for you to accomplish your ideas? Do key individuals stand in the way of your goals?

FOCUS ON THE BIG IDEA
•

Once you know your audience and are clear about your objectives and purpose, you are ready to start organizing your presentation. The first step is to find your focus. This is the Big Idea of your material, the power punch, the one thing you want your audience to walk away with. Back to our marketing plan example: Most marketing plans have several sections and are supported by reams of documenting research and facts. But you probably only have twenty to thirty minutes to summarize the plan in a way that builds support and will gain the board's approval. What is it about the plan that will capture their imagination? A new theme? A new program? A high payoff possibility?

How you translate your material—your message—into benefits for the audience determines its effectiveness. You need to structure your presentation so that it supports your one Big Idea. Of course, your message will contain more than one idea but they should all reinforce the primary focus.

One way to make sure you are clear on your focus is to develop a basic outline of your presentation. (You might want to skip forward to chapter 17 and read the section on mindmapping as it is an ideal technique to use when you are beginning to organize your material.) Begin by listing no more than five independent ideas that the audience must understand for the objectives to be accomplished. Then outline your plan for presenting the necessary detail and persuasive material needed to allow your audience to understand those points. This gives you a rough outline of the content of your message.

GETTING THEIR ATTENTION

▪

There are three major sections of a presentation: introduction, main body, and conclusion. Your first step is to get the audience's attention and convince them to listen to you. This happens in the introduction—and this is where many beginning speakers lose their audience. Grab them with something vitally interesting to them. Give them an interesting story or example that ties into your focus. Use a strong, meaningful quotation or a startling statistic.

Be succinct, use simple graphic language, and most of all, never apologize! If the airline lost your bag and you're in yesterday's clothes . . . if you're a last-minute substitute for the best speaker in the country . . . if you have the flu and a 101° temperature, don't mention it. Don't apologize for the way you look or sound, don't apologize for not being the best speaker in the world, don't apologize because your slides are upside down . . . don't apologize for anything! The minute you apologize, your ability to influence your audience is decreased. You want to do everything you can can to make sure none of those negatives happen, but if they do, go on. Start your speech with power. Make your audience think they're going to be informed, entertained, or enlightened. Don't let them think they're getting inferior goods, leftovers, or anything except your best.

It's important to write out your introduction completely, word for word. This part of your presentation is too important to leave to chance, hoping you have the right words when you get there. It also acts as a security blanket. If you can get through those first few minutes, the butterflies will settle down and the rest of the presentation will flow more easily. The introduction should take 5 to 15 percent of the allowed speaking time, and it should prepare the audience for the main points of the presentation, which will come later.

Here are the main elements that are generally included in the introductory part of a presentation.

- **BEGIN YOUR TALK WITH A BANG:** an attention-getter. An anecdote or joke can ease and relax both the audience and the speaker, but only use what is appropriate and relevant.
- **NEXT, WHAT'S IN IT FOR THEM?** Involve the audience by letting listeners know that your information is relevant to their needs.
- **INCREASE YOUR CREDIBILITY** by relating something about your background and expertise.
- **PRESENT YOUR AGENDA,** keeping in mind the familiar slogan: "Tell them what you are going to tell them, tell them, and then tell them what you just told them."
- **WHAT DO YOU EXPECT OF THE AUDIENCE?** At the beginning of your presentation, tell listeners about the question-and-answer session at the end, or the ensuing reception, or the cards you want them to fill out before they leave.

ICE-BREAKERS
▪

In many presentations to smaller groups, it's helpful to do an opening ice-breaking exercise. This exercise sets an emotional climate for the presentation. It also gets people talking and involved with the focus of your message. The most common ice-breaker is having people introduce themselves and explain their reason for attending the presentation. Simple games that are fun and get people involved are an excellent way to get a session started. If you can start off with a little humor, people will relax, open up, and be more ready to listen. (If you're presenting an action plan to deal with nuclear war, a humorous ice-breaker might not be appropriate.)

The three most important criteria for a good ice-breaker are that it be:

SHORT—five to ten minutes
APPROPRIATE—have something to do with the topic
PARTICIPATIVE—be something that each person can, and wants to, get involved with.

THE MAIN MESSAGE

▪

Once you've gotten the audience's attention, you need to deliver what you promised in the shortest, most interesting way possible. Two things to keep in mind as you structure your message is the attention cycle of your audience and pacing.

It can be discouraging to look into the audience only to note the number of persons with drooping eyelids and slumping bodies. Obviously, their attention span has fizzled. There are ways that you, as a presenter, can bring them back up, leaning forward with interest. First, you have to understand the basics of the attention cycle. Studies have shown that material at the beginning and end of a presentation will be remembered more than the material in the middle. Our attention span only lasts for a short time and then it tapers off. When we sense the end of a message, we pull our attention back in time to catch the last material. Fluctuation of the attention cycle is one of the main reasons we put such emphasis on the introduction and conclusion.

But how do we hold people's attention during the main body of our message? Simple, we create a lot of mini-cycles with beginnings, middles, and ends instead of having one big cycle that lasts through the entire presentation. We do this with pacing.

You should plan a change of pace every 10 to 15 minutes so that you can break up your talk into mini-cycles and keep attention riveted. You can do this by including appropriate humor, stories, exercises requiring people to move their bodies (even if it's just raising their hands), or calls for a verbal response. Keep these change-of-pace exercises as physical as possible if your presentation occurs after lunch when much of our energy is diverted to our digestive system.

In addition to changing your pace frequently, there are four techniques you can use to help your listeners remember more of your message. These are:

▪ **REPETITION:** Let the beginning of your presentation whet their appetites for the main message and the wrap-up reinforce the main points of the message and call for action. Main ideas should be stated more than once—using different words to keep the presentation from being redundant or boring.

- **ASSOCIATION/CONNECTION:** Using stories and analogies that connect your ideas to something the listener already understands will assist him in grasping and remembering your message.
- **INTENSITY:** Your tone of voice can reflect the passion you have about your message. You can also convey the emotional content of your message by telling gripping, relevant stories and by relating the message to the lives and values of the individuals in the audience. You can add intensity to your visual aids with the use of color and pictures or illustrations.
- **INVOLVEMENT:** Your presentation should appeal to as many senses as possible, because people have different methods of processing information (i.e., visual, auditory, emotional). Use visual aids, hand gestures, sound effects . . . anything that gets the audience involved with the message. Group participation exercises such as small group discussions, exercises, or workbooks are extremely helpful for increasing memory and understanding.

These memory supports keep attention at a high level and help people remember your message. Other techniques you can use to sharpen your presentation include:

- **EXAMPLES**—an appropriate example can quickly and powerfully transmit your message.

- **STATISTICS**—when used sparingly and presented simply, statistics can add drama and credibility to your message.

- **COMPARISONS**—can help your audience evaluate different options quickly and logically.

- **TESTIMONY**—the personal story or tribute of a credible person can make your message more believable.

Remember that the purpose of your presentation is not to present all you know about a subject—it's to present what your audience needs to know in a way that meets your personal ob jectives as well as theirs.

CONCLUSION

Many speakers have a dynamite opening and a powerful, interesting message only to drop the ball at the end. You need a strong wrap-up. It serves an important function for the audience. This is where you will sum up and stress the main ideas you want the audience to remember. You call for and encourage appropriate action.

Your conclusion should repeat your main ideas: don't expect the audience to remember a point which they have heard only once. You can signal a wind-up of the presentation with a phrase such as: "Let's review the main points we've covered." When you indicate the conclusion, you give the audience a chance to reaffirm that they know and understand the main points covered during the session. Your conclusion should be strong, succinct, and persuasive. Many speakers consider this section almost as important as the introduction and they write it out word for word.

PRACTICE AND VISUALIZE SUCCESS

You know your audience. You know your material. You've written a dynamite speech. The last step is to practice delivering it. The following guidelines may assist you in the process.

REHEARSE ALOUD. Do this in order to check your timing (you read out loud slower than you read in your mind), and to make sure your presentation flows and sounds the way you want it to.

REHEARSE AT LEAST FOUR OR FIVE TIMES. You should feel comfortable explaining all of your ideas. Don't try to memorize your speech, however, or you may end up sounding stale, as if you are reciting or reading.

REHEARSE IN THE ACTUAL LOCATION OF THE PRESENTATION, if possible. It is better to work out the technicalities of visual aids, outlets, and positioning during a rehearsal instead of on the day of your presentation.

TIME YOURSELF DURING REHEARSAL. During your last few rehearsals, time yourself so that you can make sure you stay within the amount of time allotted for your presentation.

REHEARSE IN FRONT OF PEOPLE. Get used to public speaking through rehearsing with family or friends. Ask them to explain what they heard. This will give you a chance to make sure your message is clear. Ask them if your visual aids are effective and if they make your message more understandable. Ask them what you can do better.

Once you have rehearsed your presentation and feel comfortable with the material, visualize yourself presenting it successfully. Olympic athletes use visualization to reach their peak performance. Studies have shown that visualized practice has almost the same effect as actual practice. Visualizing a successful conclusion to any activity gives you a better chance to experience success. Each time you experience success, you become more confident and more expert in your delivery.

While you are comfortably seated, close your eyes and visualize your entire presentation. See the room and imagine yourself walking to the front of the room and being greeted by a warm round of applause. See the audience and feel them anxiously awaiting your message. Hear yourself begin. Your voice sounds confident and strong. Mentally go through your entire presentation. See the audience rise and give you a standing ovation when you finish. Feel your pleasure as people come up after the presentation to tell you how well you did and how important the message was to them. Bask in your success. Repeat this exercise until you feel confident and well prepared.

VISUAL AIDS

As you're preparing your presentation, one of your main concerns should be the visual aids you use. In addition to hearing your message, if the members of the audience can have the important points emphasized with good visual aids, they will remember much more of your message. Another reason to pay special attention to your visual aids is that they are the most dramatic part of your presentation. Your audience will be deeply impressed by your visual aids—whether that impression is good or bad depends on how well you prepare.

Visual aids can help you appear more confident, more professional, and more of an expert. They can add color, humor, and images that you could never convey in words. However, if poorly done, they can undo everything you might accomplish with your words.

The most frequent mistake made with slides and overhead transparencies is putting too much information on one image. Each visual aid should focus on one idea. Try to visually reinforce the idea you're presenting with a chart, graph, cartoon, picture, or illustration. The second most frequent mistake made is using the visual aid as a cue card and reading the information. The audience can read faster than you can talk so this is deadly boring!

The size and formality of your audience determine which type of visual aid will be most effective for you. Flip charts and white boards are best with small, informal groups; overhead transparencies work well with medium-sized, formal groups; and large, formal audiences generally respond best to slides or very professionally done overhead transparencies. Here are some simple Do's and Don'ts for each type of visual aid.

FLIP CHARTS

It looks so easy . . . a blank pad of paper on an easel and a pen in your hand. Ahhh . . . the power of the pen. But that pen can explode on you if you don't follow a few simple Do's and Don'ts.

Do . . .
- Print large enough to be read at the back of the room (don't assume it can be read—go back and check it)
- Write down only the key points using key words
- Give the audience a moment to read the page before turning it
- Pencil in information beforehand if you want, and/or pencil notes in the margins
- Post key sheets (each with a brief but descriptive title) on the wall for added emphasis and clarity
- Keep a blank sheet between pages of prepared material to prevent "bleeding"

- Use wide, felt-tip watercolor markers in strong, bright colors. Throw the pens away the second they start running out of ink or squeaking

DON'T . . .
- Read the page
- Turn your back to the audience
- Put too much on one page
- Stand in front of the easel when speaking

OVERHEAD PROJECTORS

Flip charts are most effective for small, informal groups. For a more formal group, you might want to use an overhead projector. Well-done transparencies can be as effective as more expensive slides. Too often, however, someone copies a written document onto a transparency and assumes that it will work. You can put more information on a transparency than you can a slide but you can't show a complete balance sheet or five-year P&L and expect your audience to comprehend any part of it! This is not the place to show memos or lengthy textual material. When using overhead transparencies, remember:

DO . . .
- Make them legible
- Use colored pens to highlight information during the presentation
- Frame transparencies (use the frame for notes)
- Check alignment and focus before your talk
- Make sure you have extra bulbs

DON'T . . .
- Crowd information
- Read from the screen
- Turn out the lights

SLIDES

Slides are the best visual aid to use at large meetings since they allow the widest range of graphics and provide the best quality.

They do have one major drawback—unless you have rear projection, they require a darkened room. People go to sleep in dark rooms!

If you need a dark room in order to get the full effect of your slides, you may want to group them into one short, visually interesting period rather than showing them throughout your presentation. When using slides:

DO . . .
- Check equipment
- Present one idea per slide
- Use a dark background and light lettering
- Use six lines, maximum, per slide, up to six words per line
- Change slides every 15 to 20 seconds
- Use build-up slides for complex points ("Build-up slides" add a new point on successive slides until the entire point shows on the final slide. For example, slide #1 would show point A; slide #2 would show A and B; slide #3 would show A, B, and C, etc.
- Use bar and pie charts
- Use special effects for *emphasis*—not just because you can
- Keep the slides simple

DON'T . . .
- Turn out the lights any longer than necessary
- Crowd information
- Read the slides
- Turn your back to the audience
- Distract attention with a pointer
- Back up to previous slides—use copies if you need to repeat a point

Use a title slide before each major section. You will impart a professional, "corporate" image if you use a standard border and logo and the same color background.

Make charts and graphs as straightforward as possible, and vary these with slides of text, illustrations, special effects, etc. Text must be basic and direct.

Check equipment beforehand or you could be setting yourself up for embarrassment and worse. Use a remote control device if you are controlling the presentation; otherwise, make sure the person controlling the slides knows your script.

Your ability to speak in front of groups is one of the most important professional skills you can develop. To truly develop the skill, however, you have to practice it in front of a real, live audience. Force yourself to find opportunities to speak. Volunteer at your professional organizations, civic clubs, or church or temple. You might even consider joining Toastmasters—it offers you a weekly speaking experience in a supportive, educational environment.

As we stated at the beginning of this chapter, the ability to make public presentations is the number one predictor of the level of professional success. A more immediate determinant of success in the workplace is the ability to conduct effective meetings. The next two chapters will guide you through an explanation of what it takes to plan and lead meetings that produce the results you want.

15

MEETING MAGIC

Scene 1:
"Are you going to the staff meeting?"
    "Do I have a choice?"
"Not much. Two long, boring hours."
    "Every Friday afternoon. Just like clockwork."
"One of these days we'll figure out why."
    "It's his way of making sure we don't leave early."

Scene 2:
"Time for the new product development meeting."
    "OK. I'm anxious to see what information was collected this past week."
"The agenda says Smith from New Materials is giving a report. Maybe there's a new development."
    "I've got some data to share that might give us a lead. Good, let's go."

Which meeting scene is most familiar to you? Do you approach a corporate meeting expecting just another annoying waste of time? Do you walk away from it wondering why you wasted your time? If so, you know firsthand how frustrating inefficient meetings are. Most managers spend 25 to 30 percent of their time in meetings and studies show that the average cost of a meeting runs over $1,000. Since it's rare to have a meeting-free day, for most organizations, the total cost of meetings quickly adds up to a major expense.

Meetings are currently the most expensive communication activity in the corporate world—more costly than word processing, computers, paperwork, or multitudes of phone calls. Consider the salaries of those in attendance, preparation costs, travel expenses, and the price of materials, facilities, and equipment used during the meeting. Even if an organization conducted only two meetings a week, the total annual cost for those gatherings would run well over $104,000.

Perhaps even more costly than the loss of time and money is the reduced morale that happens when people are forced to sit through boring, poorly planned and conducted meetings. When unproductive meetings occur regularly, people with demanding schedules begin to avoid attending. Yet these are the very individuals whose participation may be most important.

The primary reason meetings don't accomplish their objectives is lack of advance planning and preparation. Even though executives spend a significant portion of their time in meetings, studies show that 78 percent have never received training on how to plan, organize, and conduct a meeting.

When meetings are well-managed, they are an effective and essential tool for communication within the organization. Important decisions are made, ideas are generated, and information is shared. Meetings are a critical part of team building and as team spirit grows, the company benefits as the group's ability to work together and make decisions grows.

There are six basic functions that meetings perform better than any other communication technique:

▪ **SHARE KNOWLEDGE**—Meetings provide a forum where individual information and experience can be pooled. The group revises, updates, and adds to what it knows.

- **ESTABLISH COMMON GOALS**—Meetings help every member of the team understand the goals and objectives of the group and how his individual efforts will affect those objectives.
- **GAIN COMMITMENT**—Meetings gain consensus on decisions and foster commitment. An agreement and sense of responsibility to implement and support the decisions is created.
- **PROVIDE GROUP IDENTITY**—Meetings define the team. Those present belong to the team, those absent do not. Attendees develop a sense of collective identity.
- **TEAM INTERACTION**—Meetings are often the only occasion where the group works as a team.
- **STATUS ARENA**—Meetings give group members a chance to determine their relative status.

You may not achieve any of these functions at any one specific meeting but if none of these functions are important to you, you may want to choose a different, less expensive communication method.

This chapter will show you how to plan, conduct, and follow up on meetings. Meetings do not have to be a waste of time. When well-planned and implemented, they offer enormous benefits.

GUIDELINES FOR EFFECTIVE MEETINGS
•

The fundamentals of successful meetings are not complicated or difficult to follow. Even so, meetings that are tedious and unproductive are evidence that these guidelines are being overlooked.

Here are the basics for a productive meeting:

1. NEED. Hold only those meetings for which there is a demonstrated need. Weekly status updates require a meeting only when five or more people need the information. You can speak to three or four people individually and save a lot of time. Regularly scheduled staff meetings may not be necessary if you have a small staff and have opportunity for frequent interaction. Meetings are ideal when you need to solve problems that are complex or affect many people, exchange technical information, or explain a complex policy, procedure, or situation.

2. PURPOSE. Every meeting must have specific, stated objectives and a broad purpose. Attendees need to know the meeting

190 · MEETING MAGIC

topics beforehand, in writing, so that they can come prepared.

3. ATTENDEES. Invite only attendees who can contribute or who have a serious need to know. The more people who attend a meeting, the longer it will take to accomplish your objectives. The ideal size for a working meeting is five to seven people.

4. AGENDA. Agendas are an absolute must for every meeting. While having an agenda is the most critical element of effective meeting management, 75 percent of all meetings have no preplanned agenda. If possible, distribute the agenda 48 to 72 hours prior to the session. Use an agenda even for last-minute meetings. The meeting leader can write an agenda on a flipchart or whiteboard or the agenda can be developed with the attendees as the first action of the group.

Agendas not only help the attendees come prepared, they force the meeting leader to organize his thoughts and priorities. A good agenda addresses issues in order of importance and allocates time to each issue.

5. CHOOSE A GOOD MEETING PLACE. The room should offer proper ventilation, comfort, accessibility, and the necessary equipment. It should also be free from distractions and interruptions.

6. START AND END ON TIME. Meetings should begin and end punctually. This sends a message to participants that their time is respected and that they are expected to respect the meeting time. You might consider beginning the meeting with an uncomplicated activity so that those who still arrive late can catch up. Avoid "recapping" for latecomers.

7. STICK TO THE AGENDA. Although you want to encourage participation, new issues should be noted and held over for a later meeting. If you let the meeting get sidetracked, you will have difficulty meeting the goals and objectives established. If critical issues arise which prevent resolution on an agenda item, they can be noted and that item can be rescheduled for a later meeting. If a new item is so critical that it needs immediate attention, poll the attendees for an agreement to address it at the current meeting. The agenda is a contract with the attendees; it should not be changed without their concurrence.

8. ENCOURAGE PARTICIPATION. Attendees should feel comfortable enough to offer opinions or suggestions openly.

9. LEAD A BALANCED, CONTROLLED DISCUSSION. Support members in expressing their opinions, even on volatile, highly charged issues, but discourage arguments. Do not let any one person dominate the meeting.

10. SUMMARIZE AND DISTRIBUTE MINUTES. Recap the decisions and any actions planned as a result of the meeting to make sure that everyone is in accord on the proposed action details: *who* is to do *what* and *when*. Make sure that each attendee receives written minutes no later than two days following the meeting.

You can help ensure consistently productive meetings by following a meeting policy based on the above. A succinct one-page set of guidelines should be printed, distributed, and most importantly, followed. The easiest way to encourage the adoption of these guidelines is to demonstrate them. As people see the effectiveness of meetings increase as a result of following the guidelines, they will begin to implement them also.

Managers at the Western Center of General Dynamics follow a meeting policy, knowing that this saves the company money, helps personnel learn to lead and participate in effective meetings, and improves morale and team spirit because objectives are met through good meeting dynamics.

These are the meeting guidelines used at the Western Center:

- All meetings start and end on time, with a maximum length of ninety minutes.
- Each participant has a commitment to making the meeting successful.
- A clear objective is established for the meeting and the agenda is followed.
- Common courtesy and caring are emphasized. Issues, not people, are criticized.
- A positive orientation of "We are here to help" is established.

PREPARING FOR AN EFFECTIVE MEETING
∎

The success of a meeting is directly related to the amount of time invested in preparation beforehand. Before planning the meeting, you should understand what type of meeting it will be. The type of meeting affects how many people attend, the structure of the meeting, and the meeting objectives. Here are the basic types of meeting:

- **INFORMATION EXCHANGE**—Information exchange meetings provide a forum for disseminating one message to a large group of people. This is important when the information is controversial or complex, has strong implications for attendees, or if it needs to be conveyed in person. A meeting to explain a new profit-sharing policy would be an example of this type of meeting.

  This type of meeting is also used for status meetings which generally feature progress reports on all projects under the scope of the attendees.

  These reports keep the group posted on the current status of projects it is responsible for. Information exchange meetings can be relatively large in attendance. The format typically includes formal presentations with questions and answers from other attendees. Audiovisual equipment may be required.

- **BRAINSTORMING**—These sessions generally precede problem-solving meetings when it is important to generate alternative solutions. Participation of all attendees is critical and it is important to have a broad mix of attendees. Brainstorming sessions should not have more than seven attendees.

- **PROBLEM SOLVING**—The objective here is to pool the knowledge, wisdom, and experience of the attendees and to identify the best possible solution to the problem. In order to meet that objective each attendee needs to understand the problem and each participant should have a part to play in solving the problem. Brainstorming should be used to identify possibilities. Every participant should be encouraged to contribute. After a solution is agreed upon, it should be analyzed for weaknesses. Consider both the positive and negative aspects before taking action. These sessions should have no more than five to seven participants and should be very informal and participative.

- **PROJECT PLANNING**—Planning and implementation meetings are primarily held to determine logistics and responsibility allocations. They can be somewhat larger than a problem solving session. It is important to document decisions, action items, and responsibilities.

- **TRAINING**—Training sessions are ideal when they are limited to fifteen to twenty attendees, require participation and involvement, and give people a chance to learn from their peers.

DETERMINE THE PURPOSE

•

The meeting leader needs to recognize and fine-tune the specific purpose for the meeting. For instance, if the general topic is training needs, the manager might break it into more specific subtopics such as: identifying primary training needs for each department; determining which could be done in-house; establishing priorities; and developing a strategy for training. The process of fine-tuning the purpose might determine a need for more than one meeting.

Too often the purpose for a meeting is vague or, even worse, bogus. Here are a few examples:

- **THE WEEKLY STAFF MEETING**—Ostensibly to bring everyone up to speed, too often it's a ritual done because the manager thinks she should. Because the meeting doesn't have a compelling purpose, it's usually accompanied by groans, no-shows, and stragglers.
- **RAH-RAH**—Many managers think meetings are cheerleading sessions, a time to motivate the troops. It doesn't take long for the "troops" to see through this.
- **POLITICAL HAY**—Some managers try to use meetings as a time to show how smart they are or how important their department is.

The first question a meeting leader should be able to answer is, "Why are we having this meeting?" Until the meeting leader is completely clear about the purpose of the meeting, there is no way the meeting will be efficient and effective.

SET OBJECTIVES

•

The meeting leader should have a written set of objectives for the meeting. These should be objectives that can only be accomplished by bringing together a group of people. If one person can accomplish the objectives, there's no point in having a meeting. Here are some common objectives:

- **MORE ACCURATE INFORMATION.** Since messages become standardized in a meeting, management can ensure that everyone receives the same information in the same way. As companies grow and communication tends to get more complicated, this function of meetings becomes even more important. However, for simple messages which do not require interaction, memos are a much more cost-effective method of distributing a standardized message.
- **EFFECTIVE COORDINATION OF ACTIVITIES.** Meetings bring people together and help them understand how they fit within the company. Presenting the "big picture" helps each individual understand the importance of change and how to implement it.
- **IMPROVING THE FLOW OF COMMUNICATION BOTH UPWARDS AND DOWNWARDS.** Meetings connect top management with employees, allowing management to report on what the company has accomplished and to explain future changes. Employees have a chance to ask questions, seek clarification, and understand the decision processes involved with changes. They may also offer suggestions and ideas for consideration by management.
- **FACILITATING THE DECISION-MAKING PROCESS.** Attendees bring with them the pieces of information necessary to solve a problem. Once a solution is identified, those who will implement it should be present to add their ideas and suggestions.
- **TRAINING.** Training meetings ensure more uniform training of employees and provide an interactive forum where participants can learn from each other.
- **BUILDING MORALE.** The sense of teamwork is revitalized at meetings in an environment of purpose and commitment. Meetings provide an excellent forum for recognizing achievements of the group and individuals.

SELECT PARTICIPANTS
▪

When deciding who to invite to a meeting, choose only those persons who have a reason to participate. Under no circumstances should someone be included simply because it's political or his "feelings might be hurt if not asked." Those attending should:

- have thorough knowledge of the meeting subject matter and be ready and able to make a valuable contribution
- have the power to make a decision
- be responsible for implementing decisions or bringing a project to the next stage
- represent a group that will be affected by decisions made at the meeting.

The size of a group should also be a factor when selecting participants. Although informational meetings do not require limits on attendees, consider the following size guidelines for other types of meetings:

- a meeting to identify a problem should be limited to 10
- problem-solving meetings are best accomplished with no more than 5 to 7.
- training sessions should involve 15–20, less if hands-on instruction is part of the curricula.

Between 4 to 7 people is generally ideal for any meeting, 10 is tolerable, and 12 is stretching the limit. Meetings tend to be more productive when the number of participants is low. In large group meetings, there is less opportunity for individuals to participate and consensus decision making becomes extremely time-consuming and frustrating.

Here are two ways a leader can pare an attendee list down to size:

- Analyze the agenda to see if everyone needs to be present for each item. It might be possible to divide the agenda into two parts, so that some people need only stay for the first section and others can arrive for the second.

■ Consider whether two separate smaller meetings might be more appropriate. If a large group must be included to reach a decision-making goal, try to hold meetings of smaller subgroups beforehand. After the subgroup has reached an agreement regarding the issue, a representative can attend the final decision-making meeting. Later, the representative can relay the final decision back to the first group.

In general, meetings with large numbers of attendees should be kept as short as possible to meet the objectives. Large meeting groups may need to implement formal procedures such as Robert's Rules of Order to ensure that each attendee has the chance to participate.

PLAN THE AGENDA
■

As mentioned previously, the agenda is the single most important component of meeting planning. A well-thought-out agenda distributed prior to the meeting will provide participants with purpose and direction. It prepares participants in advance and helps to create a solid structure for the meeting.

The meeting leader can ask participants to submit agenda items if she wants to promote group involvement and avoid surprises at the meeting. A written agenda is useful, because it:

■ enables participants to come supplied with the right materials
■ provides a framework which supports the flow of the meeting and keeps a time frame for the discussion of each topic
■ keeps the group on track with a written reminder and focuses the group's attention
■ lets all participants know who has been invited.

Make sure the agenda is succinct and direct, but avoid making it too brief or vague. In general, keep the agenda and meeting short. It is better to schedule two or three shorter meetings and keep the number of items per meeting to five or six than to try to cover everything in one monster meeting.

The agenda should cover the following points:

- the date, start time, and finish time (generally not more than two hours)
- where the meeting will be held, and, if necessary, how to get there
- the topic and subtopics to be covered, including a brief description of each
- a brief indication of the reason for the inclusion of each topic
- how much time will be allotted to each topic
- a list of participants.

Each item on the agenda should be relevant to the purpose of the meeting. Ask yourself the following questions when considering whether or not to include an item:

- Does the item support one of the meeting objectives?
- Is the item of concern to all group members?
- Does the group have the authority to handle the issue?
- Is the subject appropriate to the level of the group?
- Does the group have all the data it needs to discuss the topic?

Unless you can answer yes to the first four of these questions, drop the topic. If you answered no to number five, refer it to a subcommittee or staff member for research. The topic can be added to the agenda once the necessary information has been gathered.

Additionally, the agenda should explain the meeting objectives and what questions and issues are likely to arise. If one item is of special interest to the group, it is often best to single it out for special mention in a covering note. Meeting leaders should consider identifying each item with: "For information," "For discussion," or "For decision" so that attendees are aware of the purpose of each.

MANAGING THE ENERGY CYCLE
•

Meeting leaders who expect to have effective meetings must be aware of energy cycles. Meeting energy is affected by attention cycles, interest in topics, complexity of topics, the number of topics to be addressed, the scheduling of those topics, and the level of participation of attendees. Every meeting has an energy cycle that can be managed and enhanced by a perceptive leader. Here's a guide for timing:

- The early part of the meeting tends to be more lively and creative than the end of it, so items requiring more imaginative ideas, mental energy, and clear heads should be addressed early in the meeting.
- Any items of absolute priority should be first on the agenda, avoiding the possibility of getting stuck on low-payoff topics.
- In the absence of critical, high-priority items, one scheduling option is to address first those items which can be brought to closure quickly and easily, leaving the rest of the meeting for lengthier items.
- Consider reserving a controversial, high-interest item till the end of the session. This way, useful work can be accomplished before the topic comes up. The high interest level in that item will keep attention from lagging.
- Items can be grouped in a way that allows people to cycle in and out of the meeting as they are needed. Changing the make-up of attendees automatically raises the energy level as fresh faces and new voices appear.
- If the meeting will be long, with many agenda items, consider alternating working items with reporting items in order to avoid boredom.
- Try to find a unifying item to end the meeting. If any of the items on the agenda have been divisive, it's particularly important to bring the group back into harmony.

SET THE TIME AND PLACE
▪

It is important to choose a time and place that enhances the meeting and its objectives. Poorly timed meetings can create resentment even before they begin and meetings held in hot, stuffy rooms sap energy from the participants. The three most common times for meetings are as follows:

- **NOON**—This popular meeting time is disliked by some people because it interferes with their lunch. This can be partially compensated for by providing lunch.
- **MIDMORNING**—This is probably the most popular time for meetings as it gives participants time to gather their thoughts, take care of leftover work, and get departments started on the current day's assignments.
- **LATE AFTERNOON**—Some people like to hold late afternoon meetings because they feel that the nearness of quitting time will pressure people to come to closure.

Most meeting leaders find that the midmorning meetings are best for working meetings where it is important for participants to be at their best. Lunch and afternoon meetings are more appropriate for status and information exchanges. Experience shows that Mondays and Fridays are the worst days to hold a meeting. The proximity to the weekend catches people at a time when they may not be fully engaged in work priorities.

The length of the meeting is also important. Most meetings should not last more than two hours. If they do, schedule a coffee break every ninety minutes so that people can stretch, call their offices, get refreshments, etc. This is the best way to ensure that longer meetings retain their effectiveness.

The primary consideration when choosing a room for a meeting will, of course, be the size of the group. The room should be quiet, well ventilated, and the appropriate temperature. As much as possible, it should be distraction-free and comfortable. Also consider the ease of accessibility for the greatest number of people. The meeting location should offer conveniently located restrooms, a water fountain, and telephones.

ROOM ARRANGEMENT

•

There are basically seven different styles for arranging participant seating. Each arrangement affects the pattern of communication.

THEATER STYLE—rows of chairs are arranged in a semicircle facing the stage or podium. It is appropriate for large informational meetings. The leader takes the role of the lecturer,

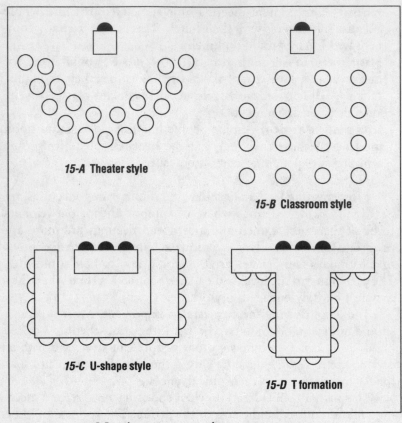

Meeting-room seating arrangements

and the semicircle design allows for some group interaction and question-and-answer sessions.

CLASSROOM—this arrangement has rows of tables and chairs facing the front of the room. It is used with a lecture format and it allows limited opportunities for group interaction. This style works well for informational, limited-interaction meetings with medium-to-large groups. The tables facilitate the handling of materials and taking notes.

U-SHAPED STYLE—the leader or leaders sit at a separate table at the front of the U-shaped participants' seating area. This style is appropriate when participants need to spread out materials such as worksheets. The setting focuses all the attention on the leaders, since the large space in the middle isolates members from one another.

These three arrangements are used primarily with large group meetings, while the following four are used for smaller group meetings.

T-FORMATION—the head table is attached to the end of the main participants' table. This gives participants closer face-to-face contact. The attention is focused on the leaders, who are clearly set off from the rest of the group. This formation only works for a small number of participants and is often used when there is a panel of leaders or experts who sit at the head table.

POWER CHAIR—this arrangement has the chairperson presiding at the end of the table. This popular arrangement focuses the attention on the leader and gives her the ability to retain tight control over the agenda and meeting.

When the leader wants participation, she can utilize one of the two equalizing patterns—democratic or round table. Here, the leader sits among the participants. This is most effective when the leader knows what she thinks about a problem and wants to foster an environment in which others can be creative while she

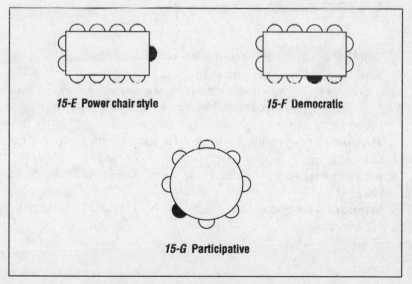

15-E Power chair style   15-F Democratic

15-G Participative

Conference-table seating arrangements

maintains a low profile, not wanting to lead others with her opinions. The manager should choose the seating style which best serves the purpose and type of meeting she is planning.

DEMOCRATIC—in this arrangement the chairperson sits on one side of the table and the ends are left open. While the leader can still maintain control, there is an appearance of openness. It is easier for participants to communicate with each other rather than directing all comments toward the leader.

ROUND TABLE—the most participative pattern. In this arrangement everyone is equal and encouraged to participate as a full partner, minimizing status and power.

FACILITIES CHECKLIST
▪

The best-planned meeting can be destroyed by logistics gone askew . . . the overheated room, the burnt-out light bulb in the overhead projector, insufficient chairs, and so on. There are hundreds of details that go into an effective meeting and the failure of any one of them can derail the session. Here is a checklist to help you remember these details:

- **ROOM SETUP**—Reservations for room made? Enough chairs? Podium needed? Thermostat located and working?
- **AUDIOVISUAL EQUIPMENT AND MATERIALS**—Projectors? Flip charts? Microphones? Display materials? Tape recorders? Pens? Extra bulbs? Light switches located?
- **HANDOUT MATERIALS**—Adequate number of copies for distribution? Staff support for handing them out?
- **REFRESHMENTS**—Coffee, tea, soda? Cookies, fruit? Sandwiches?
- **MISCELLANEOUS**—Pads? Pencils? Ashtrays? Marking pens? Name cards?

While it's true that many meetings waste a great deal of everyone's time and seem to be held for historical rather than practical reasons, it doesn't have to be true. There is great benefit to be gained from bringing people together in an environment that encourages them to share their ideas, feelings, opinions, and suggestions. This chapter has concentrated on how to *plan* an effective meeting. The next chapter will discuss how to *conduct* an effective meeting.

16

CONDUCTING POWERFUL MEETINGS

Scene 1:
"What a waste of time!"
"Right! I know it's Dan's meeting but he never shuts up! The one time I tried to say something he cut me off."
"And, he laughed at Sarah's idea and it sounded intriguing."
"What a jerk!"

Scene 2:
"I can't believe everyone bought our idea!"
"Especially since Joe wanted to go the other way. He really encourages everyone to say what they think."
"I can't believe the number of ideas that came up."
"Some of them might have potential for the future."
"Joe's meetings always seem worthwhile."

Are your meetings Scene 1 or Scene 2? When you call a meeting, you want something from the participants—information, ideas or suggestions, agreement on a decision, or commitment to an action. Your success in achieving your objectives depends not as much on what you know but how much you and the other participants know at the end of the meeting and how much commitment to the objectives is developed during the meeting. The dynamic meeting leader never calls a meeting for frivolous reasons. He respects the time and intelligence of the participants and he does everything possible to make the meeting effective and interesting.

The previous chapter gave a guideline on *preparing* for an effective meeting—determining the purpose for the meeting, preparing an agenda, inviting the attendees, setting an appropriate time and place. This chapter focuses on the skills needed to be an effective meeting leader.

DYNAMIC MEETING LEADERSHIP
■

The first step of dynamic meeting leadership is to know what you want to accomplish during the meeting. Once you know what you want to accomplish, you need to bring those objectives into alignment with the objectives of the attendees. The most productive way to begin the meeting is with a review of the agenda and the meeting goals. The leader makes copies of the agenda available in case anyone forgot to bring his. This initial discussion gives everyone an opportunity to ask questions, offer suggestions, and express opinions about why they are there.

The most important role of the meeting leader is to function as the group facilitator. A good facilitator understands how groups interact, knows how to stimulate participation, and maintains control of the meeting process. The most observable aspect of the group process is communication. Observations of communication patterns will reveal important clues about what's going on.

Meeting facilitators should ask these questions while observing the group:

- Who's doing the talking? For how long? How often?
- Who's not talking?
- Who are people looking at when they talk?
- Who talks after whom, or who interrupts them?

- What style of communication is used (assertions, questions, tentative statements)?
- What tone of voice is used?
- What is being said nonverbally through body language, posture, gestures, or seating arrangements?
- Who are the followers?
- Are people listening carefully to others?
- Are minority opinions being solicited and respected?

These observations can give the facilitator clues about what actions to take: when to step in and encourage a response from a nonparticipator and when to discourage someone who may be monopolizing the discussion; when to ask or encourage questions to stimulate a more open discussion; when to calm the waters if vocal tones and body language start to become overly hostile; when to ask for a summary or further explanation if members seem to be lost or confused; and when to move on or table a discussion for a future meeting if an issue cannot be resolved.

The group leader should put people at ease with his opening remarks, setting an appropriate climate for the meeting. The meeting should begin on a positive note, communicating both verbally and nonverbally the leader's respect for each member. The leader should make sure that the participants know each other. Take the time for brief individual introductions if people are from different organizations or groups. If there is a visitor or observer, make sure he is introduced and the participants are told his purpose for being there. Group dynamics can be derailed by an unfamiliar presence, especially if there are sensitive or controversial topics being discussed.

Good meeting facilitators always:

- **ESTABLISH A CLIMATE FOR SHARING.** Maximize participant comfort by: holding the meeting in a comfortable facility; providing name tags, if necessary; arranging chairs so that each person can see the others; encouraging everyone to speak; protecting the rights of individuals to have dissenting opinions and to change their opinions.
- **EXPLAIN THE GROUND RULES.** Let attendees know what you expect of them. Check their understanding and acceptance of the rules.

- **SET GOALS.** Develop meeting goals with the group and refer to them often as the meeting progresses.
- **EXPLAIN AGENDA.** Announce items to be covered, and the structure and process of the meeting. A written agenda emphasizes the meeting focus and aids the participants in discussing the proper item. Whenever practical, allow group members to participate in agenda setting.
- **STAY TASK-ORIENTED.** Focus on tasks, not personalities or irrelevant issues.
- **LET EVERYONE BE HEARD.** Acknowledge all ideas. Not all ideas must be used or even judged, but all ideas must be heard.

Meeting leaders should be aware of the five common meeting phases. While all meetings go through these stages, the amount of time spent in each can vary widely. The leader who understands these phases can use the dynamics to make the meeting more productive. Here is a brief description of the five common phases:

- **SOCIAL**—The first few minutes are when the group acknowledges each other socially. Typically, this time includes chatting about personal, family, and work interests. While this is not a productive part of the meeting it is important time as it sets a friendly interactive tone.
- **CATHARSIS**—If an agenda contains controversial, complex, or even interesting topics, chances are that there will be diverse opinions and objectives regarding the outcome. It's very important to let attendees express opinions, reservations, and objections early in the meeting to defuse hostility. The dynamic meeting leader might open the meeting by saying, "Let's take ten minutes to get any objections out in the open," or "Does anyone have any concerns about the agenda or our objectives for this meeting?" If this is not done, repressed negative emotions can interfere with the productivity of the meeting.
- **LEARNING**—In this stage, participants listen and acquire information. It's important to watch for fatigue or boredom in this phase. If the material is dry, technical, or presented in an uninteresting manner, try to have a change-of-pace break every ten to fifteen minutes. This can be done by simply stopping and asking for questions, requesting an opinion on some aspect of the presentation, or summarizing the key points.

- **POLICY MAKING**—Information is summarized and decisions are called for. This consensus-seeking stage is often the most challenging for meeting leaders. Successful implementation of decisions generally requires a genuine commitment by everyone involved. Decisions can be forced on meeting participants but commitment can't be. It's important for leaders to make sure everyone expresses their opinions in this stage and that the group works its way through to a decision they can all agree on.
- **ACTION**—Implementation procedures are agreed upon and future committee actions are decided. It's important to accurately document all decisions and actions and make sure that responsibility for each action step is determined.

MINUTES

■

If a meeting is important enough to be held, it's important enough to have the decisions and action items recorded. Meeting minutes make sure that important points and decisions are recorded accurately, without misinterpretations. Taking notes should not be the responsibility of the meeting leader. The trend today is to have a participant serve as the secretary and record necessary items on the flip chart as the meeting is progressing. When using a flip chart, designate one blank page as "Action Items," and record all such items or assignments on it.

Minutes developed on a flip chart or overhead projector are helpful in that they allow review by participants *during* the meeting. If it isn't possible to develop the minutes as the meeting is progressing, they should be produced and distributed as soon as possible after the meeting (not later than two days after) so corrections can be provided before memory erases the details of the meeting. Remember to keep minutes short and succinct: one page is ideal. This is a summary, not a word-for-word transcript.

Minutes should contain the following information:

- Time and the date of the meeting, where it was held, and who chaired it
- Names of all present and an indication of members not in attendance

- All agenda items (and other items) discussed and all decisions reached
- If a task was agreed on and assigned, indicate the person responsible for the task
- The ending time (important, because it may be significant later to know whether the discussion lasted fifteen minutes or six hours)
- The date, time, and place of the next meeting.

ENCOURAGE PARTICIPATION

■

Nothing affects the productivity and outcome of a meeting more than the participation of the attendees. The purpose of calling a meeting is to benefit from the combined information, wisdom, and experience of the participants. If the attendees are not sharing their ideas and opinions, the purpose of the meeting isn't being met and you run the risk of making inferior decisions. Here are several ideas for encouraging participation:

ASK FOR PARTICIPATION. The first step is for the leader to express his commitment to group participation. He should ask for participation and demonstrate rewarding verbal and nonverbal behavior for individual participation. Every person should be treated with courtesy and all ideas and contributions should be acknowledged even if they run counter to the leader's opinions and beliefs. "That's a good question," "Thanks for sharing that," "Interesting point," or "I'm glad you mentioned that," are all comments that will encourage additional contributons of ideas and opinions.

ASK SPECIFIC QUESTIONS to individuals to encourage them to get involved. Before opening up the discussion to everyone ask, for example, "Sarah, how do you feel about the budget figures?"

RESIST DOMINATING. Resist the temptation to give anyone your informed opinion up front. This will immediately cause reluctance by some who might disagree. Instead, keep a low profile on issues where you want the honest opinion of others. It is easy for a leader to dominate a meeting but if you only wanted your opinion, you wouldn't need a meeting.

DEMONSTRATE ACTIVE LISTENING. Set an example by

listening carefully to each speaker, taking notes, asking for clarification, paraphrasing the remarks, and asking for validation that you understood the message.

BREAK THE GROUP INTO SUBGROUPS to discuss the agenda items, with a spokesperson for each subgroup reporting back to the overall group. If there are more than seven participants in a meeting, or if the participants are varied in expertise or rank, there may be a hesitation to participate because of the fear of being wrong or looking foolish. Small groups of three to four are less threatening and give each person more opportunity to participate.

DISCUSS PARTICIPATION. If nonparticipation is a serious problem, ask the subgroups to discuss ways to get the whole group to participate more. Openly discussing the meeting process helps people understand that you are serious about generating discussion and sharing of ideas.

USE THE BRAINSTORMING FORMAT. Tell the participants it's a brainstorming session where everyone is asked for ideas and no criticism is allowed. Make it fun. Tell them to give you their stupid ideas as well as the ones they think are good. Tell them that, in this very special meeting format, quantity of ideas is more important than quality. Explain that you can always go back and evaluate the ideas later. The brainstorming format often gets people actively involved and interested.

AVOID "POWER" SEATING ARRANGEMENTS. Be careful when choosing a room arrangement for the meeting. Certain types of seating styles are more conducive to group interaction. If the leader wants to encourage participation, she should not position herself in a dominant position, such as behind a podium or at the head of the table.

ENCOURAGE PROBLEM-SOLVING

■

If your meeting has a problem-solving agenda, you need to be able to keep the group focused on the problem-solving process. The first step is to set an example by focusing on the facts and understanding points of disagreement rather than getting bogged down in personalities and politics. Try to keep different points of view in balance as much as possible and avoid having one person or group dominate the discussion. You may have to ask specifically for other points of view if the quieter members are not expressing their opinions. Never assume that silence means agreement; more often it signals some level of disagreement with the dominant theme of the discussion.

Effective problem-solving meetings generally follow a pattern. Early in the discussion, the group will be trying to understand the nature of the problem. In this phase, the meeting leader should encourage factual, nonevaluation discussion of the problem symptoms. All possible solutions should be identified without evaluation. It is important to identify all possible solutions in order to be able to select the solution that best fits the needs of everyone involved. Only then should the discussion become evaluative as the group begins to weigh the possibilities.

The challenge in problem-solving meetings is to keep the group from rushing to adopt a solution. Too often someone suggests a solution that seems to fix the problem. If no one sees an immediate drawback, the solution is adopted and the group goes on to the next item or to an implementation plan. There are two hazards to this approach:

SOLVING THE WRONG PROBLEM. If the problem wasn't completely explored, it may not be defined adequately. The suggested solution might solve only part of the problem or it may fix the wrong problem altogether!

NOT FINDING THE BEST SOLUTION. When the search for possible solutions ends too soon, you may wind up with a mediocre solution when a brilliant one was available and would have been found with a little more discussion.

Here is a general framework for problem-solving meetings:

- Statement of the problem
- Review of background and objectives
- Idea and solution generation
- Discussion of pros and cons of each selected solution
- Summary of the discussions
- Consensus on a decision
- Agreement on plans to implement the decision

KEEP DISCUSSIONS ON TRACK

▪

Meeting attendees depend on the leader to control the meeting, keep it on track, and deal with disruptive elements. Meeting leaders need to be able to recognize and know how to deal with the three general types of meeting participants—what we call the "3 Hs": helpfuls, hostiles, and ho-hums.

HELPFULS—Helpful participants are enthusiastic, sometimes to the point of dominating the meeting. Meeting leaders need to acknowledge and show their appreciation for their help while tactfully encouraging them to let others speak. Allow this type to maintain their eagerness but do not let them take over and prevent others from contributing.

HOSTILES—Negative participants can damage the productivity of the group, unless appropriately handled. They may work independently on paper work, talk while others are speaking, or continually interrupt the leader with negative comments. The meeting leader must remain calm when addressing the negative participant. If you have a meeting policy as suggested in the previous chapter, you might want to review the policy and emphasize any points appropriate to the situation. You can reemphasize the need for everyone to participate and to respect the opinions of other participants. You can also address the hostility directly with a comment such as, "John, you seem to be having difficulty with this subject. Would you like to share your thoughts?"

Most important: don't try to argue. Instead, ask the other participants to react to the hostile's point of view.

HO-HUMS—These are actually nonparticipants, who probably include the majority of meeting attendees. Draw these people into the discussion by addressing them by name and asking them open-ended questions. Word your question carefully; don't put them on the spot, just ask for their ideas or opinions.

You can also stimulate participation by requesting a show of hands on an issue or by asking people to write down their ideas on the topic being discussed. Try to get people involved in the meeting's preparation—ask for suggested topics, supporting documentation, and names of possible additional participants.

There are several types of behavior which can lessen the effectiveness of meetings. Here are a few examples of behavior types commonly found at meetings:

THE BLOCKER—Blocking can be conscious or unconscious but it effectively stops the progress of the meeting. The blocker generally succeeds in focusing attention on himself rather than the issue by leading the group off on a tangent and/or continuing to make objections at every possible point.

THE AGGRESSOR—deflates others' status; attacks the group or its values; jokes in a barbed or self-concealed way. The aggressor wants his own way on every issue.

THE AGENDA HIDER—This member is also disruptive because he brings a hidden agenda to the meeting. He wants to achieve a specific result that he never brings out into the open so he supports or blocks an issue using superficial reasoning. When hidden agendas are present, there is a lack of openness and honesty and core issues are seldom addressed.

THE JOKER—This person shows his contempt for the agenda (or his personal lack of interest) through joking, teasing, and disruptive humor.

THE DOMINATOR—The attention seeking behavior of this person can cause disinterest in the rest of the group. The dominator always wants to have the last word, keeping many of the more passive members from speaking up. Members get reluctant about speaking up out of annoyance or the fear of being constantly interrupted.

THE AVOIDER—The avoider strays off subject to avoid commitment or conflict. He may pursue special interests not related to the meeting or prevent the group from facing up to controversy through his avoidance tactics.

THE HELP SEEKER—This person uses the group to solve his own problems, which are unrelated to the group's goals. This person often starts a comment with, "While I've got you here . . ." and then proceeds into a description of his problem and away from the issue facing the group.

Guidelines for handling these dysfunctional behaviors include:

- Confronting the participant in a caring way, being careful to concentrate on the behavior, not the person.

- Pointing out the effects that the dysfunctional behavior is having on the meeting.
- Suggesting alternative behaviors that might be more satisfying for all concerned.

There is a natural tendency for meetings to get sidetracked— discussion on one topic goes too long, someone brings up a new topic that seems to need immediate attention, a participant is called out of the room, or discussion of a topic stalls for lack of important information. All of these are common challenges faced by meeting leaders. The leader must identify and stay committed to the common objectives of the meeting. The best way to prevent being sidetracked is to maintain a sense of urgency and a clear desire to reach the most appropriate conclusions as quickly as possible.

The leader needs to keep the discussion focused on issues, and to minimize interruptions, disruptions, and irrelevant comments. When discussion begins to ramble or go off on a tangent, the leader needs to intercede and get the discussion back on track. Effective meeting leaders develop an arsenal of nonverbal gestures such as the not-so-subtle stare, a raised eyebrow, or a gentle frown, that help them silently communicate their desire to get back on track.

Leaders may wish to exercise different levels of control for different types of meetings. Normally more control is exercised when:

- The meeting is oriented more toward information exchange
- The topic generates strong, potentially disruptive feelings
- The group is moving toward a decision
- Time pressures are significant

There is a wide range of techniques to use if you wish to exert more control over the meeting. You may, for example, permit participants to speak only when you call on them. Another control technique is to comment on or summarize each statement. This prevents interaction, and confrontations, between other individuals. You may also use a flip chart or blackboard to summarize ideas, increasing the formality and decreasing the number of direct exchanges. At times you may want to employ formal parliamentary procedures such as Robert's Rules of Order.

Some of these techniques are obviously not necessary for smaller group meetings. Also consider that although these techniques offer a high degree of control, they do not prevent participants from developing strong feelings, sometimes precisely as a result of their being stifled in the first place.

Other less rigid methods can prevent the increased tensions which sometimes arise during more controlled meetings. If the meeting starts to fall off track, a simple glance at the clock can be a reminder that it is time to return to the agenda. Another way to mark progress is periodically to summarize the group's progress, then ask the group if they would prefer to continue the present discussion or to move on in the interest of time.

A short break can revitalize people's willingness to concentrate on the problem. It also serves to cut off old conversations, making it easier to start new ones. It is important that the leader neither overdirect nor underdirect the meeting. The highly structured leader (the most common type) often unintentionally curtails participation in an effort to move quickly and stay on schedule.

At the beginning of the discussion of any item, the leader should make it clear what the objective is for that particular topic. All participants need to understand the issue and why they are discussing it. Someone should introduce the topic, give an overview of why the item is on the agenda and its importance, the current situation, what the needs are, and some indication of lines of inquiry or courses of action that have been suggested or explored, as well as arguments on both sides of the issue.

ENCOURAGE A CLASH OF IDEAS
■

Good meeting leaders maintain a climate of constant inquiry in which all assumptions (including theirs) can be questioned and tested. They encourage different points of view, critical thinking, and constructive disagreement. They stimulate creativity and counter the group's desire to reach an early consensus. Productive meetings often involve conflict . . . but it should be a clash of ideas, not personalities.

Most meeting leaders will eventually face a situation when voices are raised and tempers flare. While disagreement can be productive, it's important not to let personal hostility escalate out of control. The leader can calm the situation by asking a neutral participant a question requiring a factual answer or by asking someone to recap or summarize both sides of a situation. The leader could recap the points for and against the issue on a flip chart.

THE PERILS OF "GROUPTHINK"

Meetings are held to focus a variety of ideas and opinions on a topic. One of the critical pitfalls of meetings, even in meetings that appear to be working well, is groupthink. This is especially prominent in groups that meet together over long periods of time. Once groupthink begins to occur, the group no longer explores the depths of an issue. They stay on the surface and opt for easy solutions. They don't challenge ideas and recommendations. Here are some of the causes of groupthink:

ILLUSION OF TOGETHERNESS—this is the perception that everyone is in agreement. The group begins to take pride in its lack of disagreement and ability to come to rapid decisions.

CONFORMITY PRESSURES—dissenters are discounted as not being "team players." Dissention is seen as an unhealthy attack on the group.

SELF-CENSORSHIP—group members keep quiet about negative factors affecting decisions and fail to question the direction of the group.

TIME PRESSURES—time pressures can block deep examination of issues and make people grab at easy solutions and avoid the interpersonal processes that make constructive disagreement possible.

In order to prevent groupthink, the leader should:

LEGITIMATIZE DISAGREEMENT—the leader should promote an atmosphere where members feel free to disagree. Openness has to be encouraged and minority viewpoints need to be given careful consideration. Members should be encouraged to play devil's advocate and silence should not be taken as agreement.

ENCOURAGE DIVERSITY OF VIEWPOINT—ask for different ideas. Solicit new views. Ask people to point out hidden risks or unrecognized assets.

GENERATE IDEAS BEFORE EVALUATING THEM—Divide discussions into two phases—generation and evaluation. Prohibit evaluation during the generation stage. Free input of ideas and suggestions should be encouraged and the group should focus on complete understanding of the problem rather than leaping to an easy solution.

DISCUSS THE PROS AND CONS OF EACH SOLUTION—in the evaluation phase, weigh the assets and liabilities of each solution.

THINK THROUGH AN IDEA MORE THAN ONCE—make it a habit to review decisions after enough time has elapsed for them to cool off. Involve as many people as possible in the decision-making process.

EXAMINE THE GROUP PROCESS—analyze how the group is dealing with an issue, as well as what the issue is. After each decision is made, examine the process the group used to make it.

REACHING A DECISION

■

There are two major ways for groups to reach a decision at a meeting: voting and reaching a consensus. Voting is the most common choice when a group is large or split over an important decision. The advantage of this option is that it results in a guaranteed decision. It has its drawbacks, however, namely that it creates a win-lose situation for group members, who are required to have a public commitment to the position. Voting can cause certain members to be identified by their minority position on a decision. This often results in them trying to balance their account on the next decision.

On the other hand, consensus is generally a more effective decision-making procedure, but it is more difficult and frequently more time-consuming. The biggest advantage of consensus decision making is that it allows all points of view to be heard, and usually results in a decision that is more whole-heartedly supported by each member. This is especially vital when it comes to implementing the decision later on. Members are less likely to sabotage the decision when they believe their positions have had a complete hearing.

One way of making sure that consensus has been reached is to ask each member if they agree with the decision—anything less than "Yes" is considered a "No." A person who says, "Well, I basically agree, but . . ." needs to continue the discussion. He has unresolved reservations or unexpressed disagreements.

A discussion should be closed once it has become clear that (a) more facts are required before further progress can be made, (b) the issue needs the views of people not present, (c) members need more time, (d) events are changing and likely to alter or clarify the basis of the decision quite soon, (e) there is not going to be enough time at this meeting to go over the subject properly, or (f) two or three members can settle the matter without the involvement of the entire group.

At the end of the discussion of each agenda item, the leader should give a brief and clear summary of what has been agreed on. The summary should involve a recap of each action item accepted by a participant. That person should confirm his acceptance of the task.

ENDING THE MEETING
■

As the end of the meeting nears, the leader should press for a conclusion. The last few minutes should be used to summarize highlights and decisions, and to restate all agreed-upon assignments and deadlines. Always conclude the session on a positive note, for instance, thanking participants for their attendance and contributions. It is important that everyone feel that the meeting accomplished its objectives. If the group needs to meet again, save time by scheduling the meeting while the group is right there.

POST-MEETING FOLLOW-UP
■

Take five minutes to evaluate the meeting. Determine what the session accomplished, how the results or findings fit into overall company objectives or plans, and what should be the next logical step. Ask these questions:

Were the goals of the meeting met?
Did everyone participate adequately?
Were the physical arrangements satisfactory?
What could have been done better?

Remember to distribute the minutes as soon as possible.

Being able to conduct a meeting effectively is a critical communication skill. The benefits of a well-planned and conducted meeting are enormous: identification of solutions to problems, shared ideas and information, development of action plans that have group commitment, and improved team cohesiveness and morale.

V

WRITTEN COMMUNICATION

As soon as you move one step up from the bottom,
your effectiveness depends on your ability to reach
others through the spoken or written word.

—PETER DRUCKER

Writing abilities are as visible as a person's wardrobe. The impressions you leave through your written work last even longer, however, as memos, reports, and letters are read and often reread. You may be bright, ambitious, and hardworking and yet have a handicap which will stall your career climb on the lower rungs of the ladder: poor writing skills. By developing your writing skills, you will be able to persuade, direct, and influence the course of your organization and the direction of your career.

Poor writing smothers even the most important messages. The reader may spend more time interpreting the message than acting upon it. Writing well takes practice, effort, and a bit of talent. In the end you want your writing to be organized and coherent: not open to multiple interpretations. You want your reader to understand your message, not point at it and exclaim, "What does *this* mean?"

The ingredients of writing are content, style, technique, and format. This next chapter will help you understand how to powerfully focus your content and to use each of the most common business formats (memos, letters, and reports) effectively. The last chapter will give you guidelines on style and how to avoid some of the most common writing mistakes.

PUTTING YOURSELF AHEAD OF THE PACK

Grasp the subject, the words will follow.

—CATO THE ELDER

Good business writing is more about clear thinking than it is about writing style. Writing can only be as good as the thinking that precedes it. You must know what you want to say, what your objective is in saying it, and why it's important for your audience to read it. Organizing a writing project is very similar to organizing a presentation. The good writer is just as aware of her audience as a good public speaker is.

One technique that can help your organize your thoughts and content is mindmapping. This whole-brain, visually-interesting version of outlining helps you pull together all your ideas, memories, associations, and connections in a quick "mind dump." It has none of the constraints that make the Roman numeral form of outlining so stale and dry. Instead, mindmapping allows information to flow more freely from mind to page, streaming off naturally into organized branches.

According to recent brain/mind research, the mind's attention span is extremely short—between five to seven minutes depending on subject matter and level of interest. The mind works best in these short bursts of activity. Mindmapping takes advantage of the mind's tendency to work in short, intense "mind bursts" by allowing you to "dump" your ideas and thoughts onto paper in just a few minutes. Mindmapping is like a personal brainstorming session. It gives you a chance to make new connections with the information and organize it into its primary pieces or branches and the appropriate subtopics and details. It helps you quickly explore your topic creatively.

Mindmapping is extremely easy to use. Here are the basics:

- **FOCUS**—Print the central idea in a circle or box in the center of the page.
- **FREE ASSOCIATION**—Allow your ideas to flow freely without judgment.
- **CONNECT IDEAS**—Print key ideas or thoughts on lines connected to the center focus.
- **BRANCHES**—First branches are key ideas, related ideas are connected as sub-branches.
- **KEY WORDS**—Print key words only: mindmapping is a form of brain shorthand and needs only a few key words to capture an idea.
- **SYMBOLS/IMAGES**—Use any symbols or images which make sense to you.
- **COLOR**—Use color to stimulate your thought processes and to help you organize the material.

Mindmapping allows you to get information down on paper the way your mind handles it rather than in a rigid outline form. Each mindmap is a unique product of the person who produces it—there are no right or wrong mindmaps, no rigid outline forms. If you would like more information on how to use this powerful technique, see *Mindmapping, Your Personal Guide to Exploring Creativity and Problem-Solving* by Joyce Wycoff.

After you have mindmapped the subject of your memo, report, or letter, you should have a clear idea of your main focus. Focus in your business report or memo is your objective—it is the "why" of why you are bothering to write at all. Most business writing has its purpose buried. There is no focus: no goal, no call for action, no desired end result. If you do not provide the focus, you

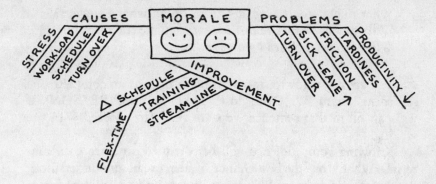

17-A

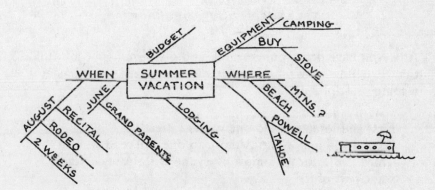

17-B

Examples of mindmapping.

force your reader to ask questions about your message which you should have answered *before* sitting down at your word processor. Ask yourself:

Who is my audience?
What do I want them to do?
What reasons will they have for *not* wanting to do what I want them to do?

What might stop the reader from doing what I suggest?
Will someone other than the reader make the decision?
What are the politics involved?

You are not ready to start writing until you can complete this sentence: I want (WHO) to do (WHAT) because (REASON). If you can fill in that sentence, you are ready to proceed with the writing.

Knowing your audience will help you to organize your material so that it has the best chance of being read and understood. Put yourself in your reader's shoes, listen, and you will be better received. Do not be condescending. Phrases such as, "As you can clearly see" (How do you know I can?) and "I am sure you will agree" (Why are you so sure?) can only serve to turn your audience off.

TELEGRAPH YOUR MESSAGE
•

After you have done your research and organized your information, it is time to write out your message. Keep these business writing principles in mind:

First and foremost: No one wants to read it!
Second and important: Almost no one will read all of it!
Third and critical: Almost everyone will misunderstand some part of it!

No one exclaims, "Oh wow! A new report for me to read!"—except with sarcasm. In the business world, a written message is usually a call to do something, to make decisions, to add to an already overcrowded schedule. Too often we blow it from the first line. *Per your request, please find enclosed the report on the possible involvement of management in a . . .* Yawn. Z-z-z-z.

You are competing for the time of busy people. Unless you are the chairman of the board or president, you probably have about thirty seconds to grab the interest of your reader. Just as we buy magazines based on the front-page headline or picture, we are more likely to read a memo that captures our attention.

Otherwise, the magazine stays on the stand and the memo ends up in the "To Read" cemetery.

Borrowing from the journalism and advertising trades, energize your writing with headlines; subheads; bullets; short, crisp, active words; visuals; powerful persuasion; and dynamic delivery. Telegraph your message. Grab the reader's attention.

HEADLINES ARE GOLDEN. They must never be boring. Don't waste a headline with *Summary of Benefits* when you could have stated: *Three Million in Savings*. When writing a report, proceed in this order: start with the headlines, then plan the graphics and subheads and, perfecting those, add the main body. This is the best way to maintain focus and flow in your writing.

VISUALS SELL YOUR MESSAGE. Pictures, graphs, or illustrations will help you get an idea across quickly or emphasize a particular point. Keep these suggestions in mind when incorporating graphics:

- Graphs and charts have more impact than tables.
- Each graph, chart, or picture should make only one point. Better to have several graphs, each making one point, than one confusing graph with little impact.
- Add color if at all possible.
- Keep the graph or picture as close to the related text as possible.

SHORT IS BEST. Short words . . . short sentences . . . short paragraphs. The trick is to write them without sounding like a second-grade primer. Your words can be crisp, punchy, colorful, musical, poetic, and graphic. They can lift, stomp, drag, kick, and breathe life into your work. Short sentences are active and quickly understood.

FORMAT FOLLOWS FUNCTION

•

The format of what you are writing should fit its function. If you receive a memo and your response is a short note or decision, you may want to just jot your response on the memo and send it back. But if you are responsible for presenting an analysis of a new market, you will need a formal report complete with charts, graphs, and documentation.

Making the format fit the function of your writing seems simple, but all too often a brief request triggers a three-page memo. Review the following hierarchy of communication formats so that you are sure your situation fits the requirements:

VERBAL—informal conversations where no documentation is required

HANDWRITTEN—informal communication requiring a minimum of documentation

MEMOS—broad communication (to more than three people) where formal documentation is required

REPORTS—broad communication required; they involve complex issues requiring supporting documentation, and decisions need to be documented

BUSINESS LETTERS—written communication generally to people outside your organization, serves several different functions and provides documentation

MEMOS: USE AND ABUSE

•

Memos are most often boring, confusing, unnecessary, or all of the above. The first thing you should ask yourself is if you really need to write it at all. Can you phone the people involved and *talk* to them? ATI Medical, Inc., (150 employees, $14 million sales) abolished memos and only occasionally writes PAPCOES (reverse acronym for "enunciations of corporate policies and procedures"). President Paul Stevenson states, *Everyone has learned to talk to each other*. Talking to people has wonderful advantages over writing: you get immediate feedback; you strengthen your social contacts; and you save trees.

Eliminating written communication probably is not practical or even desirable for most organizations. Whenever possible, however, talk to people and save your written communications for complex issues requiring extensive explanation or documentation.

When you do decide to write a memo, it should facilitate, simplify, and accelerate internal communication. When used effectively, memos provide a simple method to communicate an identical message to several people. In effect, memos are a meeting on paper. Use them to give instructions, ask for information or action, to announce or clarify a new policy or procedure, announce changes or personnel transfers, or as "covers" for lengthier material such as reports.

Memos are an appropriate method of giving instructions to a number of people. Putting directions in writing, when done clearly, prevents misunderstandings about what is to be done, who's responsibility it is, and the date it's due.

Memos should be short (one page for most). Use every possible trick for quick communication including: headlines, short paragraphs, bullets, bolding of important points, and a modified outline format. A common heading for memos is the following:

Date:

TO:
FROM:
SUBJECT:
ACTION REQUIRED:

"To" should include all intended recipients of the memo. The form of address depends on the culture of your organizations. Some companies use Mr./Mrs./Ms. and titles; others use only first names.

"From" includes your name and phone number.

The "Subject" of your memo should be specific. Clarify it, including only the relevant information: who, what, when, where, how, and why. This line should instantly give the reader enough information to know how to deal with it. A memo with the subject *New Marketing Plan Review Meeting* will receive a much different response than one with the subject *Salary Freeze Policy*.

The "Action Required" line makes it clear to the reader that the writer expects an action. It also helps the writer consider the purpose of the memo. If you are writing too many "Info Only" memos, it's time to rethink your communication policy. If you refer to an earlier memo, include it, preventing inconvenience for the receiver.

Keep your message brief, informal, and simple. Keep the specific readers' needs and circumstances in mind. Clarify the purpose and be specific about the actions the reader should take and when. Avoid words with double-meanings, hidden agendas, jokes, or jargon. Artificial embellishments, fancy words, and wasteful sentences have no place in the office memo. Short and informal, a memo should never be written so hastily that it is ambiguous. Write it well, and avoid misunderstandings, hurt feelings, and time spent correcting errors.

REPORTS—MORE THAN LONG MEMOS
•

Many people get anxious at the thought of writing a business report. Reports are generally long and they deal with complex, often controversial, subjects. They require a great deal of research and critical thought. Perhaps even more anxiety-producing is the realization that business reports generally influence major company decisions. The people who determine your future in the organization will read it, and a well-written report can enhance your opportunity for advancement. Conversely, a poorly thought out and written report leaves a black mark that may be difficult to overcome.

The business report is a highly organized, fact-oriented document. You should use headings, subheadings, bulleted points, and supporting detail to support any conclusions. Use a variety of graphs and charts to help the reader understand the data you are presenting.

Know the purpose of your report before you begin writing. Is it a white paper for information only? Will it recommend a specific solution?

As with every other form of communication, you should also know your intended audience. Make sure you don't insult their intelligence by presenting in detail information they already know, or confuse them with terms they may not be familiar with. Here are some excellent questions to ask yourself before you proceed with your report:

- What is the familiarity of the reader with the problem?
- What expertise does the reader have in this area?
- What conclusions are of importance to the reader?
- What are the preconceived notions of the reader?
- Why was the report requested?
- What does the reader need to know in order to make a decision?

You should also be thoroughly familiar with the ramifications of your suggestion and any drawbacks to it. Few solutions are perfect—make sure you understand the limitations of yours. The purpose of the report, the proposed solution, and the intended audience will all affect the strategy you choose for your report. You should understand your strategy before you begin to write. Here are three typical strategies:

MOST IMPORTANT TO LEAST IMPORTANT. This strategy works well when the decision or action is logical and not highly political and the readers are objective.

LEAST CONTROVERSIAL TO MOST CONTROVERSIAL. Builds support gradually and is best used when the decision is expensive, controversial, politically sensitive, or when the readers are emotionally attached to a different solution than the one proposed.

NEGATIVE TO POSITIVE. Works well when readers are familiar with the problems involved with the situation and the proposed solution. It establishes a common ground and puts the positive argument last in a place of strength.

Business reports are fact-oriented and should not include opinion. If you want to add your personal opinions, they can be included in the cover letter. Opinions in the body of your report will make it seem less factual and objective.

Informal business reports have a fairly standard organization:

INTRODUCTION—This is similar to the opening of a presentation. It is where you grab the reader, introduce the key issues, and give the reader a sense of who, what, where, when, why, and how. It should give the reader the background of the problem, state the problem clearly and indicate why its solution is important to the reader, and define the scope and limitations of the proposed solution.

TABLE OF CONTENTS—Make it easy for the reader to find key information. In a ten-page report, it's not critical, but in a hundred-page report, a great deal of time can be wasted looking for information. Reports are often reviewed in meetings and it can be frustrating trying to find a key point.

MAIN BODY—This is where the writer presents the findings from the research, analyzes the data, evaluates the possible solutions, and develops a rationale for selecting the proposed solution. This section is often broken down into the following subsections:

BACKGROUND MATERIAL AND FACTS

The two functions of this section are to give readers essential background material they may lack, and to clarify the report writer's understanding of the situation (which may well differ from the perceptions of others).

STATEMENT OF PROBLEM

This section explicitly defines the problem (as opposed to the symptoms) to be solved.

ANALYSIS

This section contains the logical thought processes used to develop the solution; it is designed to persuade the reader regarding the advantages of the solution and thoroughness of the writer's analysis. This section could be further divided into such topics as alternatives considered, objectives for solution, evaluation of alternatives, alternatives rejected, or assumptions.

SOLUTIONS AND IMPLEMENTATION

This final section details solutions to the problem.

CONCLUSIONS AND RECOMMENDATIONS—the entire report leads up to this point. No new information is presented but the key ideas are recapped and summarized in a way that reinforces the validity of the recommendation.

APPENDICES—data that is too lengthy or complex should be in this section. The body of the text can reference data in a particular appendix without bogging the reader down with the entire set of data. It is not unusual to have the body of a report be a few pages of text backed up by hundreds of pages of detailed data.

BUSINESS LETTERS—YOUR MESSENGERS TO THE OUTSIDE WORLD

•

Malcolm Forbes once said, "Most business letters don't make it." In his typical, direct style he continued, "It's totally asinine to blow your chances of getting whatever you want with a business letter that turns people off instead of turning them on." He said that most business letters fall into three categories: stultifying if not stupid; mundane (most of them); and first-rate (rare). His primary recommendation for reaching the first-rate level is to know what you want and to be able to write it down in one sentence.

Business letters are your written contact with people outside the organization. Unlike telephone conversations, letters document your communication, providing a long-lasting record which can be referred to whenever necessary. There are many different reasons for writing a business letter and each purpose dictates a slightly different style and tone. Some common reasons are:

- to request specific information or action from someone outside the company
- to provide information to someone who requests it
- for ceremonial purposes (congratulations, thank-yous, commendations)
- to exchange ideas, handle arguments, present a point of view, or explain why an action was taken or why a requested action was rejected
- to sell goods or services or to provide information about the company

You are representing your company when you write a business letter. Get to the point quickly. Be clear, courteous, and concise.

Your first paragraph is where you hook your reader's attention and get her involved with your purpose. This is not the time for mumbling, stuttering, or vagueness. This is where you persuade the reader to consider your ideas. Give the reader a clear idea of the benefits your proposal brings to her or why you need the information she has.

Write so that the reader enjoys reading it. Write the entire letter from *her* point of view. Answer questions and objections she might have. Be positive. Be nice. Be natural.

Conclude by urging the reader to act upon your solution. You should get your message across in one or two pages. If not, add an appendix of materials. Read your letter out loud to see if it sounds natural, pleasant, and clearly addresses your purpose.

Good business writing is a combination of clear thinking, good organization, and effective presentation. This chapter has given you a technique—mindmapping—to help you think through your writing project and organize it effectively. It has also given you a guide to using the three most common formats in business writing—memos, reports, and business letters. The next chapter will help you improve your style and avoid some of the most common pitfalls in writing.

IT'S A MATTER OF STYLE

Colors fade, temples crumble, empires fall, but wise
words endure.

EDWARD THORNDIKE

What kind of memos and reports do you absolutely dread reading?

Those with sentences so long you get lost along the way? Those that strangle you with confusing phrases, technical terms, acronyms, and words that only a dictionary could love? Those that ramble for pages without a break or even a sense of where they're going?

You've probably seen them all . . . and maybe worse. These are the memos, letters, and reports that you want to pass along to someone else to read, no matter how important the information inside may seem to be. The overwhelming temptation is to set it aside in the "To Read" file, or, better yet, the circular file.

How do you keep your written work from receiving the same treatment you've often been tempted to give others? The last chapter gave you an overview of how to organize your thinking and structure as well as how to use the right format. This chapter will help you understand the basics of style and how to keep your memos, reports and business letters out of the circular file and in the hands, and minds, of your readers.

Style is what makes the difference.

WHAT IS STYLE?
■

Hemingway had style. Stephen King has style. Does that mean you have to be a professional writer to have style? No. In fiction, "style" is used to describe a distinctive voice in writing . . . a certain grace with words that sets the truly great writer apart from the rest. In business writing, we're talking about something much more basic. In business writing, the style we're looking for emphasizes clarity, conciseness, and readability more than eloquence.

THE BIG THREE: CLEAR, CONCISE, READABLE
■

The clarity of your writing rests on the foundation of clarity in your thinking which we discussed in the last chapter. It is also affected by the words you use, the voice you choose, and your level of formality. Clear writing demands a high level of preparation. If you lack confidence when you write, it shows up in the use of passive voice, jargon, indirect expressions, and lengthy, unfocused writing. In business writing, you need to say what you want to say directly rather than tiptoeing gently around the bush. Most readers won't tiptoe around the bush with you and it makes you, the writer, seem to be hiding something.

DON'T MUDDY THE WATER
■

Once you are confident about what you want to say and have it well organized and structured, there are three ways to improve the clarity of your writing: use active voice, avoid jargon, avoid indirectness.

USE ACTIVE VOICE—Active voice is open and up-front. Business writing is about action—it requests action, suggests action, encourages action. If you want people to act, use active rather than passive voice. Example:

> *Passive:* It is suggested that you have a meeting called at your earliest convenience.
> *Active:* Please call a meeting ASAP.

We get into passive voice primarily in two ways: hiding the subject and using a "be" verb or past participle of an active verb. Here are two examples. The subject of the sentence is highlighted and the verb is underlined:

> *Passive: There* <u>seems</u> to be a need to review our health plan.
> *Active: We* <u>will review</u> our health plan.

Did you have trouble finding the subject of the first sentence? So would a reader who would be left with a vague impression and no sense of action.

> *Passive:* A new phone system *was chosen* by the committee.
> *Active:* The committee *chose* a new phone system.

Notice that it's the same basic verb—chose—but the passive voice uses the past participle form. The active sentence is clean, clear, and simple. Active voice is much closer to the way we talk. As a writer you are talking with your reader through the written word. If you were talking to a coworker, you would say "I suggest" and not "it is suggested." The active voice not only adds vitality to your writing, but it is more direct, forceful, and personal.

Active voice depends on action verbs. Decide. Talk. Meet. Sell. Start. Buy. Merge. Choose. Hire. Fire. Plan. Negotiate. Make. Build. Ask. These are a few of the action words of business. They telegraph meaning when they aren't surrounded by muddy, indirect phrases.

Passive voice is a shield to hide behind. It is flat and dull, and you should only resort to it when you want to soften bad news, you want to avoid responsibility for some occurrence or remain detached, or you do not know who the main "actor" is in a sentence.

AVOID JARGON—every profession has its terminology, acronms, and jargon. When everyone understands the terms, it provides a quick and efficient shorthand. When everyone doesn't understand the terms, it creates miscommunication and misunderstandings. It's almost impossible to avoid jargon and acronyms, and when you are writing for people within your organization, you are probably safe. If there is any doubt that your readers will understand a term or acronym, define the term the first time it is used, or find a different way of expressing your idea. Example:

> *Jargon:* The LOE required to respond to the RFP is too high.
> *Translation:* The level of effort required to respond to the request for proposal is too high.
> *Plain English:* We can't afford to bid on this project.

BE DIRECT—Say what you mean. If you try to hide behind indirect expressions, people will either not understand what you're saying or they'll figure it out anyway and just think you're a poor writer. Examples:

> *Indirect:* It is suggested that you have a meeting called at your earliest convenience regarding the possibility of determining the feasibility of implementing a new marketing plan.
> *Direct:* Please call a meeting ASAP to discuss a new marketing plan.

People generally go into indirect mode when they're hedging. Common hedging words are: seem, appears, might possibly be, could be. These words and phrases indicate a lack of confidence and a fuzziness of thinking. They do not inspire confidence and action in your reader.

Writing is an act of communication. We are trying to pass a message from one mind to another. It is our job as a writer to make the message as clear as possible to the reader. The more active, jargon-free, and direct our writing is, the more the reader will understand what our message is.

SHORT IS BEST

The second goal of business writing is conciseness. We are not writing the Great American Novel; we are transmitting information or requesting action from people who have little time or inclination to read what we're writing. If we're asking someone to take action and we can clearly convey that request in one paragraph, great! Business writing is not a college term paper with a fixed page requirement. We want to state our business in the clearest and shortest way possible. Cut out all the fluff and improve your chances of having your memos and reports read and acted on.

SHORT WORDS. Start with short words. Big words are no substitute for clear thinking and often they aren't as powerful as short, punchy, crisp, lean, exact, sharp, tight, and to-the-point small words. Here are a few examples of big words that have smaller alternatives. You may want to use the big word but consider the little one:

> Circumvent—avoid
> Viable—workable, useful
> Dialog—talk, conversation
> Scenario—plan
> Interface with—meet with, work with
> Optimize—make the most of
> Sufficient—enough
> Utilize—Use

SHORT PHRASES. Just as we often opt for a long word when a short one would do, we have developed a lot of wordy phrases that need to be trimmed back. Here are some examples:

> With reference to—about, regarding
> On the grounds that—because
> Explore every avenue—analyze
> In accordance with—by, following

To tell the truth—(avoid this one; it sounds like a lie is coming)
To the best of my ability—(eliminate)
Hold a discussion—discuss
Take action—act
At this point in time—now
Decision-making process—decide

SHORT SENTENCES. Short sentences are active. They have punch. They telegraph. While all sentences can't be short, watch out for these three tiny words: and, but, or. They often lead into long sentences full of dependent clauses and twists and turns that lose the reader. The most interesting writing uses a variety of sentence length with the short sentence being used as the power punch. Look at a recent memo or report and count the words in three or four sentences. A common guideline is 17 words. It's OK to go over that limit occasionally, but if all your sentences are more than 17 words, your readers are going to go brain dead. (This last sentence contained 26 words. It could have been two sentences: It's OK to go over that limit occasionally. However, if all your sentences are more than 17 words, your readers are going to go brain dead.)

SHORT PARAGRAPHS—There are two reasons for short paragraphs: one idea and white space. **One idea:** Powerful paragraphs transmit one idea. Each sentence in the paragraph develops the idea. When that idea is complete, go to the next idea in the next paragraph. **White space:** Take a lesson from the advertising folks. White space sells. The space between paragraphs gives the reader time to process information and makes it easier to transition to the next idea. Short paragraphs broken by white space please the eye more than an unbroken mass of words on a page.

SHORT WRITING—If you can say it in one page, don't take two. Brief is better. Short has more chance of being read. However, short is not easier. It is much harder to write a one-page memo than to ramble on for two. It requires clear thinking and clear writing. But it is worth the effort.

Business is about productivity and efficiency. Business writing that is clear and concise promotes those ideals. Business writing is almost never about entertaining the reader. Reading memos is not a leisure-time activity. Respect your reader's time by saying what you need to say as clearly and concisely as possible.

TELEGRAPH

■

Once your message is clear and concise, telegraph it to your reader's mind with a powerful layout. Make it as easy to read as possible. Your two main tools to readability are highlighting and white space.

HIGHLIGHTING: Use bolding and italics to highlight key ideas and introduce new topics, and bullets to emphasize list items . . . for example:

- **BOLDING AND ITALICS**—key ideas and new topics
- **BULLETS**—emphasize list items

Caution: use these tools sparingly. When you are speaking in public, you can use your voice to emphasize certain ideas. When you're writing, you're using these highlighting mechanisms in the same way you would use your voice. Just as you wouldn't try to emphasize every word to your audience, you don't emphasize every word on the page. *Also,* if you *try* to **emphasize** *too* many words, **it** becomes *visually* **chaotic** and *makes* the **reader** want to quit *reading.* Another emphasis tool is the exclamation point! In business writing it should be used very infrequently! Frequent use is the mark of amateur writing! Or a disturbed mind!

WHITE SPACE: Again, white space makes a page more readable. Use it to produce a page that is clean and attractive. Use wide margins and a break between paragraphs. It is much easier to read narrow columns than wide lines. Wide margins also make it easy for the reader to make notes as he reads. It makes the page look clean and professional.

ADDITIONAL READABILITY TIPS: These are housekeeping tips to make your memos and reports more readable.

- **LIMIT UPPER CASE**—We normally read upper and lower case text. While upper case may be used OCCASIONALLY for emphasis, long blocks of text in upper case are very difficult to read. It is almost always better to use bolding and italics for emphasis and save upper case for titles and headings.
- **NUMBERS**—Numbers should be written in a way that makes them easier to read. $4 million is easier to read than $4,000,000.

- **PAGE NUMBERS**—Mandatory for reports of more than three pages. Trying to discuss unnumbered pages has ruined many meetings.
- **HYPHENS**—Before we had word processing, we seldom thought about breaking a word at the end of a line. The only purpose for hyphenation is to even out spacing. Hyphens do not improve readability. Avoid them if you can and if you can't, review them carefully to make sure they do not break the flow of words.
- **AVOID RIGHT JUSTIFICATION**—This technique of aligning typed lines at the right margin is popular because it is used by magazines and newspapers. This makes it look "professional." However, they use it because it packs more words into a smaller space and saves paper. The uneven spaces between words created by right justification make reading more difficult and should be avoided when possible.

If you can use these guidelines to help you write clearly and concisely in a readable format, your writing will become far more powerful and effective. And as your memos and reports become more powerful, you will begin to have more of an impact on your organization. The following paragraphs will give you a few more tips to help your writing style.

AVOID SEXISM
▪

A recent study of 500 college students (50 percent male and 50 percent female) showed that when they read a story using he, him, or his *where the subject could be male or female,* 65 percent of the study group assumed the subject was male. Recently, people have been sensitized to sexism in writing; therefore, you should avoid sexism whenever possible. However, using awkward constructions such as he/she or (s)he can break the flow of your writing and lessen readability.

Here are some ways to avoid sexism without sacrificing readability:

- Specify the person you are discussing.
- Use plurals. For example:

A manager should listen to his staff.
Managers should listen to their staffs.

- Alternate gender: he/his and she/her. In a long report, you could alternate gender by sections. In short works, it would be better to just occasionally use the feminine pronoun except where it would be confusing.

  The employee picked up his check.
  A manager should listen to her staff.

- Substitute less-offensive words: person for man; synthetic for manmade; representative for spokesman; worker for workman; labor hours for man hours.

HUMOR
■

Humor can be effective in informal writing. However, unless you are positive that the humor will not give offense, it's better not to use it. If you are a boss writing to your staff, humor directed at yourself can establish a warm, human tone. If you are an underling, humor directed at yourself might be perceived as a lack of self-confidence or weakness.

Even if you are extremely good at humor, you should limit it in your business writing. People will come to expect it and your serious communications will be more difficult.

PUNCTUATION
■

Punctuation is another way we approximate in writing what we can do with our voice in speaking. Punctuation creates pauses, clarifies meaning, and adds rhythm to our writing. Reading is like listening: the more fluent and lyrical the words, the more willing the reader to read on. Writers use punctuation to control the timing and pace of their work.

- The period stops the sentence. The semicolon creates a pause between two halves that could be separate sentences. And, the comma is a brief rest before going on.
- Dashes separate an important aspect of a larger idea—such as our discussion of punctuation—and draw attention to it.

- The colon is a pause longer than a semicolon but not as long as a period. The most common uses of colons are to introduce a list or serve as a link between an introductory statement and an important point.
- Parentheses tell the reader that the enclosed information is useful but not vital or directly related to the main point of the paragraph.

Two punctuation marks affect the tone of a paper: the question mark and quotation marks. Questions are unassuming and can add a warm, easygoing tone to your writing. Questions facilitate transitions, too (e.g., How are we going to do it?). Quotation marks not only enclose direct quotes, but set off and denote words or phrases used in a special sense.

EDITING
■

You have not finished your report until you have edited it thoroughly for typos, misspellings, and errors in numbers or dates. Whether you write one memo a month or forty, you should have a minimum of three reference books: a good dictionary, a thesaurus, and a style guide. Keep these by your desk and do not hesitate to refer to them. The time you take now to double-check a spelling or find the right word will make all the difference later.

Here are a few of the "classics":

- *The Elements of Style* by William Strunk, Jr. and E. B. White (New York: Macmillan, 1979).
- *Manual of Style* (Chicago: University of Chicago Press, 1969)
- *The American Heritage Dictionary of the English Language* (Boston: American Heritage and Houghton Mifflin, 1969).
- *The Synonym Finder* by J. I. Rodale (Rodale Press, Inc., 1978) *Lists over one million synonyms.*

COMMON ERRORS
■

We make many word errors—words with the wrong meaning, imprecise words, redundant words, out-of-date words. Know your words, and when in doubt, check a dictionary. Certain words are confused with others over and over again, and this in turn confuses the reader. Here are a few common culprits:

- It's vs. Its—It's is a contraction of "it is." Its is the possessive form of "it."
- Imply vs. Infer—Imply means to suggest indirectly. Infer means to draw meaning out of something.
  He implied that he wanted to go.
  I inferred from his actions that he wanted to go.
- I.e. vs. e.g.—i.e. (*id est*) means "that is." E.g. (*exempli gratia*) means "for example."
- Appraise vs. Apprise—Appraise means to measure, to assess the value or nature of something. Apprise means to inform in detail.

STYLE STRATEGIES

∎

Once you thoroughly understand style you can select the style that fits your reader and the type of writing situation you face. These situations generally fall into the following four categories:

- **POSITIVE SITUATIONS:** where you are saying yes or relating good news
  Style: Personal, at times Colorful
- **SITUATIONS WHERE YOU ARE ASKING SOMETHING OF THE READER:** where you are giving instructions or persuading someone to do as requested
  Style: Active, at times Personal and Colorful
- **INFORMATION-CONVEYING SITUATIONS:** where you are passing along factual, detailed information
  Style: Impersonal
- **NEGATIVE SITUATIONS:** where you are delivering information that the reader would prefer not to know
  Style: Passive, Impersonal

Here is a list of the highlights of each style:

ACTIVE STYLE

- use when you want to be forceful, confident, and sure as in action requests or when you are saying no firmly but politely to an employee
- active verbs
- short sentences
- direct statements that start with the subject
- first person—*I want, We need*

PASSIVE STYLE

- use when you are in a negative situation or are in a lower position than the reader
- avoid the imperative—never give an order
- subordinate the subject to the end of the sentence or bury it completely
- attribute responsibility for negative statements to nameless, faceless, impersonal "others"
- use long sentences or dense paragraphs to slow down the reader's attention to sensitive or negative information

PERSONAL STYLE

- use when you are relating good news or a persuasive action-request
- refer to people by name (first name, when appropriate) instead of by title
- use personal pronouns (especially "you" and "I") when you have positive things to say
- incorporate short, informal, and conversational sentences, with contractions if necessary
- ask the reader direct questions
- include personal notes and references

IMPERSONAL STYLE

- use in negative and information-conveying situations, and especially in technical and scientific writing

- refer to people by title or job description if necessary, not by name (particularly first name)
- avoid using personal pronouns, although a faceless "we" may be appropriate
- use passive verbs
- use longer sentences including complex sentences and long paragraphs

COLORFUL STYLE

- use for highly persuasive writing such as sales letters or for good-news situations
- use more descriptive adjectives and adverbs
- use metaphor and simile when appropriate
- use unusual words or slang

Memos, reports, business letters are a critical part of an organization's communication environment. As you develop your ability to write in a clear, concise, forceful style, you will improve your personal effectiveness and the productivity of your organization. "Style," as it applies to business writing, is not as mysterious as it sounds. It is more a matter of common sense: understanding the needs of your reader, as well as your own objectives, and then presenting your message clearly and concisely in a readable format.

Wrap Up: Putting It All Together

We have come a long way since the first chapter. First we covered the basics of interpersonal communications, and learned about the four styles and the different "languages" they speak. You learned how to identify your own style and the style of those around you and how to adapt your communication in order to speak to others in their language.

We then examined various listening and questioning techniques and strategies to give you a greater ability to uncover the problems and needs of those around you. Active listening was explored through the CARESS model so that you would be better able to be sensitive, attentive, and responsive to other people during the communications process. You were also given a simple model for resolving conflicts with others.

The full area of nonverbal communications was covered to provide you with a deeper sensitivity to what other people are really communicating and how they are actually feeling. In this regard, we covered the topics of image, body language, vocal tone, and communicating with time and space. These nonverbal communication techniques send a powerful message before you utter your first word.

In the section on group communication, you were shown how to organize and deliver public presentations and given a detailed guide on how to plan and conduct effective meetings. And the last section gave you valuable insight on how to make your written communication telegraph your message to your readers.

In short, you have just been exposed to a total picture of communication and given specific techniques for delivering your message to others powerfully and effectively.

People generally respond to new experiences in one of five ways. First, you might integrate the new experience with past experiences easily because the new experience is seen as pleasant and compatible. Second, the new experience might be rejected totally because it is perceived as too threatening. Third, you can isolate the new experience from what you are presently accustomed to and thereby treat this experience as an exception to the rule. This allows you to continue acting and thinking as you customarily have done. Fourth, you might distort the new experience to make it "fit" your past experiences. Fifth, you may perceive the experience as a new reality and change your old ways of thinking and acting to conform to a newly expanded or newly perceived reality.

The most productive of the five responses listed is the last one. By reacting in accordance with this response, you undergo a positive behavioral change. You do not accept everything that you have read, of course. Instead, you take what makes sense to you and weave it into your current "reality." Nothing that you have seen in this book is cast in concrete. What segments you use and how you use them will determine your personal effectiveness—now and in the future.

It would make us extremely pleased if, after reading this book, you went out and started practicing these new communication techniques. It won't be easy and will require more practice, as well as some mistakes, to lead to greater success in communicating with others.

Remember the time you first learned how to drive a car? Before you learned how, you were what we call an unconscious incompetent. That is, you didn't know how to drive the car, and you didn't even know why you didn't know how to drive it.

When you first went out with one of your parents, a friend, or an instructor to learn how actually to drive the car, you became a *conscious* incompetent. You still couldn't drive the car; but because of your new awareness of the automobile and its parts, you were consciously aware of why you couldn't drive it. From this step, you at least had the awareness of what you had to do to acquire the competency to drive.

With some additional practice and guidance, you were able to become competent in driving the car. However, you had to be consciously aware of what you were doing with all the mechanical aspects of the car as well as with your body. You had to be consciously aware of turning your blinker signals well before you executed a turn. You had to remember to monitor the traffic behind you in your rearview mirror. You kept both hands on the wheel and monitored your car's position relative to the centerline road divider. You were consciously aware of all these things as you "competently" drove.

Think of the last time you drove a car. Were you consciously aware of all the things we've discussed? Of course not! Most of us, after having driven for a while, progress to a level of unconscious competency. This is the level where we can do something well and not even have to think about it. It comes somewhat naturally.

The foregoing example holds true for communicating with others. You need to go through the competency processes to get to the highest level—the unconscious competence level. This is where you can communicate naturally and effectively. However, you have to pay a price to get to the level of unconscious competence: Practice, practice, practice.

When you were learning to drive the car, you acquired your competency through practice. For some of you, effectively communicating with others may require a significant change of behavior. After persistence and practice, and as you approach the unconscious competency level, your interpersonal communication skills will increase beyond its previous level to a new and higher plateau.

If you've decided to accept the challenge of more effectively communicating with others, the payoffs are certainly well worth your efforts. With so much to learn about, you are probably confused as to where to start. Our advice is that you first assess your current situation. How well do you probe? Listen? Read body language? Give and receive feedback? Communicate effectively with time and space?

As you determine your current situation and compare it with your new objectives, identify those areas that need work. There may be a number of areas that need work, but take care to set priorities on problem areas according to how much attention they need. Work on those problem areas first that need the most help. As you become more competent in these areas, go on to the lower-priority areas. Specifically develop an action plan to improve those areas that will help you in your quest to become better at communicating with others. Define what has to be done to accomplish your action plan. Set up an implementation schedule, and establish commitment to follow it through according to the scheduled completion times. Set the goals and establish your criteria for success; determine how and when to measure your performance in improving your interpersonal communication skills. Constantly monitor the results, and take corrective action where necessary.

Your new action plan might include further professional help in the form of seminars, books, or tapes. Keep informed of other learning devices that will help you improve any or all of the skills discussed in this book. Your plan may also include a more detailed review of relevant portions of this book when appropriate.

Whatever your goals and objectives, make sure you have an action plan with a specific implementation schedule and a method for tracking results. Otherwise, you may get too caught up in trying to do too much at one time and not grow with any specific skill. This will undoubtedly lead to frustration on your part and the ultimate decision to quit your self-improvement program.

Correctly used, interpersonal communication skills will allow you to interact with others, as well as solve problems in an open, honest atmosphere of trust and helpfulness. You will gain more support from others. You will deservedly feel an increased pride in your new and successful communication style.

You needn't wait; you can start to apply communication skills immediately. The path has been mapped. Where you go from here depends on your determination and persistence in applying these skills.

BIBLIOGRAPHY

CHAPTER ONE

Adler, Ronald B. *Interplay: The Process of Interpersonal Communication, 4th edition,* (New York: Holt, Rinehart & Winston, 1989).

DeVito, Joseph A. *Messages: Building Interpersonal Communication Skills,* (New York: HarperCollins Publishers, 1989).

DeVito, Joseph A. *The Interpersonal Communication Book, 5th edition,* (New York: HarperCollins Publishers, 1988).

Haney, William V. *Communication & Interpersonal Relations: Text and Cases,* sixth edition, (Homewood, IL: Richard D. Irwin, Inc., 1992).

Huseman, Richard, James Lahif, and John Hatfield. *Interpersonal Communication in Organizations,* (Boston: Holbrook Press, 1976).

Hybels, Saundra. *Communicating Effectively, 2nd edition,* (New York: McGraw-Hill, 1988).

Mader, Thomas F. and Diane, *Understanding One Another: Com-*

municating Interpersonally, (Dubuque, IA: William C. Brown Publishers, 1990).

Myers, Gail E. *The Dynamics of Human Communication: A Laboratory Approach, 6th edition,* (New York: McGraw-Hill, 1991).

Pearson, Judy. *Interpersonal Communication: Concepts, Components & Contexts, 2nd edition,* (Dubuque, IA: William C. Brown, Publishers, 1990).

Rogers, Carl and F. J. Roethlisberger, "Barriers and Gateways to Communication," *Harvard Business Review,* Vol. 30, July–August, 1962: 46–62).

Ruben, Brent D. and Richard W. Budd. *Human Communication Handbook,* (Rochelle Park, NJ: Hayden Book Company, 1975).

Stewart, John. *Bridges Not Walls: A Book About Interpersonal Communication, 5th edition,* (New York: McGraw-Hill, 1989).

Stewart, John and Gary D'Angelo. *Together: Communicating Interpersonally,* (Reading, MA: Addison-Wesley Publishing Company, 1975).

Trenholm, Sarah. *Interpersonal Communication,* (Belmont, CA: Wadsworth Publishing Co., 1988).

Verderber, Rudolf. *Communicate,* (Belmont: Wadsworth, 1975).

Verderber, Rudolf. *Inter-Act: Using Interpersonal Communication Skills, 5th edition,* (Belmont: Wadsworth, 1989).

CHAPTERS TWO, THREE, AND FOUR

Alessandra, Tony, Ph.D., and Michael J. O'Connor, Ph.D. *PeopleSmart,* (LaJolla, CA: Keynote Publishing Company, 1990).

Driver, M.J., K.B. Brousseau, and P.L. Hunsaker. *The Dynamic Decision Maker,* (New York: Harper & Row, 1990).

Englesman, Ralph G. "Sizing Up Social Style," *Real Estate Today,* (August, 1975).

Harvey, John H., and William P. Smith. *Social Psychology: An Attributional Approach,* (St. Louis, MO.: C.V. Mosby, 1977).

Homans, George Caspar. *Social Behavior: Its Elementary Form,* (New York: Harcourt Brace Jovanovich, 1961).

Jabubowski, Patricia, and Arthur Lange. *Responsible Assertive Behavior,* (Champaign, IL: Research Press, 1976).

Jung, C. G. *Psychological Types* (London: Pantheon Books, 1923).

Kildahl, John P., and Lewis Wolberg. *The Dynamics of Personality,* (New York: Grune & Stratton, 1970).

Littauer, Florence. *Discover the Real You by Uncovering the Roots of Your Personality Tree,* (Waco, TX: Word Books, 1986).

Mehrabian, Albert. *Silent Messages,* (Belmont: Wadsworth, 1971).

Novak, Alys. "Mirror, Mirror on the Wall, Who's the Most Successful Executive of All," *Executive West,* (March, 1974).

Rose, Arnold. *Human Behavior and Social Process,* (Boston: Houghton Mifflin, 1962).

Tagiuri, Renato, and Luigi Petrullo. *Person Perception and Interpersonal Behavior,* (Stanford, CA: Stanford University Press, 1958).

CHAPTER FIVE

Alessandra, A.J., Phil Wexler, and Rick Barrera. *Non-Manipulative Selling, Second Edition,* (New York: Prentice-Hall Press, 1987).

Barbara, Dominick A. *The Art of Listening,* (Springfield, IL: Charles C. Thomas, 1965).

Barker, Larry L. *Listening Behavior,* (Englewood, NJ: Prentice-Hall, 1971).

Bostrom, Robert N. *Communicating: Speaking & Listening,* (Edina, MN: Burgess International Group, 1988).

Burley-Allen, Madelyn. *Listening: The Forgotten Skill,* (New York: John Wiley & Sons, 1982).

Caldwell, Taylor. *The Listener,* (New York: Doubleday & Co., 1960).

Gordon, Dr. Thomas. *P.E.T. Parent Effectiveness Training: The Tested New Way to Raise Responsible Children,* (New York: New American Library, 1975).

Goss, Blaine and Dan O'Hair. *Communicating in Interpersonal Relationships,* (New York: Macmillan Publishing Co., 1988).

Johnson, Wendell. *Your Most Enchanted Listener,* (New York: Harper, 1956).

Katz, Robert L. *Empathy*, (New York: The Free Press of Glencoe, Macmillan Co., 1963).

Koile, Earl. *Listening As a Way of Becoming*, (Waco, TX: Regency Books, 1977).

Montgomery, Robert. *Listening Made Easy*, (New York: AMACOM, 1981).

Morley, Joan. *Improving Aural Comprehension*, (Ann Arbor, MI: University of Michigan Press, 1973).

Nelson-Jones, Richard. *Human Relationships: A Skills Approach*, (Pacific Grove, CA: Brooks/Cole Publishing Co. 1990).

Nichols, R.G. *Active Listening*, (Atlanta: The Behavioral Science and Marketing Division of Learning Laboratories, Learning Laboratories, Inc.).

Nichols, R.G. "Listening Is a 10 Part Skill," *Nation's Business*, (July, 1957).

Nichols, R.G., and L.A. Stevens, *Are You Listening?*, (New York: McGraw Hill, 1957)

Nichols, R.G. "Do We Know How To Listen? Practical Helps in a Modern Age," *The Speech Teacher*, Vol. 10 (March 1961): 118–124.

Oakland, Thomas and Fern C. Williams. *Auditory Perception: Diagnosis and Development for Language and Reading Abilities*, (Seattle, WA: Special Child Publications, 1971).

Pearson, Judy Cornelia and Brian H. Spitzberg. *Interpersonal Communication: Concepts, Components, and Contexts*, Second Edition, (Dubuque, IA: William C. Brown Publishers, 1990).

Reik, Theodore. *Listening With the Third Ear*, (New York: Arena Books, 1972).

Rogers, Carl. "Active Listening," in Cohen, Allan R., et al., *Effective Behavior in Organizations*, (Homewood, IL: Richard Irwin, 1976) 277–290.

Rogers, Carl. *On Becoming a Person*, (Boston: Houghton Mifflin Co., 1961).

Rogers, Carl. *Client Centered Therapy*, (Boston: Houghton Mifflin Co., 1951).

Sartain, Harold D. *The Relevance of Listening: An Individualized Course*, (Westinghouse Learning Press, 1975).

Steil, Lyman, Larry Barker, and Kittie Watson. *Effective Listening*, (Reading, MA: Addison-Wesley Publishing Co., 1983).

Steil, Lyman, Joanne Summerfield, and George deMare. *Listening: It Can Change Your Life,* (New York: John Wiley & Sons, Inc., 1983).

Tubesing, Donald A. and Nancy Tubesing. *Tune In, Empathy Training Workshop,* (Milwaukee, WI: Listening Group, 1973).

Weaver, Carl. *Human Listening,* (New York: Bobbs-Merrill, 1972).

Wilkinson, Andrew, Leslie Stratta, and Peter Dudley. *The Quality of Listening,* (New York: Macmillan, 1974).

CHAPTER SIX

Alessandra, Wexler, and Barrera. *Non-Manipulative Selling.*

Dillon, J.T. *The Practice of Questioning,* (New York: Routledge, 1990).

CHAPTER SEVEN

Hunsaker, P.L. and A.J. Alessandra. "Giving—and Getting—Feedback," *Working Woman,* (April 1987), 30–35. Reprinted in *Traditions and Trends,* (American Express), 1987.

Robbins, Stephen P. *Training in Interpersonal Skills: Tips for Managing People at Work,* (Englewood, NJ: Prentice-Hall, 1989).

Sussman, Lyle and Sam Deep. *The Communication Experience in Human Relations,* (Cincinnati, OH: South-Western Publishing Co. 1989).

CHAPTER EIGHT

Gibson, Jane Whitney and Richard M. Hodgetts. *Organizational Communication: A Managerial Perspective,* (Academic Press, Inc., Harcourt Brace, 1986).

Hunsaker, J.S, P.L. Hunsaker, and N. Chase. "Guidelines for Productive Negotiating Relationships," Reading in Gordon, J.R., *Human Resource Management,* (Needham Heights, MA: Allyn and Bacon, 1986), 518–521.

Mader and Mader. *Understanding One Another: Communicating Interpersonally.*

CHAPTER NINE

Alessandra, Wexler, and Barrera. *Non-Manipulative Selling.*
Hunsaker, P.L. "Projecting the Appropriate Image" *Supervisory Management,* (May 1989), 26–30.

CHAPTER TEN

Alessandra, Wexler, and Barrera. *Non-Manipulative Selling.*
Ekman, Paul. "Face Muscles Talk Every Language," *Psychology Today,* September 1975:36–39.
Fast, Julius. *Subtext: Beneath the Surface & Between the Lines of Workplace Communication,* (New York: Viking Penguin, 1991).
Gibson, Jane Whitney and Richard M. Hodgetts. *Organizational Communication: A Managerial Perspective,* (Academic Press, Inc., Harcourt Brace, 1986).
Hunsaker, P.L. and Hunsaker, J.S. "Reading Between the Lids: Learning Eye Language to See What Clients Won't Say," *Registered Representative,* (July 1985), 66–69.
Nierenberg, Gerard I. and Henry Calero. *How To Read a Person Like a Book,* (New York: Pocket Books, 1971).
Nierenberg, Gerard I. and Henry H. Calero. *Meta-Talk: Guide to Hidden Meanings in Conversations,* (New York: Simon and Schuster, 1973).
Weiss, Brian. "The Invisible Smile," *Psychology Today,* September 1975: 38.

CHAPTER ELEVEN

DeVito, Joseph A. *The Interpersonal Communication Book,* Sixth Edition, (New York: HarperCollins Publishers, 1992).
Hunsaker, P.L., "Reading Voice Message: What Clients Are Really

Saying When They Say What They Say," *Registered Representative,* (April 1985), 62–70.

CHAPTER TWELVE

Athos, A.G., and J.J. Gabarro. "Communication: The Use of Time, Space, and Things," Chapter 1 in *Interpersonal Behavior: Communication and Understanding in Relationships,* (Englewood Cliffs, N.J.: Prentice-Hall, 1978).

Dalton, C., and M. Dalton. "Personal Communications: The Space Factor," *Machine Design,* (September 23, 1976).

Englesman, Ralph G. "Unscrambling Nonverbal Signals," *Best's Review—Life/Health Insurance Edition* (April, 1974).

Hall, E.J. *The Silent Dimension,* (New York: Doubleday, 1959).

Hall, E.J. *The Hidden Dimension,* (New York: Doubleday, 1966).

Hunsaker, P.L., "Communicating Better Through Proxemics," in Huseman, R.E., *Readings in Business Communications: Strategies and Skills,* (Hinsdale, IL: Dryden Press, 1980, 1984).

CHAPTER THIRTEEN

Athos, and Gabarro. "Communication: The Use of Time, Space, and Things."

Hunsaker, P.L. "Talking with Time," *Registered Representative,* (September 1984), 77–80.

CHAPTER FOURTEEN

Gatto, Rex P. *A Practical Guide to Effective Presentation,* (Pittsburgh: GTA Press, 1990).

Hunsaker, Johanna B., and Phillip L. Hunsaker. "Notes on Effective Presentations," *Industrial Management,* (March–April, 1985).

Hunsaker, J.S. and P.L. Hunsaker. "Effective Presentation Skills," *Industrial Management,* (March 1985).

Level, Dale A., Jr., and William P. Galle, Jr. *Managerial Com-*

munications, (San Diego, CA: Business Publications, Inc. 1988).

Robbins, Stephen P. *Training in Interpersonal Skills: Tips for Managing People at Work,* (Englewood Cliffs, N.J.: Prentice-Hall, 1989).

Sussman and Deep. *The Communication Experience in Human Relations.*

CHAPTER FIFTEEN

Bormann, Ernest G. and Nancy C. Bormann. *Effective Small Group Communication,* (Broken Arrow, OK: Burgess Publishing, 1988).

Gibson and Hodgetts. *Organizational Communications.*

Hunsaker, P.L. "Using Group Dynamics To Improve Decision Making Meetings," *Industrial Management,* (July–August 1983), 19–23.

Sigband, Norman B. "Meetings with Success," *Personnel Journal,* (May, 1985).

CHAPTER SIXTEEN

Driver, M.J., K.B. Brousseau, and P.L. Hunsaker. *The Dynamic Decision Maker,* (New York: Harper & Row, 1990).

Robbins, Stephen P. *Training in Interpersonal Skills: Tips for Managing People at Work,* (Prentice Hall, 1989).

CHAPTER SEVENTEEN

Forbes, Malcolm. "Exorcising Demons from Important Business Letters," *Marketing Times,* (March/April, 1981).

Hunsaker, J.S. and P.L. Hunsaker. *Strategies and Skills for Managerial Women,* Second Edition, (Cincinnati, OH: South-Western Publishing Co., 1991).

Huseman, Richard C., James M. Lahiff, and John M. Penrose, Jr. *Reading and Applications in Business Communications: Strat-*

egies and Skills, Second Edition, (New York: CBS College Publishing, 1985).

Wycoff, Joyce. *Mindmapping: Your Personal Guide to Exploring Creativity and Problem-Solving,* (New York: Berkeley Books, 1991).

CHAPTER EIGHTEEN

DeVito. *Messages.*

Huseman, Lahiff, and Penrose. *Readings and Applications in Business Communication.*

INDEX

Accommodation, as strategy for managing conflict, 96–97
Accuracy, and time, 161–63
Acknowledge, and listening, 59, 62
Acknowledging, and nonverbal feedback, 83
Across the table arrangement, 153, 155
Action, 208
and listening, 55
Active listener, 58
attitude of, 67–68
Active listening, at meetings, 209–10
Active style, of business writing, 246
Active voice, in business writing, 236–38
Adaptability, to styles, 45–50
Advice on How to Form a Good Combination of Blood Types (Nomi), 21
Affection, and vocal qualities, 138
Agenda

for meetings, 190, 195, 196–97, 207
for presentation, 178
Agenda hider, 213
Aggression, vs. assertiveness, 99
Aggressor, 213
Agreement checking, and asking questions, 71
Ambiguity, and questions, 77
Americans, as noncontact group, 151
See also North Americans; South Americans
Analysis, and reports, 232
Anger, and vocal qualities, 138
Angle of approach, and personal space, 156
Appendices, in reports, 232
Arabs, as contact people, 151
Arms, and language gestures, 126
Assertiveness, as component of collaboration, 99

Association/connection, and message, 180
Assumptions, and effective feedback, 87
Astonishment, and vocal qualities, 138
Athos, Dr. Anthony, 144, 161
ATI Medical, Inc., 228
Attendees, at meetings, 190
AT&T study, 169
Audience
  for business writing, 226
  for presentation, 174–75, 177–178, 183
Audiovisual equipment and materials, 202
Authority, and gesture clusters, 130
Avoidance, as strategy for managing conflict, 96
Avoider, 213

Background material, for reports, 232
Big Idea, of presentation, 176–77
Blame, as strategy to avoid, 105
Blocker, 213
Body language
  and customer service, 132
  and employee/manager relationship, 131–32
  and mixed messages, 83
  and negotiations, 132
  as nonverbal communication, 121–23, 131–34
  and salespeople, 132–33
  See also Gesture clusters; Language gestures
Body postures, 114
Bolding, as style, 241
Boredom, 125, 131, 138
Brainstorming, 192, 210, 224
Branches, and mindmapping, 224
Breathing, and listening, 61
Bullets, as style, 241
Business letters, 228, 233–34
Business writing, 223–34
  business letters, 228, 233–34
  format follows function in, 227–228
  memos, 228–30
  and message, telegraphing, 226–227
  and mindmapping, 223–24
  reports, 230–32
  and style, 236–47

CARESS model, 58–68, 248
  acknowledge, 59, 62
  concentrate, 59–62
  exercise emotional control, 59, 64–65
  research, 59, 63–64
  sense the nonverbal message, 59, 65–66
  structure, 59, 66–67
Carson, Johnny, 70
Catharsis, at meetings, 207
Challenger tragedy, 56
Cheerfulness, and vocal qualities, 138
Cheerleading sessions, 193
Christmas, 165
Churchill, Sir Winston, 170
Cicero, 170
Cigarette smoking, 128, 130–31
Clarifying, and closed questions, 74
  See also Feedback
Clarity, 137
  of style, 236–39
Clash of ideas, at meetings, 215–16
Classroom arrangement, for meetings, 200
Climate, for sharing, 206
Closed questions, 72–74
Clothing, and image projection, 115–16
Coaction seating, 153
"Cold shoulder," as rejection, 129
Collaboration, as strategy for managing conflict, 98–99
Color, and mindmapping, 224
Colorful style, 247
commitment, and meetings, 189
Common goals, and meetings, 189
Common ground, and redirecting reaction, 65
Communication barriers, and conflict, 93–94
Communication breakdown, 18, 21
Comparing, and structure, 67
Comparisons, as presentation techniques, 180
Competition
  and conflict, 94–95
  and listening, 55
Concentrate, and listening, 59–62

Conciseness, of style, 236, 239–40
Conclusion
  of presentation, 181
  of report, 232
Confidence, and gesture clusters,
  130
Conflict, 91–108
  common sources of, 93–95
  and confrontation continuum
    strategies, 100–104
  five behaviors for resolution of,
    106–7
  four phases of, 95–96
  nature of, 92
  strategies to avoid, 104–6
  strategies for managing, 96–99
  three basic components of, 92–93
Conflict of interest, 93
Conformity pressures, at meetings,
  216
Confrontation, as component of collaboration, 99
Confrontation continuum strategies,
  100–104
  diplomatic disagreement, 101
  feelings statement, 103
  firm confrontation, 102
  gentle confrontation, 101–2
  I-statement, 101
  reflection, 100–101
  and specifics, 102–3
  timing, 102
Connect ideas, and mindmapping,
  224
Connection. See Association/
  connection
Contact people, vs. noncontact people, 151–52
Controlling people
  behavior of, 29–31
  directors as, 47
  and one-dimensional adapting, 50
  vs. supporting people, 22, 26–27
  thinkers as, 48
Control techniques, at meetings,
  214–15
Conversation stimulation, and asking
  questions, 71
Coordination, at meetings, 194
Corner-to-corner arrangements, 153
Creative problem-solving, as component of collaboration, 99
Cupping, as language gesture, 125

Customer service, and body language, 132

Dalton, Charles and Marie, 152
Decide to listen, 61
Decision-making, at meetings, 194,
  217–18
Defensiveness, 127–28, 138
Definitions, and effective feedback,
  86–87
Democratic arrangement, for meetings, 202
Diplomatic disagreement, as confrontation continuum strategy,
  101
Direct vs. indirect writing, 238–39
Directing, and closed questions, 74
Directors, 37–39, 152
  adapting of, 46
  adapting to, 46–47
  as controlling people, 47
  as direct people, 47
  at a glance, 39, 43–44
Direct people
  directors as, 47
  vs. indirect people, 22–26, 30
  and one-dimensional adapting, 49
  socializers as, 47
Disagreement, legitimatized at meetings, 216
Disbelief, and vocal qualities, 138
Discussion, at meetings, 190–91,
  212–15
Domination, 209
  as strategy for managing conflict,
  97
Dominator, 213
Doubt, and gesture clusters, 129
Dressing. See Clothing
Dyad arrangements, for interpersonal space, 152–53
Dysfunctional behaviors, at meetings, 212–14

Editing, 244
Emerson, Ralph Waldo, 61
Emotions, vocal projection of, 137–
  138
Empathy, and conflict resolution,
  107
Empathy statements, 63–64
Employees
  and accommodation, 97

Employees (*cont.*)
    body language of, 120–21, 131–132
    and effective feedback, 88
    listening of, 55–56
    and personal space, 158, 159
    See also Manager/employee relationship
Energy cycle, and meetings, 197–98
Enthusiasm, 138
    and gesture clusters, 131
    and image projection, 118–19
Enunciation, 141
Environment, noise in, 15, 17
    See also Work environment
Environmental barriers (external), to listening, 60, 61
Equality, and conflict resolution, 107
Errors (common), in style, 244–45
Evaluation, and gesture clusters, 128–29
Evaluative listener, 57–58
Examples, as technique, 180
Exercise emotional control, and listening, 59, 64–65
Expanding, and open questions, 74
Explanatory presentation, 173
External environmental barriers, to listening, 60, 61
External speaker-related barriers, 60
Extroverts vs. introverts, and interpersonal space, 156
Eyebrows raised, 124
Eye contact, 114, 124
    and listening, 62
Eyes, and language gestures, 124–25

Face, and language gestures, 125
Facilities checklist, at meetings, 202
Fact feedback, 83–84, 86
    examples of requests for, 84
    statements, 83
Fact finding, and closed questions, 73
Feedback, 78–90
    fact, 83–84, 86
    feeling, 84–86
    keys to effective, 86–90
    nonverbal, 82–83
    positive and negative, when to use, 88
    types of, 80–86
    verbal, 80–82
    withholding, 88–90

Feeling feedback, 84–86
    examples of requests for, 85
    statements, 85
Feeling-finding, and open questions, 74
Feelings statement, as confrontation continuum strategy, 103
Felt conflict, 95–96
Firm confrontation, as confrontation continuum strategy, 102
First impressions, 110
    and image projection, 112–17
Flip charts, as visual aids, 183–84
Focus, at meetings, 224
Follow-up, after meetings, 218–19
Forbes, Malcolm, 233
Force, as strategy to avoid, 106
Format follows function, in business writing, 227–28
Free association, and mindmapping, 224
Freud, Sigmund, 122–23
Frustration, and gesture clusters, 130
Funnel technique, of formulating questions, 75–76

General Dynamics, Western Center of, 191
Gentle confrontation, as confrontation continuum strategy, 101–2
Gesture clusters, as nonverbal communication, 126–31
    boredom or impatience, 131
    confidence, superiority, authority, 130
    defensiveness, 127–28
    enthusiasm, 131
    evaluation, 128–29
    frustration, 130
    nervousness, 130–31
    openness, 127
    readiness, 129–30
    reassurance, 130
    self-control, 131
    suspicion, secrecy, rejection, doubt, 129
Goals, at meetings, 207
    See also Common goals
Greece (ancient), 21
Grooming, 114
Ground rules, for meetings, 206
Group arrangements, for interpersonal space, 153, 155

Group communication, *See* Presentation; Meetings
Group identity, at meetings, 189
Group process, at meetings, 217
"Groupthink," at meetings, 216–17

Hall, Edward, 151
Handout materials, at meetings, 202
Hands, and language gestures, 125–126
Handshake, importance of, 114
Handwritten communications, 228
Heading, for memos, 229
Headlines, importance of, 227
Helpful participants, 212
Help seeker, 213
Hemingway, Ernest, 236
Highlighting, use of, 241
Hippocrates, 21
Hitchhiking theory, 62
Ho-hums, 212
Hootiloo, 212
Humor, 243
Hygiene. *See* Grooming
Hyphens, use of, 242

Ice-breakers, for presentation, 178
Ideas, 217
  and paragraphing, 240
  See also Connect ideas
Identity. *See* Group identity
Image projection, 111–19
  and enthusiasm, 118–19
  first impressions, 112–17
  and knowledge breadth, 117–18
  and knowledge depth, 117
  See also Symbols/images
Impatience, 138
  and gesture clusters, 131
Impersonal style, 246–47
Implementation, of reports, 232
Indexing, and structure, 66
Indirect vs. direct writing, 238–39
Indirect people
  vs. direct people, 22–26, 30
  and one-dimensional adapting, 49
  relaters as, 48
  thinkers as, 48
Inflection, and vocal quality, 137
Information, 245
  and meetings, 192, 194
  transfer of, 71
  verification of, 72

Information Age, 70
Instructional presentations, 173–74
Intensity, and message, 180
Interaction, and conflict, 94
  See also Team interaction
Interdependency, and conflict, 94
Internal listener-related barriers, 60
Internal physical barriers, 60
Internal psychological barriers, 60
Interpersonal communication. *See* Personal styles
Interpersonal space, as personal space, 150–55
  Intimate Zone, 150, 151
  Personal Zone, 150, 151, 152
  Public Zone, 151
  Social Zone, 150, 151
  strategies, 152–55
Intimate zone, 150, 151
Introduction,
  to presentation, 177–78
  to reports, 231
Introverts vs. extroverts, and interpersonal space, 156
Involvement, and message, 180
I-statement, as confrontation continuum strategy, 101
Italics, use of, 241

James, William, 11
Japan, 21
Jargon, 238
  See also Language simplification
Joker, 213
Joyfulness, and vocal qualities, 138
Jung, Dr. Carl, 21

Kennedy, John F., 112
Key words, and mindmapping, 224
King, Stephen, 236
King of the Mountain game, 146
Knowledge breadth, and image projection, 117–18
Knowledge depth, and image projection, 117
Knowledge sharing, at meetings, 188

Language gestures, as nonverbal communication, 123–26
  arms, 126
  eyes, 124–25
  face, 125
  hands, 125–26

Language gestures (*cont.*)
  legs, 126
  posture, 126
  sitting, 126
  walking, 126
Language simplification, and effective feedback, 88
Latent conflict, 95
Latins, as contact group, 151
Leaders
  and interpersonal space, 153, 155
  at meetings, 205–8, 214
Leaning back, as language gesture, 125
Learning, at meetings, 207
Left lookers, 124–25
Legs, and language gestures, 126
Limited resources, and conflict, 93
Listener
  active, 58, 67–68
  evaluative, 57–58
  marginal, 57
  and reception problems, 17–19
  See also Nonlistener
Listening, 54–68
  barriers to, 60–61
  benefits of better, 56
  and CARESS model, 58–68
  four levels of, 56–58
  importance of, 67
  at meetings, 209–10
  reasons for poor, 55
  and speech, 67
  and time, 67
Loaded words, 64–65
Low blows, in conflict, 105–6
Loyola University study, 54

Main body, of reports, 231–32
Manager/employee relationship, 151
  and body language, 131–32
  and nonverbal feedback, 82–83
Managers
  body language of, 131–32
  and effective feedback, 88
  image of, 116
  listening of, 55–56
  at meetings, 188
Manifest conflict, 96
Manipulation, 77, 106
Marginal listener, 57
Meanings, of words, 86–87

Meetings
  agenda for, 190, 195, 196–97, 207
  clash of ideas at, 215–16
  conducting, 204–19
  control techniques at, 214–15
  decision-making at, 217–18
  discussions at, 212–15
  dysfunctional behaviors at, 212–14
  ending, 218
  and energy cycle, 197–98
  facilities checklist for, 202
  five common phases of, 207–8
  follow-up after, 218–19
  "groupthink" at, 216–17
  guidelines for effective, 189–91
  leadership for, 205–8, 214
  minutes at, 191, 208–9
  objectives of, 193–94
  participation at, 190, 195–96, 209–10, 212
  planning, 187–203
  preparing for effective, 191–93
  problem-solving at, 210–11
  purpose of, 189–90, 193
  room arrangement for, 199–202
  six basic functions of, 188–89
  time and place for, 190, 198–99
Mehrabian, Dr. Albert, 65
Memos, 228–30
Men vs. women, and interpersonal space, 156, 158
Message
  and image projection, 112
  of presentation, 179–81
  telegraphing, in business writing, 226–27
  See also Mixed messages
Mindmapping, 67, 223–24
Mindmapping, Your Personal Guide to Exploring Creativity and Problem-Solving (Wycoff), 224
Mind-melding, 13, 14
Minimization, as strategy to avoid, 104
Minutes, at meetings, 191, 208–9
Misunderstandings, and listening, 56
Mixed messages, and nonverbal feedback, 83
Morale, and meetings, 194

Negative emotional reactions, recognizing and redirecting, 65
Negative participants, 212

Negative situations, 245
Negotiation, 132
   as strategy for managing conflict,
      97–98
Nervousness, and gesture clusters,
      130–31
Nixon, Richard, 112
Noise, in environment, 15, 17
Nomi, Toshitaka, 21
Noncontact people, vs. contact peo-
   ple, 151–52
Nonlistener, 56–57
Nonparticipants, 212
Nonverbal communication, 120–34
   body language, 121–23, 131–34
   gesture clusters, 126–31
   language gestures, 123–26
Nonverbal feedback, 82–83
Nonverbal message. See Sense the
   nonverbal message
North Americans, as noncontact
   group, 151, 152
Northern Europeans, as noncontact
   group, 151
Numbers styling, 241

Objective. See Specific objective
Open communication, 92
Openness, 107, 127
Open questions, 72–74
Oral reports, 174
Organizations, and personal space,
   158–59
Overhead projectors, 184
Overreactions, 64–65

Page numbers, 242
Paragraphs, 240
Paraphrase, and listening, 61–62
Parking spaces, 146–47
Participation, at meetings, 190, 195–
   196, 209–10, 212
Passive style, 246
Passive voice, vs. active voice, 237–
   238
Pause, as technique, 65
Perceived conflict, 95
Permission, asking, 77
Personality, and interpersonal space,
   156–57
Personal space, 142–59
   higher is better than lower, 145–
   146

in is better than out, 147
interpersonal space as, 150–55
more is better than less, 144
near is better than far, 146–47
and organizations, 158–59
private is better than public, 144–
   145
and special arrangement determinants, 156–58
territory as, 142–43, 149
things in, 147–49
and touching, 150
in work environment, 144–47,
   149
Personal styles, 20–33, 246
   determining, 31–33
   direct or indirect?, 22–26, 49
   four-type model, 21–22
   supporting or controlling?, 26–31,
      49–50
   two simple questions, 22
   See also Directors; Relaters; So-
      cializers; Thinkers
Personal zone, 150, 151, 152
Phrases, short, 239–40
Physical barriers (internal), to listening, 60
Pipe smokers, 128
Pitch, and vocal qualities, 137
Planning and implementation meetings, 192
Poker face, 125
Policy making, at meetings, 208
Political meetings, 193
Pondy, Louis, 95
Positiveness, and conflicts, 107
Positive situations, 245
Posture, 126
   See also Body postures
Power chair arrangement, for meet-
   ings, 201–2, 210
Presentation, 169–86
   agenda for, 178
   audience for, 174–75, 177–78,
      183
   Big Idea of, 176–77
   conclusion of, 181
   fear of, 169
   ice-breakers for, 178
   introduction to, 177–78
   message of, 179–81
   planning successful, 173–74,
      181–82

Presentation (*cont.*)
  rehearsal for, 181–82
  specific objective of, 175–76
  and stage fright, 170–72
  visual aids for, 182–86
Problem-solving, at meetings, 192,
    210–11
  See also Creative problem-
    solving
Proxemics. *See* Personal space
Psychological barriers (internal), to
    listening, 60
Public speakers
  characteristics of effective, 172
  developing attitudes of successful,
    171–72
Public zone, 151
Punctuation, use of, 243–44

Questions, 69–77, 209
  closed, 72–74
  feedback, testing for, 87–88
  funnel technique of formulating,
    75–76
  open, 72–74
  reasons for asking, 70–72
  strategies for formulating, 74–77
  two major types of, 72–74

Race, and personal space, 157
Rapport, and asking questions, 71
Readability, and style, 236, 241–42
Readiness, and gesture clusters,
    129–30
Reassurance, and gesture clusters,
    130
Receiving, 52
Reception problems, 15, 17–19
Recognizing negative emotional reac-
    tions, 65
Recommendations, in reports, 232
Redirecting negative emotional reac-
    tions, 65
Reflection, as confrontation contin-
    uum strategy, 100–101
Refreshments, at meetings, 202
Rehearsal, for presentation, 181–82
Rejection, and gesture clusters, 129
Relaters, 41–43, 152
  adapting of, 46
  at a glance, 43
  as indirect people, 48
  as supporting people, 48

Relationships
  defined by time, 162
  and listening, 56
  and personal space, 157
Repetition, 165
  of message, 179–80
Reports, 228, 230–32
  introduction to, 231
  least controversial to most contro-
    versial, 231
  main body of, 231–32
  most important to least impor-
    tant, 231
  negative to positive, 231
  Table of Contents in, 231
Research, and listening, 59, 63–64
Resonance, 136
Respecting, as component of collab-
    oration, 98–99
Responsibility levels, and conflict, 93
Rhythm, and vocal qualities, 137
Right justification, use of, 242
Right lookers, 124–25
Robert's Rules of Order, 196, 215
Rodin, Auguste, 128
Room arrangement, for meetings,
    199–202
Round table arrangement, for meet-
    ings, 202
Rubbing motions, 125

Sadness, and vocal qualities, 138
Salespeople
  and body language, 130, 132–33
  and funnel technique, 75–76
  and personal space, 158–59
Sales presentation, 173
Sarcasm, use of, 137
Satisfaction, and vocal qualities, 138
Scarcity, and time, 163–64
Secrecy, and gesture clusters, 129
Self-censorship, 216
Self-control, and gesture clusters,
    131
Sending, problems in, 15–17
Sense the nonverbal message, and
    listening, 59, 65–66
Sentences, style of, 240
Sequencing, 66–67
Sex, and interpersonal space, 156,
    158
Sexism, and style, 242–43
Sharing, at meetings, 206

Short is best, 227
    See also Conciseness
Side-by-side conversations, 155
Side-by-side seating arrangements,
    153, 156
Silent Messages (Mehrabian), 65
Sitting, and language gestures, 126
Situations, and style strategies, 245
Slides, as visual aids, 184–85
Socializers, 34–37, 152
    adapting of, 46–47
    adapting to, 47
    as direct people, 47
    at a glance, 36–37, 43
    as supporting people, 47
Social phase, of meetings, 207
Social zone, 150, 151
Solutions
    at meetings, 217
    of reports, 232
South Americans, as contact group,
    151
Space. See Personal space
Speaker-related (external) barriers,
    to listening, 60
Special arrangement determinants,
    for personal space, 156–58
Specific objective, of presentation,
    175–76
Specifics, and confrontation contin-
    uum strategy, 102–3
Speech
    and listening, 67
    timing in, 140
Speech speed, vs. thought speed, 55
Speed
    and listening, 55
    and vocal qualities, 137, 139
Staff meeting, weekly, 193
Stage fright, 170–72
Stanford University study, 169
Star Trek (TV show), 13
Statements
    empathy, 63–64
    in reports, 232
    See also I-statement
Statistics, for presentations, 180
Status, at meetings, 189
"Steepling," 125
Stevenson, Paul, 228
Structure, and listening, 59, 66–67
Style, in business writing, 236–47
    active voice, 236–38

clarity of, 236–39
common errors in, 244–45
conciseness of, 236, 239–40
direct vs. indirect, 238–39
and editing, 244
and humor, 243
jargon, avoiding, 238
and punctuation, 243–44
and readability, 236, 241–42
and sexism, 242–43
strategies of, 245–47
    See also Personal styles
Style languages, 20–21, 22, 33
Subgroups, at meetings, 210
Superiority, and gesture clusters,
    130
Supervisors
    and accommodation, 97
    and funnel technique, 75
    and personal space, 158, 159
Supporting people
    behavior of, 27–29
    vs. controlling people, 22, 26–27
    and one-dimensional adapting,
        49–50
    relaters as, 48
    socializers as, 47
Supportiveness, in conflicts, 107
Suspicion, and gesture clusters, 129
Symbols/images, and mindmapping,
    224

Table of Contents, in reports, 231
Task-oriented meetings, 207
Team interaction, at meetings, 189
Teamwork, at meetings, 194
Technical terms. See Language sim-
    plification
Telegraphing, 241
Telephone, vocal quality on, 139
Territory, as personal space, 142–
    143, 149
Testimony, in presentation, 180
T-formation arrangement, for meet-
    ings, 201
Theater style arrangement, for meet-
    ings, 199–200
Things, in personal space, 147–49
    bigger is better than smaller, 147–
        148
    clean is better than dirty, 148
    expensive is better than cheap,
        148

Things (cont.)
  more is better than few, 148
  neat is better than messy, 148
  personal is better than public, 149
  very old or very new is better than recent, 148
Thinker, The (Rodin), 128
Thinkers, 39–41, 42, 152
  adapting of, 46
  as controlling people, 48
  at a glance, 41, 43–44
  as indirect people, 48
Thought speed, vs. speech speed, 55
"3 Hs," at meetings, 212
Three "Vs," of communication, 13, 14, 19, 20
Time, 160–65, 182, 190
  and listening, 67
  for meetings, 198–99
  three major variables of, 161–65
Time pressures, at meetings, 216
Timing, 102
  in speech, 140
Togetherness, at meetings, 216
Touching, and personal space, 150
Training, and listening, 55
Training sessions, 192–93, 194
Trust building, and asking questions, 71
Tuning in, as effective feedback, 88

Understanding
  as component of collaboration, 98–99
  and listening, 56
Unloading, and conflict, 105
Upper case styling, 241
U-shaped style arrangement, for meetings, 200–201

Verbal element, 14, 16, 20, 228
  See also Conflict; Feedback; Listening; Questions

Verbal feedback, 80–82
Viewpoint, diversity of, 217
Views of others, and asking questions, 71
Visual aids, 227
  flip charts, 183–84
  overhead projectors, 184
  for presentation, 182–86
  slides, 184–85
Visual element, 14, 16, 17, 20
Visualize calm, as redirecting technique, 65
Vocal element, 14, 16–17, 20
Vocal qualities, 135–41
  and emotions, projection of, 137–138
  five aids for assured, 140
  seven major, 136–37
  and speed, 139
  using, 139–41
  and volume, 137, 139
Volume, and vocal qualities, 137, 139

Walking, and language gestures, 126
Weekly staff meeting, 193
Western Center, of General Dynamics, 191
White space, value of, 240, 241
Winking, 124
Women vs. men, and interpersonal space, 156, 158
Words, 239
  loaded, 64–65
  meanings of, 86–87
  See also Key words
Work environment, personal space in, 144–47, 149
Written communication. See Business writing
Wycoff, Joyce, 224

Yale University study, 140

ABOUT THE AUTHORS

TONY ALESSANDRA, PH.D., CPAE

Recognized by *Meetings & Conventions Magazine* as "one of America's most electrifying speakers," Tony's natural wit combined with his knowledge, experience, and education has captivated audiences in over 1000 keynote speeches worldwide. His clients include Fortune 500 giants, smaller companies, and professional associations. Relationship Strategies, Customer Service, and Collaborative Selling are his most often requested idea-packed topics.

While working his way through college as a salesman, Tony earned his B.B.A. (Notre Dame), M.B.A. (U. of Conn.), and Ph.D. (Georgia State U., in 1976). He taught marketing and sales at the university level for eight years before becoming a full-time professional speaker in 1979. Since then, Tony has authored 10 books, including *Non-Manipulative Selling, The Art of Managing People, Publish & Flourish*, and *People Smart*. His expertise is also featured in several award-winning audio and video training programs, including *The Power of Listening* film.

Tony lives in La Jolla, California, with his wife, Sue, and their four children.

To reach Tony, contact:

Alessandra & Associates, P.O. Box 2767, La Jolla, CA. 92038. (800) 222-4383 or FAX (619) 459-0435.

PHILLIP HUNSAKER, PH.D.

Dr. Hunsaker is an internationally recognized consultant, seminar leader, speaker, author, teacher, and researcher in the areas of management and organizational development. He has worked with a wide variety of organizations in both the public and private sectors to increase personal, group and organizational effectiveness.

Dr. Hunsaker has published five books and over one hundred publications, including numerous articles in academic and professional journals. He is a Professor of Management and Director of Management Programs in the School of Business Administration at the University of San Diego. He also serves as a consultant to management for Decision Dynamics Corporation and as a faculty member for the University of California—San Diego Leadership and Management Program, and the Institute for Quality and Productivity. He can be reached by writing to the School of Business Administration, University of San Diego, Alcala Park, San Diego, CA 92110; or by telephoning (619) 260-4870.